Taking the King

By

John Cannon

CONTENTS

Introduction

1   Taking the King's shilling
2   Mainstream Ganges
3   "Away Aloft"
4   Shotley Routine
5   Topical Topics
6   Farewell to Shotley
7   My first Draft
8   HMS Courageous
9   The Royal Visit
10   "The Admiralty Regrets"
11   H.M.S.Dorsetshire
12   Leaving Plymouth
13   The 'Richelieu'
14   DURBAN S.A.
15   Sea raiders in the Atlantic
16   Simonstown
17   Patrolling the Atlantic.
18   Sink the Bismarck
19   HEBBURN on TYNE
20   THE LAST COMMISSION
21   MALAYA
22   The Japanese cometh
23   Easter Eggs
24   An unwelcome return
25   Dundee
26   A funny shaped coal burner
27   The Seychelle Islands.
28   H.M.S.Gambia
29   Beating the Retreat
30   HMS Drake - Devonport

Introduction

In Napoleonic times the Navy's insatiable demands for more and more men, especially in times of war, changed the choice of optional enlistment to one of compulsory 'volunteering'. Pressing was necessary to satisfy the demand for sufficient manpower to sail the large square-rigged warships of the day. Well-paid seamen, armed with cutlass and cudgel, were organised into press gangs to accommodate the needs of the Navy. Their method of recruitment was brutal, and indiscriminate, with a total disregard for the suitability of the men they 'pressed'. Whorehouses and Alehouses provided a main source of procurement. Inebriated men, and those with their breeches down, were restricted in escaping and fell easy prey to the notorious press-gangs. The term 'pressed' had its origins in the voluntary acceptance of 'prest', the King's shilling, to seal a contract binding a man to a period of service with the Fleet. Although living conditions for the average worker ashore meant existing on a mere pittance, men were reluctant to enlist for the harsh and often cruel life at sea. There was always an adventurous few that volunteered for service, lured by the promise of prize money and free liquor. Scarcely anyone joined out of a patriotic desire to serve the King. Ships' captains, alarmed at the large number of sickly 'pressed' men who died soon after going to sea, continually petitioned the Admiralty to find alternative methods of recruitment.

In 1756 James Hanway, a governor of the Foundling Hospital, and Sir John Fleming, a Bow Street magistrate, formed the Marine Society for vagrant and starving boys willing to go to sea. Before going to a ship the boys received a basic education and were provided with adequate clothing and bedding. They were only allocated to ships that would guarantee the welfare conditions laid down by the Society. Maintained by public subscription the charity proved popular. It could be said that it was the blueprint for the future training of youngsters preparing for a career at sea. Other establishments sprang up to become equally famous. Arethusa, the fourth ship to carry the name, became a training ship for destitute boys in 1873. The Shaftesbury Homes later took over the Arethusa, and kept it going until 1932. The Royal Hospital School at Greenwich was another such school. Founded for the education of sons of seamen, particularly those who were orphaned, it moved to Holbrook, Suffolk, in 1934. It is one of the few still operating today, albeit in a revamped form. Warspite was also an important training ship for boys, prior to their entry into the Royal Navy.

'Pressing' ceased with the ending of Napoleonic War in 1815, although the 'Right to Press' remained on the statue book as a contingency measure. A commission set up to deal with the recruiting problem, recommended better pay and conditions for men who volunteered for the Navy, and formal training for Boy Seamen. In 1847 a start was made when the Brig H.M.S. Rolla was allocated specifically for training boys. This was followed a year later by the Brig H.M.S. Nautilus, stationed at Devonport to attract West Country youths into the Service. It was so successful that in 1850 a third Brig, H.M.S. Wizard, was added and located at Cork. 1853 saw the introduction of Continuous Service, and the need for 'pressing' finally faded. The improved conditions attracted men and boys in large numbers. Boys trained to high standards in the training ships were much sought after, when seagoing captains became aware of their future potential as skilled and disciplined seamen. In 1854, to increase the number of junior recruits, H.M.S. Illustrious was moored at Portsmouth for the purpose of training 250 boys, followed in 1855 by H.M.S. Implacable (330 boys) at Devonport. In 1862 H.M.S. Boscawen (350 boys) positioned at Southampton, H.M.S. Wellesly (200 boys) at Chatham, and H.M.S. St.Vincent (300 boys) at Portsmouth. A further ship, H.M.S. Impregnable was based at Devonport in 1863. H.M.S. St.Vincent and H.M.S. Impregnable in due course became shore establishments (Stone Frigates). In 1927 when the land based St.Vincent was opened, 450 boys went from H.M.S. Ganges to establish the new school.

H.M.S. Ganges was undoubtedly one of the most elitist, and notorious, names in Boys Training Ships. It was originally an 84 gun ship, and one of the first in the navy to be built of teak instead of the traditional oak. The work was carried out in 1821 at Bombay, by the famous Parsee master building dynasty of Jamsetjee Wadia. It was the fourth ship to carry the name and had the distinction, under Rear-Admiral Sir Robert Baynes, to be the last sailing ship to serve as a seagoing flagship.

In 1865,' Ganges' was fitted out as a boy's training ship at Devonport and arrived to anchor in St. Just Pool at Mylor, and Falmouth in 1866. Later, in 1899, the ship was again refitted at Devonport before moving under sail to Sheerness. On the 11th.November 1899 again under sail but assisted by the tugs Alligator and Hearty she arrived at Harwich, where she remained until 1906. In 1903 the Admiralty, concerned at the lack of facilities on the old wooden 'Ganges', decided to build a shore establishment to house 2000 boys at Shotley, on the other side of the river from Harwich. First known as The Royal Training Establishment, because shore bases were not referred to as 'ships' until 1927, it carried the notoriety and later the name of its predecessor until 1939, when boy entrants were replaced by adult 'Hostility Only' recruits for the duration of the war. The Shotley site was considered an ideal site, situated well away from the distracting influences of a major town. Shotley opened on 4th.Oct.1905 for the first intake of boys. It was never intended to be a haven for sensitive youngsters; the lifestyle was strenuous and demanding, mentally and physically. The purpose of the strict and harsh treatment of the recruits was to turn out disciplined, responsible, fit and confident young men. The methods employed had the desired effect. Boys matured quickly as their chests filled out and their muscles developed. The harsh routine was a good test of an individual's endurance for a future life at sea. A discipline, enforced by punishment, was necessary to maintain a firm control of the hundreds of high-spirited, mischievous and venturesome boys who considered flogging a fair price to pay if they were caught smoking a cigarette. Fifteen year olds who eagerly stood on the 11" 'button' at the top of the mast, 150 feet high above the ground only holding on by gripping the lightening conductor between their knees, needed strict supervision under a watchful eye.

I speak from personal experience when I say that we sixteen year old survivors of H.M.S.Courageous, the first warship to be sunk by enemy action in the Second World War with the loss of over 500 men, attributed our survival to a disciplined training to act positively and without panic in an emergency. Our endurance was further tested a few years later when we were nineteen-year-olds. Sunk by the dive-bombers of the Imperial Japanese Navy in the Indian Ocean, we searched for scraps of flotsam and hung on for thirty-three hours before being rescued.

Hospital Schools like Greenwich combined with H.M.S.Ganges to produce famous 'boys' like Admiral Sir Philip King Enright and Rear-Admiral Sir Benjamin Charles Stanley Martin KBE.CBE.DSO.RN. From their humble beginnings, and lack of social connections, they overcame all the obstacles to reach high rank. It was the time-honoured tradition for each generation of 'old' boys to accuse their successors of having it easy compared to them. Subsequent administrations were blamed for going soft on discipline to the detriment of the fledgling sailors. Men who had known Shotley before my time made their views known about the classes of 1938. I accept that we were given many small privileges denied to them, like being allowed to wear gym shoes when going 'over the mast'. They climbed the rigging in their bare feet even in the coldest months of winter. Pointing out to them that we still scrubbed and hosed down the roadways in our bare feet with trousers rolled above our knees as icy gusts of easterly winds blew around our legs, failed to impress them. Invidious as it might seem I feel I am justified to compare the treatment of pre-war boys with that of the post war period. When the recruitment of boys was discontinued during the war, to be replaced with conscripts, it was inevitable that the introduction of adult - 'hostilities only'- recruits in 1939 would bring about major changes. The transformation severed the link of continuity with the traditional past and the accepted strict treatment of boys. The mould of pre-war training was finally broken for ever.

After the 1939-45 war Ganges reopened to enlist boy entrants but it was never the same. It is not difficult to recognise the newfound comforts of the reshaped 'Ganges' of the post war to the harsh era of earlier times. When Shotley eventually reverted to its historical role, the new intakes inherited a wellbeing from the conscripts that was unknown luxury to their predecessors. Smoking, which had been a flogging offence in 1938, was permitted. Enhanced pay and leave with 1st Class Boys being allowed weekend leave. Improved recreational and living conditions in the form of central heating, hobbies block and electrically operated bowling alley and an extended library were just some of the comforts. Females, an unknown sight at one time, were evident in the shape of WRENS. Whatever their age, shape or size, they would have enhanced the general appearance of the pre-war training ship and given many a boy's fantasies food for thought. Another big change was the new approach to the catering arrangements and the variety of the menu. A communal dining hall ensured the food was served hot and plentiful. Previously the 'cooks' of the mess had a distance to walk in the open air from the galley to their mess, which meant the food was more often served partly cold.

H.M.S. Ganges finally closed on October 28th.1976, when the White Ensign was lowered for the last time. Gone but not forgotten is an apt phrase because 'Ganges' lived on in the memories of the thousands of aspiring young 'jacks' that once walked up the Long Covered Way at Shotley.

that we were kindred spirits making for the same place so we introduced ourselves. Our small talk was interrupted by the arrival of a smartly turned-out young sailor who asked if we were for 'Ganges'. We eagerly answered in unison that we were. It was evident that he was of some standing because on his uniform sleeve he had a stripe, an anchor and a crown. In the weeks to follow I was to learn that he was one of a rare breed known as an Instructor Boy. Only boys of exceptional ability achieved this prestigious position, for which they remained behind at the training ship, after their classmates had gone to sea, to assist the Instructors. When they did go to sea they carried special recommendations of attainment to their future commanding officers that enhanced their promotion. "Right then, follow me". He spoke with the authority of someone who expected to be obeyed without question. The little party trailed after him until we reached the waterfront jetty where a pinnace was waiting to ferry us across the river to our new home. Nobody had much to say as the boat chugged it's way laboriously to the other side. Having lived most of my life around boats, I felt at ease with the rise and fall of the swell under my feet.

When we landed on the Shotley foreshore the Instructor Boy pointed towards a large complex of bleak structures behind tall iron railings. "That's it, your ship for the next nine months". The first sight of H.M.S. Ganges was a terrible disappointment; it looked like a prison and not what I had conjured up in my mind. The stark buildings and inhospitable atmosphere bore no resemblance to the majestic warship I had expected. Once I overcame the disappointment that my ship was in fact a collection of brick buildings, I started to view the surroundings with considerable interest. Little did I realise as I walked through the rear gates of the 'Stone Frigate' that my world was about to be turned upside down, and remain that way for some time. The only consolation was knowing it would be happening to thousands of others as well. H.M.S. Ganges, before the Second World War, was a frightening introduction to life in the navy. It was an experience that left an indelible mark on the minds of all those who passed through the portals of this infamous training establishment. As we walked up a long covered colonnade, with mess buildings on both sides, I felt conspicuous in my sports jacket and flannel trousers. Groups of young 'blue-jackets' loitering outside their messes took great delight shouting ribald remarks. Most of the jibes were about where we came from. Someone shouted. "Any of you from London"? One of my companions replied in all innocence. "Yes. I'm from London". "Well go back to the 'Smoke' you bloody Cockney git!" was the reply, bringing howls of laughter from the crowd. Then someone else called out "Hey mush! you out of Dartmoor". Realising what to expect I kept my mouth shut, especially when a lad of my own age asked me if I had been in Borstal with him, and another asked what it was like doing a stretch in Sing-Sing. I made a mental note to punch him in the mouth when we met on more equal terms. The Instructor Boy was unperturbed by the verbal tirade showered on us. He had heard it all before and knew that within a few weeks another batch of new entrants would receive similar catcalling from some of us.

At the top of the long covered way we came to a small section of roadway, bounded by offices. The Instructor Boy saluted, explaining that this was the Quarter Deck and in future we must salute and move at the double on it. Saluting the Quarter Deck was an age-old tradition in the navy, going back to medieval times when England was a Catholic country and early sailing ships had a crucifix mounted there. Men coming on board ship turned towards the

Quarter Deck and doffed their hats or touched their forelocks as a mark of respect. Although a crucifix was no longer displayed, saluting towards this part of a ship continued the showing of respect. It might have seemed strange to some newcomers but, whenever practical, it was the long-standing practise to use shipboard terminology and procedures in shore establishments. My time in the Sea Scouts, and the many visits to warships had not been wasted. Although I was already aware of many nautical terms, but there was a tremendous amount I still had to learn. The new language with unique expressions would soon be picked up with daily usage. Dormitories would be known as messdecks, lavatories the 'Heads' and the ground would be the deck.

Walking out through the gates would be 'going ashore'. Whistling was forbidden for a variety of reasons. 'Colours', was raising the White Ensign everyday, to be flown at the same permitted hours as a ship at sea. Most of the strange terms came from the early days of sail, words like 'slops'. Originally it meant the wide breeches worn by seamen during the 17th.and 18th.centuries.

Clothing contractors became known as slop sellers and the name continued to refer to clothing issues. When the Admiralty introduced regulated dress for seamen it also provided it's own clothing store that retained the name 'Slops', meaning regulation issue. The official nautical vocabulary of definitions seemed inexhaustible. It was only matched by the volume of everyday naval colloquialisms, some of which I have listed later in the book. The Instructor Boy collected documents from one of the offices before returning to escort us out through the main gates to another group of buildings further along the road. This smaller version of the 'Ganges', a Kite Balloon Station during the 1914-18 war, was known as the Annex. All newcomers went there for a few weeks of indoctrination. Our civilian clothes were exchanged for a set of second-hand, ill-fitting, serge trousers and jumper. In due course we would be kited out with properly fitting garments. After changing, I joined the others in the dining hall for my first meal in the Navy. I'll never forget it was faggots, which I thoroughly enjoyed and couldn't understand why some of the other lads didn't. Within days things changed and they were glad to eat everything, and anything, put before them to ease the pangs of hunger. The youngsters, between the ages of 15 and 16, came from all over the British Isles and from a variety of backgrounds. Some from middle-class homes, with prospects of good employment, were now kindred spirits with errand boys who had become disenchanted with pushing a delivery bike for a living. 'Geordie', 'Scouse', and Glaswegian Gorbal blended with the singsong of East Anglia and the burr of the West Country to create a confusing cocktail of dialects. That night each boy was shown to an iron bedstead and given two blankets and a pillow but no sheets. As we prepared to turn in, a strange mixture of night attire gave some indication of social backgrounds. It was a mixture of pyjamas, night-shirts, underpants, and 'in the buff'.

The next morning began with the first of many rude awakenings. After breakfast we were taken to the Barber's Shop to suffer the indignity of having our hair cut right down to the scalp. Walking dejectedly back to Quarters in the badly fitting clothes, the shorn locks gave us a tramp-like appearance far removed from that of proud sailor boys. There was every reason to believe the story put about that the barber had served his apprenticeship on an Australian sheep farm. It seemed pointless to mention to the 'Sweeny Todd' scalper that the last recorded pigtail to be worn at sea was on a previous H.M.S. Ganges. Petty Officers lost no time making us aware that 'Ganges' was not a refuge of tranquil seclusion. Any microscopic resemblance to a holiday camp was a gross oversight on the part of the builders. During the first few days several became homesick and suffered the added humiliation and torment of being called 'cissies' and 'mummy's boys' by the others. It applied mostly to those who came from a 'good' home. They found the bleak restricted surroundings alien and miserable. The majority, from homes that considered wall- to- wall lino a luxury, accepted the conditions and fared better. Nevertheless, in varying degrees we all experienced a culture shock during the initial stages; the introduction to 'Ganges' had a sobering effect on us. It was confusing and in some ways frightening, as we struggled to overcome a natural awe while coming to terms with the strictness of the new environment. We got very little sympathy from our Instructors who behaved as if we were all stone deaf and thought it necessary to speak to us in tones, several decibels above the accepted noise levels. The most advantaged youngsters were those who joined straight from Hospital Training Schools like the 'Warspite' and 'Arethusa'. Their previous school syllabus had a strong nautical bearing and they were well versed in seagoing subjects when they arrived at 'Ganges'. The majority were the orphaned sons of men who had served in the Navy. With the exception of the orphanage boys, few had received any encouragement to join. On the contrary, most were actively discouraged by their parents from committing themselves to a long period of continuous service. Any parental advice was philosophically disregarded. As long as boys sought adventure the Royal Navy provided the lure and inducement for them to forsake family and home for a life of challenge, discipline and obedience at sea.

The Annex had it's own parade ground to teach newcomers the rudiments of drill. It was all part of the necessary grounding 'nozzers' received to smarten them up before they were allowed to join their contemporaries in the main long pole. In desperation some grasped the poles spluttering and gasping for breath, only to be shaken off and told to swim or sink. It was a terrifying ordeal, but faced with a limited option boys learnt to move in the water at an accelerated pace. Never before had the 'dog-paddle' come to the rescue of so many near drowning youngsters.

One of the biggest thrills for me was the day I queued at 'Slops' for my new kit. Filling my kit bag with an amazing collection of clothing that catered for my every need was an indescribable feeling. As I eagerly stowed away more personal possessions then I had ever owned in my life, I really felt like a boy sailor in His Majesty's Royal Navy. I returned to the Annex in a happy frame of mind and at peace with the world. Like everyone else, the first task as a precaution against theft, was to print my name on every item of clothing using ink and a name stamp. Next, the tedious, time consuming, chore of chain stitching over the names with cottons. Black cotton was sewn on the white garments and red on the darker things. Progress was constantly checked by the Petty Officers to assess the quantity and quality of our efforts. Pity the poor soul that failed on either count. Some had a natural aptitude for needlework, others had to learn the hard way by having to laboriously unpick and re-do work that failed to pass the P.O.'s critical eye. An Irish lad struggled in vain to keep up, because most of his time was spent unpicking faulty work. He was hopeless at sewing but extremely accomplished at Gaelic dancing so several volunteered to do stitching for him if he would display his talents. On the table top, in his smooth soled 'dorm' slippers, he tapped away entertaining us as we sewed. The Instructors were puzzled by the increased output of his neatly embroidered name. One piece of kit needed special attention, our boots. Spit and polish with a lot of rubbing was the order of the day to produce toe-caps that shone like the sun. Inspections always started at the top but ended with close scrutiny at the feet to make sure lots of elbow grease had been applied to footwear. Some P.O.'s were keen enough to check the insteps to make sure they were as clean as the tops.

A Boy's Kit List

2. Blue Serge Suits	1. Oilskin Coat	2. Black Silks
2. White Duck Suits	2. Lanyards	Money Belt
2. Blue Jerseys	3. Flannel Shirts	3 Collars
4pr. Socks	2pr. Stockings	2pr. Pyjamas
2pr. Shorts	2. Short Shirts	3 Vests
3. Towels	1. Hairbrush & Comb	1 Set Boot Brushes
3. Underpants	2 Blue Handkerchiefs	1pr Overalls
2. Caps with ribbons	1 Ditty Box	1 Hat Box
2pr Boots	1pr. Dormitory Shoes	1pr Gym Shoes
1pr. Football Boots	1 Housewife (Sewing Holdall)	1 Name Stamp
1 Hammock	1 Hammock mattress	1 Mattress Cover
2 Blankets	1 Set Belt & Gaiters	1 Kit Bag
1 Seamanship Manual	1 Admiralty Pattern Knife	

On Leaving For Sea

1 No1. Serge Suit made to measure   1 Heavy Duty Overcoat   1 Gas Mask

2   Mainstream Ganges

In due course our intake was transferred to the 'Ganges' proper, to become No.59 Class Grenville Division. It was exciting to be in the mainstream of the training ship where so much was happening. Wearing white duck suits, two thousand boys paraded for Divisions every morning at 0830hrs. On Sunday, it was a half-hour later at 0900hrs in our best rig of blue serge. The Royal Marine band accompanied the parade and their rendering of 'Blaze Away', 'Rule Britannia', and 'Hearts of Oak' made the lads march tall and feel proud of their calling. After the long columns passed the saluting dais they dispersed in all directions depending on the schedule for the day. 'Ganges' had an impressive land area of approximately 150 acres with excellent playing fields and running tracks. The well-kept sports grounds accommodated football, hockey, rugby and field events of every kind. A championship size swimming pool catered for all types of aquatic activity including water polo. Expense was not spared to develop physical maturity and vigorous competitiveness. Rivalry between the Divisions was keen and actively encouraged. The establishment was virtually a self-contained village with about 80 acres of buildings covering nearly 650,000sq.ft. An additional 1400 yards long foreshore provided a jetty and moorings for the many cutters and whalers. Any misplaced illusions I had that my new Instructors in the barracks would have serene dispositions, or the discipline more relaxed, was soon shattered. It was patently obvious it was going to be even harsher and more exacting than the Annex regime.

Reveille ('Charlie') was sounded at 0630hrs, 0530hrs when it was early morning laundry. From the frantic early morning scramble to wash and dress, until 'Lights Out' at 2000hrs, we were watched and supervised. Every part of the working day was taken up with lessons of one kind or another, be it sport, school, seamanship or gunnery. 'Spiritual needs' was treated as a special subject of immense importance. It was recognised that many boys came from homes with strong religious beliefs. The Chapels were beautifully furnished by the Navy; and run by Ministers of different denominations. The Sky Pilots (clergymen) were respected for their pious calling and acted as the resident 'agony aunts' and 'sin bosuns' to council those with a problem they could not discuss with anyone else.

The Biblical version of the Ten Commandments taught by the clergy differed from the revised Shotley version, which was:-
Thou shall not lend, borrow or steal.
Thou shall not have regrets or complaints.
Thou shall not enter the mess before 1545hrs.
Thou shall not wear a vest under sports gear in winter.
Thou shall not volunteer for anything.
Thou shall not get caught having a 'drag' (smoke).
Thou shall not be adrift.
Thou shall not be last.
Thou shall always cut with your knife towards your friend.
Thou shall do unto others before they do you.

An unfortunate turn of events took place on the 31st.May 1938, when I reported sick with pains in my right knee and ankle. After a thorough medical examination I was confined to the Sick Quarters. This was a well-equipped cottage hospital, with full medical, surgical and dentistry staff to cater for sick boys. Returning to duty, and because of missed lessons, I was back-classed to No.69 Class. Thankfully I slotted into my new surroundings with ease, and without regrets.

Ganges had forty-eight messes divided into eight divisions commemorating some of the great Admirals of the past, Collinwood, Grenville, Hawke, Anson, Blake, Drake, Rodney and Benbow. My new home in No.23 Mess, Anson Division had much the same layout as the other messes. Inside the entrance was a night 'Heads' [night time lavatory] next to a washroom. There was a dining space with four stout tables and bench seats, the only furniture in the Mess. During the evenings the boys found it more convenient to sit on the floor where there was more room to stretch out. The stark bleakness encouraged everyone to spend as much time out of doors as possible when the weather permitted. The largest part of the living quarters was taken up with a dormitory. It's wooden deck had a mirror appearance from continuous waxing and burnishing with remnants of old serge uniforms. It was sacrosanct, and punishable, to walk on it with everyday footwear. Only 'Dorm' slippers or stocking feet was allowed to prevent scratching the highly polished surface. The legs of the beds lining both sides of the dormitory stood on bed-chocks [wooden blocks] for the same reason. Two coke/coal-burning stoves, one at each end, never provided enough warmth in the winter. It was worse when the dreaded Captain's inspection was due, adding to our cold comfort because the fires couldn't be lit. During the evening previous to his inspection, the insides of the stoves were whitewashed and the coals in the buckets washed. It was another small example of the many inconveniences we put up with to present a spotlessly clean image to the man who controlled our lives. His nod of approval was necessary for us to escape the wrath of our Petty Officers. "I want this place shining like a brand new shilling on a pigs backside, or else" was P.O.Rook's repeated warning when the Captain's 'rounds' were due.

In addition to the many ancillary teachers, our two Instructors Petty Officers Cardew and Rook were directly responsible for supervising the mess, controlling the general behaviour of the boys, and teaching the two main core subjects of Seamanship and Gunnery. Our course tutors remained with us for the duration of the training, and would be answerable to the Divisional Officer, Lieut.Battersby, for the standards achieved in the final examinations. Both were disciplinarians but good Instructors, with their own individual idiosyncrasies. Admittedly they could use their whistle chains, toe of their boot, or fists with great effect. Cardew took the gunnery classes and Rook the seamanship lessons. P.O.Cardew's kindest words, used all too often, were " Come here you bloody little crow". It was the warning to watch his boot before it made contact with the seat of your trousers. Needless to say Instructors and Officers were always addressed as 'Sir'. Boys stood to attention when spoken to, and all rank above Petty Officer was saluted. Thankfully our two Class Instructors were not as vindictive as some of the other Petty Officers. Physical Training Instructors in particular seemed to delight in showing their prowess with a swift clout and a kick to those who lacked courage and speed on the gym apparatus.

Punishment was inflicted, officially and unofficially. The official versions were well defined by the King's Rules and Admiralty Instructions. These were classified by numbers depending on the severity of the crime. It varied in degrees from extra work, stoppage of leave and privileges, to flogging and based on the principle that physical pain was essential if it was to be effective. Flogging was never formally abolished in the Royal Navy, although it was suspended in 1879. Unfortunately this did not apply to boy seamen and flogging was still administered at the 'Ganges' in 1939 for such severe misdemeanours as smoking cigarettes. I suppose in some ways we youngsters were grateful that keelhauling and ducking had long since disappeared officially from the records for all classes, or some Instructors might have gladly used them. Those unlucky enough to be flogged did receive concessions. They were allowed to stand at mealtimes and in class because it was too painful for them to sit down. At night they were permitted to sleep on their stomachs and endure their pain in silence. The birch, laid with precision around the buttocks, produced red-blue weal that made a backside look like a piece of raw meat and took weeks to heal. The maximum number of strokes given at any one time by the Master at Arms was twelve, and under medical supervision. It was a severe way to stress the necessity of obeying the basic rules of the ship, and boys who had been flogged said that the experience was vividly implanted in their minds forever.

Because smoking was forcefully prohibited it was seen as an irresistible challenge to pit wits against authority. The threat of flogging did not eliminate the trading and smoking of tobacco. A well organised black market flourished to supply the 'Dragger's Needs' at a price. Involvement with nicotine was an expensive affair, it cost a third of a weeks pay for a single Woodbine. This made sharing a necessity; one fag passed several 'gaspers' lips before the butt end became too tiny to puff. Then it was recycled with other fag ends to do the rounds again. Smuggling matches was an unprofitable risk, especially as getting a 'free' light was never a problem. The method passed down from class to class was to sharpen two pencils at both ends and spark them across the electricity mains in the switch box, the arcing was sufficient to light a cigarette without blowing the fuse.

A much disliked punishment was one known as 'Shotley Routine', particularly detested because it was total class 'Jankers'. It also inconvenienced the Petty Officers who were detailed to supervise it.
They resented the extra duties it created and took their spite out on the defaulters. 69 Class in the months ahead suffered the unpleasant experience of Shotley Routine that I will relate in more detail later. 'Janker' boys doing official punishment received little sympathy from the other boys, the consensus of opinion was "if you got caught, then you deserved to be punished". Unofficial punishment took many forms and Instructors could make life very unpleasant. They could instigate extra drill, doubling up and down laundry hill with a rifle and pack, doing extra work, or just a blow with the hand or a kick in the backside. The use of the dreaded 'Stonniky' was another painful reminder to any boy who failed to move faster than a weaver's shuttle when told to 'look lively'. Originally it was a ropes end topped with a large 'Matthew Walker' knot, designed and used effectively in earlier times to make seamen climb swiftly into the rigging to set sails. The use of stonnickies was officially restricted in 1890, but again this did not apply to training ships. In later years the ropes end was replaced by a length of hard rubber that was just as painful especially so when wielded with the

devastating effect of a Boer policeman's sjambok. The 'last' boy at anything ran the risk of receiving a taste of this infamous implement.

Troublesome characters unwilling to yield readily to the strict rules and discipline were categorised as a 'thorn in the side' or a 'pain in the arse'. For their trouble they received the full awesome wrath of the Instructors until they accepted the inevitable and conformed. It would be unfair to portray an exaggerated picture of fiendish Officers and Instructors motivated by the cruel instincts of sadistic bullies. They saw themselves as the keepers of long held traditions handed down for preserving. Entrusted with the continuity of time-honoured practises and customs they enforced them to the best of their ability, even if it meant Draconian discipline. In all probability outside the confines of the barracks they were kind and considerate family men who, through circumstances, led a Jekyll and Hyde lifestyle. They had a limited time to fashion a 'Ganges' boy with seamanship qualities unsurpassed by any other training establishment. The one-upmanship reputation of Shotley was jealously preserved by boys long after they had left for sea. At the end of the course the Instructors were expected to have produced morally, physically, and mentally strong able-bodied young men worthy of being an integral part of, and a credit to, the Senior Service. A large picture of a serious looking individual on the recreation space wall was a constant reminder of a previous 'Ganges' achiever. He was Rear-Admiral Thomas John Lyne who joined H.M.S. Lion at Devonport in 1884 as a boy seaman and rose through the ranks to become a Flag Officer. It was supposed to prove to us that any boy with initiative could do the same. To the budding bluejackets it was a PR exercise that didn't fool anyone; they knew the reality was something very different. The number who actually achieved high rank could be counted on the fingers of one hand. Officers came from cadet establishments like Britannia where a mixture of patronage, family connections, public school education, as well as social and professional background formed the main criterion for entry and advancement.

Most boys knew the limitations of a lower deck entry but it did not stop them trying to be the best. Needless to say we did not meet with the total approval of everyone in high places. On one occasion Admiral Edward Evans (Evans of the 'Broke') demonstrated this when he paid a visit to Shotley. His exploits as captain of the destroyer H.M.S. Broke during the First World War was legendary and made him famous. After an inspection he gave a slide show and talk about his involvement with Captain Scott's ill-fated expedition to the South Pole. Those of us selected to attend the lecture felt privileged to hear the great man's adventure story. As a Lieutenant, Admiral Evans was with the party up to the last staging post before Captain Scott made his fatal dash to the Pole. The Admiral's namesake, Petty Officer Evans, was one of those nominated to carry on with Scott and never returned. The Admiral spoke about the rigours of life on board ship, and the struggle across the icy wastelands of the Antarctic. I was in awe at his reminiscences until he came to the conclusion of his talk, then he spoilt it for me and I think every other boy present. He finished by saying "Of course when I was a lad the ships were made of wood and the men of steel, today it is the other way around". It was an odious and caustic comparison to end an otherwise exciting lecture. With hindsight he probably regretted it when the boys he demeaned were survivors of the first ships sunk when war started. Others in the hall did not survive the first six months of the hostilities.

The disastrous happenings in Europe, caused by Hitler's expansion programme during May and June 1938, brought the threat of enemy attack. Lack of readiness for war and weakened defences caused a national crisis. Fortunately, Britain still maintained a naval strength and for additional support the reserve fleet was quickly mobilised. The Navy, as in times past, would be the first line of defence and a bulwark against invasion. Harwich, once an influential naval port since early times, lost it's importance to the bigger ports of Chatham, Portsmouth and Devonport. The threat of war revived it's value as a base for the destroyer flotillas operating in the English Channel. In the 1914-18 war, German Zeppelins dropped bombs on Ganges and it was possible a similar attack could take place again. H.M.S. Ganges entered into the spirit of things by digging trenches and air raid shelters, filling sandbags, and spreading barbed wire. Contingency plans were made for many of the staff to leave at short notice if war was declared. The reservists already placed on standby for call up would replace them. The threat of war receded with the signing of the Munich Agreement on the 29th.September 1938. Chamberlain, Daladier, Mussolini and Hitler were in accord about the futility of all out war, at least for the time being. 'Ganges' returned to it's normal routine without having suffered any apparent loss of training due to the Crisis.

By now I had been promoted to Leading Boy and entitled to wear a stripe on the sleeve of my jumper. It meant an increase in pay of three pence a week [apprx.10 new pence], it also brought certain responsibilities. The well being of the Mess and the discipline of the class were amongst the many duties 'badge' boys were expected to carry out when the Instructors were not about. The P.O.s came down heavily on them if they failed to meet their obligations to the full. I shared the onus with two other Leading Boys, Jones and Gregory, and a Petty Officer Boy by the name of Dredge. The 'perk' of the stripe was to supervise someone else to do the dirty jobs instead of doing them myself.

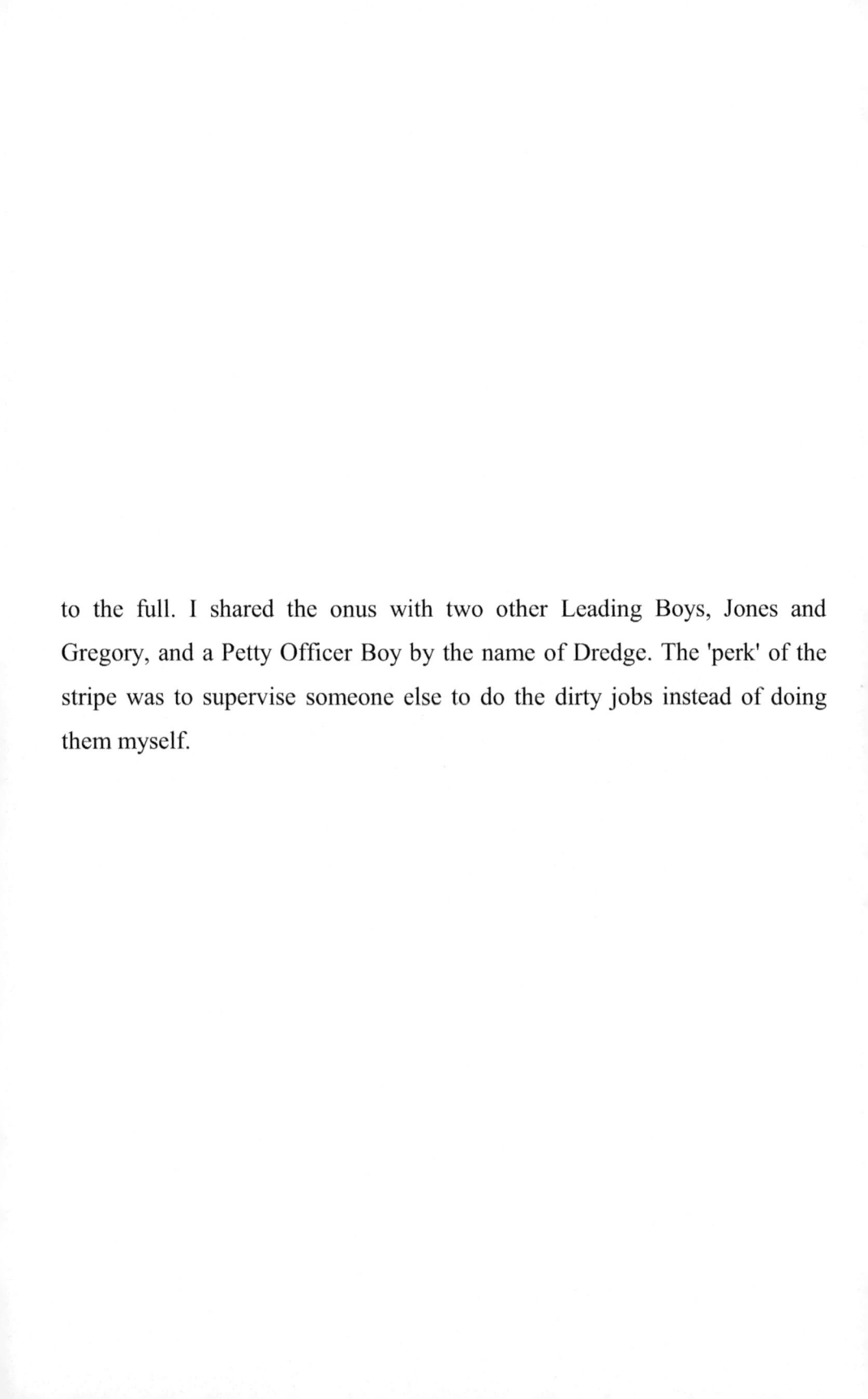

3 "Away Aloft"

Shotley's most imposing landmark, at the Quarter Deck end of the parade ground, was a fully rigged ships' mast reaching 150ft into the sky. Equally impressive was the large figurehead of a brightly coloured Indian prince in front of the mast. Mast drill was considered an essential part of our training to develop self-confidence as well as providing an awareness of ships' rigging. The mast was not a legacy of the sailing ship 'Ganges', the lower part came in 1907 from the corvette H.M.S.Cordella that paid off in 1900. The other parts came from H.M.S.Agincourt, later renamed 'Ganges' 2. My first encounter with this giant, towering high above the deck, was one of cautious respect. To most it was a vehicle of escape from the preying eyes of Instructors, to others it was an intimidating scourge. The higher I climbed the tarred rope ratlines the more exhilarating it became. Like most of the class, much of my spare time on Saturday and Sunday afternoons was spent scrambling up and down the rigging until the novelty wore off. Afterwards I climbed mainly to achieve the passing out speed for going over the mast in three minutes. At first it seemed an impossible target but with a little practise and determination it was within the capability of almost everyone. When the drill was carried out as a supervised instruction, the whole class 'fell in" at the front of the mast in lines of six abreast. On the command "man the rigging" the first line moved forward to take up positions at the ratlines between the shrouds. The next order "way aloft" sent them scurrying like agile monkeys high into the rigging determined to excel. With the Petty Officer watching it was prudent to show an eagerness to climb without signs of fear. The shrouds narrowed under the platform at the top of the lower mast, restricting the number of places in the rigging from six to three. It was crucial to get to this point as swiftly as possible and claim a place, otherwise precious time was lost. Pushing and elbowing was the name of the game, no quarter was asked for and none given.

The first real obstacle was the large wooden platform known as the 'Top'. Boys were not permitted to go through the opening in the 'Top' known as 'Lubber's hole', except in leisure periods. Even in free time it was considered cissy to take the soft option. The ropes of the Futtock rigging ran out from the shrouds to the edge of the platform aptly named the 'Devil's Elbow'. Climbing the rigging around the 'Top' meant leaning backward at 45 degrees to the ground with a straight drop down. It was difficult and time consuming to retain a foothold while negotiating the edge of the platform to reach up to the ratlines of the upper mast. Unless one went at a snail's pace or had the skills of a contortionist the only practical way was to let the legs dangle in space and rely on the strength of arm to haul the body upwards and around the edge of the 'Top'. It needed a little confidence in one's own ability, and it was not the officially prescribed way of doing it, but it worked best. The problem was still there on the descent and the solution was the same. The few who froze on the infamous elbow during the early days of training got additional early morning mast drill. Instructor Boys were sent aloft to convince the faint-hearted that a taste of the dreaded Stonniky was much more unpleasant then fear of the 'Devil's Elbow'. The howls of the timid as they felt the painful strokes could be heard across the parade ground by those on early duties. The golden rule applied 'Do what you are told whatever your feelings of fear might be, and do it now.'

On ceremonial occasions eighty-five smartly dressed young matelots manned the mast to give a splendid display. At the very top, on an eleven inch circle of wood, stood the 'button' boy. With his arms outstretched and gripping the lightening conductor with his knees, he held the position coveted by many of his contemporaries. Mast drill was a very minute part of a well-devised and professionally carried out curriculum. Apart from the many ancillary subjects the accent was mainly on school, seamanship and gunnery. At the time the Seaman Branch was recognised as the senior in the Royal Navy, making it understandable why seamanship subjects received special attention. It was a comprehensive training programme that included every facet of rope work, and every item and style of boat construction and sail. Boys were expected to know all the types of hawsers, shackles, slips, anchors and cable they would encounter on a seagoing ship.

In addition to the practical training of rowing and sailing in clinker built 32/34 ft. cutters and 27 ft. whalers, a lot of time was given to classroom subjects. This included navigation and chart plotting, flags and signals, as well as the design and construction of warships. It was hard luck for the boy who could not remember the difference between a 'crow's foot' on a log and the 'bee's knees' in a boat. With so much to cram in before the regular assessment times the seamanship manual was never far from a boy's hand. Everyone studied hard, afraid of being 'dipped' for low marks. It was inevitable that some were slower at learning and I thought it unfair to always regard them as 'back sliders'. The Instructors had little sympathy for those who struggled to make the grades. Their verbal remedy was cold comfort to the ones who were making a genuine effort with their studies. "If you stopped buggering about and read your manual more often you could pass with ease" was the Petty Officer's cure all. Fortunately I came to Ganges with a good knowledge of boats similar to the types used at Shotley. The Sloop rigged cutters and the Montague rigged whalers were identical to the ones in the Sea Scout troop at home. My recognition and familiarity with the sails and rigging didn't go unnoticed, never one to hide my light under a bushel I had no inhibitions about airing by knowledge. In due course I was allowed to select a crew and coxswain my own boat in sailing races, and I did with some merit. I had a love for sail and enjoyed the frequent visits on the water, especially when I had the tiller.

Sailing 'close hauled' in a fresh breeze, with the boat heeling to the extremes of it's accepted limits, is a wonderful feeling. Coupled with the challenge, the thrill of competitiveness, and the fact that it was an escape from the watchful eye of the instructors made sailing an attractive pastime. Rowing was less appealing, particularly when pulling against the tricky Harwich tides or when Petty Officer Cardew decided to take the boat away. He had a nasty habit of unshipping the tiller, stepping along the thwarts and whacking any unfortunate he considered was not pulling his weight or responding to commands. Failure to 'feather' the blades of the oars or simply 'catching a crab' could invoke his wrath.

The Gunnery Instructor was responsible to our Gunnery Officer, Mr.Potter, for implementing a thorough grounding in weaponry. It covered a wide range from Field Gun, .303 and .22 rifle shooting to the inevitable rifle drill on the parade ground. The Gunners had an amusing store of adjectives for anyone who fumbled a movement, always well received except by the hapless bungler. The gunnery course included 6" heavy gun drill in the

Battery. Whatever the exercise the Instructor could always vent his spleen on a class by making them sweat and ache if he wished, and he often did. Running around the parade ground with a field gun and ammunition limber before dismantling it, then carrying the sections over numerous obstacles before reassembling it and running around again, and again, could be sheer hell.

Rifle drill was always very precise and exacting. The Gunner's Mates barked their orders to put extra snap into every movement and heaven help the lad who failed to march with a stiff straight back and rifle shouldered at the right angle. "You are the Senior Service not bloody pongos or bloody 'fly' boys" [RAF]. "You, the corkscrew, straighten up you bloody crow"." If you don't want my boot up your arse you'll keep in line". These were some of the milder remarks we were bombarded with. The parade ground rang to the crunch of boots, marching and counter marching, the beat of the correct step kept by the frequent shouting of "Left, right, left, by the gunner. It was always a feeling of relief to fall out and return our rifles knowing that for another day our tired muscles could rest. That was unless mast drill, rowing or physical training instruction was not still on the day's schedule.

"Wisdom is Strength" was a fitting motto for H.M.S.Ganges. In 1939 the senior schoolmaster, Instructor Commander A.J.Low M.A., controlled a staff of forty-one schoolmasters to teach the academic subjects in the curriculum. They were mostly degree teachers whose prime object was to give boys who had not mastered Algebra, Trigonometry, English, Science and History at their previous school, another chance to do so. The school buildings were new and well designed. The classrooms were light, airy, and equipped to a high standard. It must be said that the Admiralty were extremely generous with their funding to educate the new generation of seamen coming into the Service. Discipline was never relaxed in the schoolrooms. One of my teachers, an Instructor Lieutenant, had a vile practise of throwing the blackboard eraser at anyone he suspected of talking behind his back in class. Whenever he turned from the board and raised his arm it was the danger signal for all the class to get ready to duck. He also had a nasty tendency of walking up and down the room peering over boys' shoulders as they were writing. If he spotted a bad mistake he would give the culprit a good clout, pass some facetious remark and walk on as if nothing had happened, leaving the poor soul with a tingling ear. One of his favourite sayings was "You are slow but sure, young man". Then after a short pause he would continue "Slow to learn and sure to forget". I remember an occasion when someone passed a funny remark and the other boys sniggered, but made sure to keep their heads bowed. The Teacher came down the room and said to the boy. "Methinks young man you must be a thespian".

Innocently or just 'acting green' he replied. "No sir, I'm Church of England". It was a Freudian slip that earned him a boxed ear that took on a deep shade of red.

4   Shotley Routine

On one memorable occasion as the class waited outside the mess for dinner call, a 'Crusher' was spotted on the prowl. Diligently he circled the lavatories looking for telltale wisps of smoke haze. The intricate system of look-outs to warn of approaching danger seemed to have broken down. Realising the situation, several of our class instinctively shouted "Lobs, lobs, lobs", the abbreviation for look out boys, to alert any smokers in the Heads. The 'Crusher' stopped in his tracks, abandoned stalking his prey and came over to confront a now dumbstruck 69 Class. He had lost a couple of potential 'Draggers' in the Heads but scooped up a whole class of defaulters instead, not a bad catch. There was an uncalled for expressions of triumph on his face as he eyed us in silence, aware that we were dreading what was about to happen. He was obviously a vindictive man, enjoying the spartan misery he was about to inflict. He marched us to the Regulating Office to be charged with an offence under the King's Rules and Admiralty Instructions, which put us all in Commander's report. Several of the lads willingly owned up to shouting the warning but their admissions were ignored and the class received 14 days Shotley Routine. Even those not present at the time of the incident were not excused.

Shotley Routine was an irritating punishment levied collectively on a whole class. It's sole objective was to inflict as much misery as possible. Roughly awakened long before reveille we mustered, sleepy-eyed, for extra work. Except for meals, entry to our mess was barred until bedtime. The restrictions also applied to us going into other messes, the recreation room, gym and swimming baths. It was our hard luck to be doing Shotley Routine when the weather was very chilly. Standing around outside was downright unpleasant especially as our area was open to the gusts of bitterly cold easterly winds that blew in from the sea. Mealtimes were practically non-existent; before we had time to sit down properly we were ordered outside again. Food was grabbed by the handful and eaten on the move. All privileges and pay were stopped immediately. Every spare minute was taken up with additional work or punishing drills. It was especially hurtful on Saturday and Sunday afternoons when we should have been having a 'make and mend' with the rest of the ship.

Aware of the agonising time ahead, two of our most knowledgeable 'Janker' boys offered to give us a few tips, from their personal experiences, on how to reduce the pain of punishment. The best lad was O'Grady, a tough, highly intelligent and thoroughly likeable character. He didn't have much to say for himself but he had a history of exploits that commanded the respect of the class. Over a period of time he had been flogged far more than most, as well as 'dipped' from class to class before ending up in 69. It was all part and parcel of the punishments he received for absconding and generally misbehaving. On the last occasion he was reputed to have swum across the wide river Stour with his clothes tied in a bundle on his head. The busy shipping river with it's treacherous currents would deter the most daring but not O'Grady who was a brilliant swimmer. His determination to get discharged from the navy brought him nothing but trouble. By the time he had been put through the 'grinder' and joined us he was beginning to accept that the Admiralty had no intention of discharging him. The official policy was to be, and seen to be, unyielding in their resolve to stop boys opting out of their contract. The slightest show of leniency would have been an open invitation for every boy who found the going hard to try for his ticket.

O'Grady's crash course included advice to keep our feet as close to the ground as possible when doubling for long periods. This was known as the 'Shotley Shuffle' and when properly carried out conserved much needed energy and eased the strain on the legs. It was unanimously agreed that O'Grady and his mate would lead the class on the parade ground. This way they would set the pace to ensure a steady rhythmic shuffle. On the first day we were unfortunate enough to have a nimble-witted GI who saw through the ploy. Possibly when he was a boy he had done the Shotley shuffle himself. He changed the column leaders and ordered us to lift our feet and quicken the pace. Every time the Petty Officers changed we tried it on again, sometimes with success. Dressed in canvas suits, gaiters and webbing, and shouldering a .303 Lee-Enfield rifle we had to put up with hour after hour of exhausting square-bashing, much of it not in the drill manual. The second Gunner's Mate who took us was an unmitigated bastard with ideas of crippling us all for life. In fairness to him, he could have been relaxing in his mess instead of doing extra drill duty, we were keeping him on his feet and he was going to make us pay for that. After doubling around the parade ground a forgotten number of times with our arms up stretched holding the rifle, he introduced a muscle aching, knees bend programme into the schedule. Hopping like frogs, still holding the rifles over our heads, he seemed to delight in cuffing anyone who fell over, accusing them of doing it on purpose.

When he tired of this torment he had us back doubling again. This time he made us bring our knees right up as far as we could lift them to our chins. Every sinew protested violently as we attempted the impossible and every bone felt as if it was about to break. Even after 'lights out' we didn't escape the misery. Just when we should have been getting to sleep a Petty Officer would arrive, switch on the lights, and order everyone to dress and fall in outside. Satisfied he had inconvenienced us enough, he allowed us back to bed. The loss of sleep at both ends of the day brought on a weariness that showed on our faces, but there was no let up. A bigger loss was my pay of nine pennies [4 pence in today's money]; it really was a hard blow. It might seem a small amount today but it was a weeks allowance then for a few small luxuries. When boys got their coppers it was a dash to the recreation space to splash out on a bottle of fizzy drink and two 'Charlie' cakes, known as Nelson's squares. The cakes were made of a Christmas pudding type filling between two slices of pastry. It didn't matter much what they were made of or that they seemed to be the only choice, boys never lost their appetite for them to fill a hole. After the pay day 'blow out' there was enough to buy a stamp for the letter home. The loss of pay meant that for two weeks we were to forfeit the gastronomic pleasures.

Ironically we still had to muster for pay parade with the rest of the 2000 boys. Approaching the Paymaster's table, I held out my upturned hat and called my number. In a loud voice the clerk answered "Not entitled" (known in the navy as a north-easter). I smartly replaced my hat and doubled away reflecting on the price we were paying for that warning shout. With untold relief our punishment came to an end. It was sheer bliss to 'flake-out' around the mess stoves and sing popular ditties like 'When the War Broke Out in

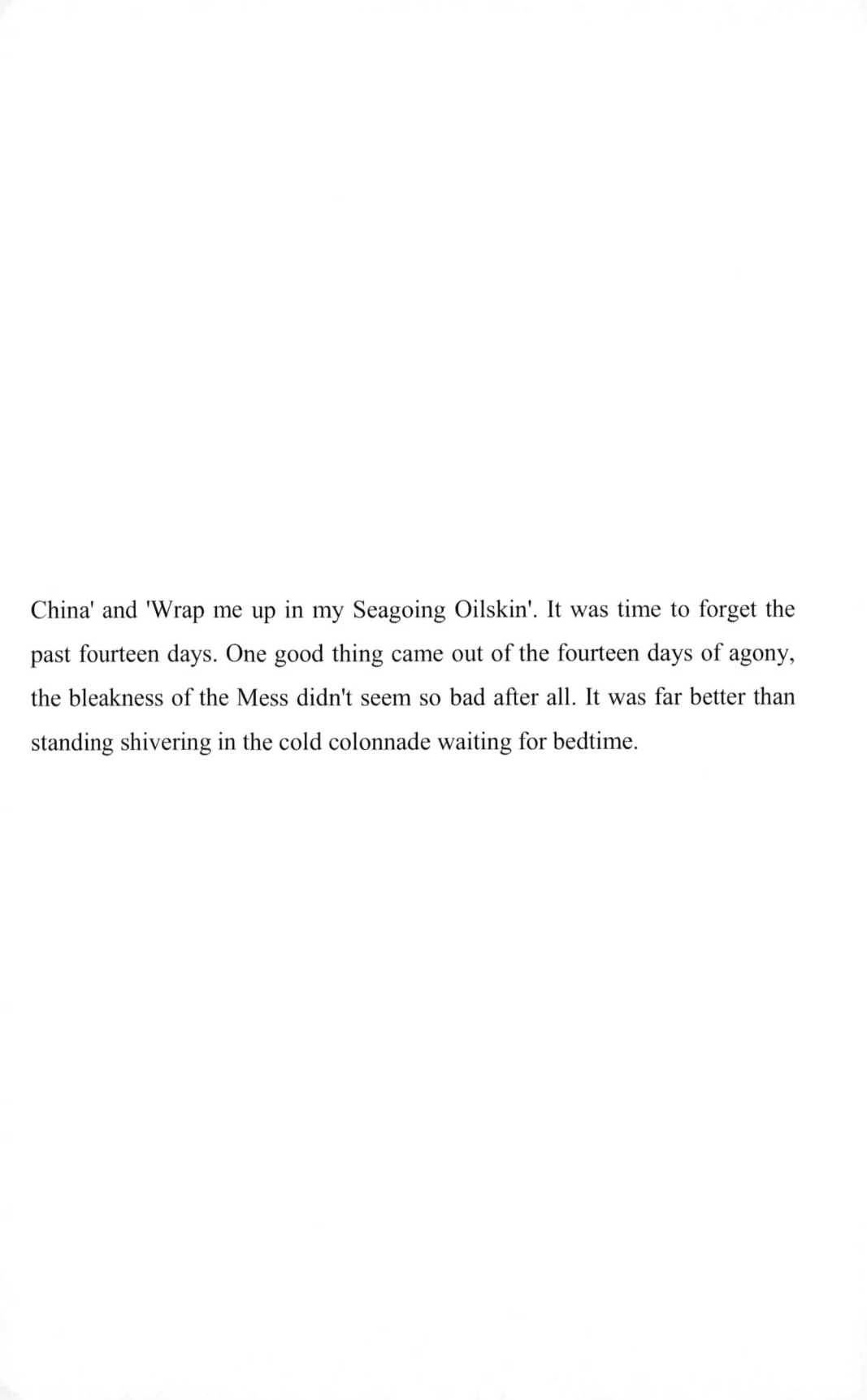

China' and 'Wrap me up in my Seagoing Oilskin'. It was time to forget the past fourteen days. One good thing came out of the fourteen days of agony, the bleakness of the Mess didn't seem so bad after all. It was far better than standing shivering in the cold colonnade waiting for bedtime.

5 Topical Topics

Next to the incessant chatter about girls and draft, the favourite babble of animated conversation centred on food and leave. Training ship 'scran' was wholesome, but for youngsters who used up considerable energy in a strenuous daily lifestyle it was never enough to satisfy. There was little need to cater for delicate stomachs; nothing was ever left on the aluminium dinner plates. We were always hungry and impatiently looking forwards to the next meal to satisfy our gigantic appetites. 'Cooks to the galley' was the most welcome bugle call of the day, it made the taste buds of two thousand boys work overtime. Mess cooks were allowed out early from lessons to collect the food from the galley and start the eagerly awaited feeding ritual. Because of the distance to some of the messes the food was often eaten half-cold, but nobody cared. Badge Boys supervised the serving to see that it was shared fairly. Human nature being what it was, they were not above giving themselves an extra spoonful. The class remained outside the Mess until the order was given to march in and sit down. Grace was said before the food disappeared at an alarming rate of knots down the throats of the hungry 'gannets'.

The role of 'cooks' was rotated to ensure every boy took his turn, including washing up afterwards, returning the dishes to the galley, and cleaning up the dining area. On Saturday and Sunday free periods, boys stood outside the galley door, volunteering to scrub and wash equipment for the cookhouse staff on the promise of some 'gash' that had been left over from the cooking. Usually only the first few were lucky but it never deterred others from waiting on the off chance of leftovers.

Few were fortunate enough to receive food parcels from home, but there was one boy in my Mess from Colchester lucky enough to occasionally get one. It always contained a tin of pears and a tin of thick Nestles cream. He annoyed the rest of us when he ceremoniously opened both tins and ate the lot. He never even offered the juice to any of the onlookers, which earned him the label of 'greedy pig'.

Leave was another subject never far from our minds. Local leave was practically non-existent during the school term. The favoured Instructor Boys had the choice of visiting either Ipswich or Harwich. Second Class boys were not allowed outside the barracks at all. First Class boys could go out once a week on Sunday afternoons for approximately two hours. With no town nearby the leave consisted of walking up the country road, around in a horseshoe and back again. The area known as Shotley Village was made up of a couple of small shops and a few houses. Before going 'ashore' we lined up dressed in our best serge uniform to be inspected and warned:

>Not to smoke.
>
>Not to go into the shops.
>
>Not to converse with females.

'Crushers' patrolled the road on bicycles to keep a watchful eye on everything that moved and especially anything that didn't. It might not have seemed worth the bother of dressing up to go for a walk but psychologically it mattered to be able to go out through the big gates. I can only remember, not intimately, one female in the village known affectionately as Shotley 'Lil'. According to the bragging of the First Class boys to their less fortunate

2nd.Class juniors, she must have put herself about with each and every one of three or four hundred lads every Sunday afternoon.

Term end leave was a generous allowance, two weeks at Easter, three in the summer and two at Christmas. 'Tids for leave' was the much used expression as boys pressed, brushed and polished their kit to look good for going home. When the day of departure approached the excitement was infectious as we packed our belongings for an early exodus the next day. Just after four in the morning we boarded buses for Ipswich railway station. As the vehicles pulled away from Shotley it was a signal for intense activity. A wide assortment of naval badges appeared for sale, to be frantically sewn on to uniforms. Where they all originated from was a mystery, although some were known to come from brothers and fathers serving in the navy, probably unaware what they were to be used for. The fact that it was an offence to wear them, having not been earned, didn't matter. They were a means of attracting impressionable young ladies during the leave. At the station, the tobacco kiosk did brisk trade with a long queue forming to take the first opportunity to buy cigarettes. It was amusing to see trains pulling out with boys hanging out of the carriage windows, cigarettes defiantly dangling from their mouths and sleeves festooned with long service badges, diver's helmets, coxswain's wheels and torpedomen's 'tin fish'. I had to settle for my Leading Boys stripe. It was the era when servicemen wore their uniforms on leave. Living in Torquay with a high density of mature naval personnel, and in close proximity to Plymouth, I would have been quickly recognised as a fraud too young to qualify for specialist badges. Away from Shotley, we took to wearing our hats on the back of our heads in a breezy manner and adopting a savoir-faire swagger. We assumed it portrayed the "I've been to exotic places and seen strange things" image that would appeal to the girls. With hindsight I'm convinced nobody was taken in by such pretentious adolescence.

Unfortunately the old saying 'All the nice girls love a sailor' did have regional differences. Before the war, sections of the general public had a love-hate relationship with sailors depending on the area. Any girl walking arm in arm with a 'Jack Tar' in the naval ports of Plymouth, Portsmouth or Chatham, could expect a few snide remarks and a loss of respect from the local inhabitants. Their long association with carefree matelots was not always remembered as the most cordial. Fathers were known to confine their daughters to the house when the fleet was in port. I vividly remember an extreme instance in 1939 when a well known seaside town put a notice in one of it's parks saying 'Dogs and sailors not admitted'. Light-heartedly the sailors complained that the dogs had been given preference on the notice board. The National Press brought the incident to public notice and the council concerned had it promptly taken down. It was a sad reflection of the low opinion some people had of the navy. Within months, war was declared and the same town was proclaiming undying support for 'our gallant navy' in the fight against that evil monster Adolf Hitler. In all fairness it had to be said that dance halls and pubs could be laid waste, by sailors, at the slightest provocation. When Jack was 'tanked up' it only needed one insulting remark about his ship to cause mayhem. It gave the Navy bad publicity it could well do without. For some a bloody brawl was the icing on the cake for a run ashore, fortunately they were in the minority. When the Fleet sailed into Tor Bay after summer manoeuvres the whole the area became a mass of blue serge uniforms that put fear into the hearts of girl's parents but plenty of money into the pockets of local traders, especially pub landlords. I never suffered any discriminations or adverse remarks in Torquay. On the contrary, people I had little contact with before I joined the navy made me welcome. I suppose being on 'home' ground made a difference.

My first leave was a momentous occasion, the feeling of total freedom was exhilarating and I enjoyed every moment of it. I must have looked good in my uniform; well at least my mother said I did. Meeting with some of my former school friends was not the same as before, the old rapport had gone. I had matured beyond their parochial chin-wagging and it bored me. We remained good pals but my interests lay elsewhere and I realised it was me that had changed not them. Dance nights at Torquay Town Hall acted like a magnet to the young people of the district. It was the place to mix and have fun, the ideal event for boy to meet girl. My quickstep lacked finesse but it didn't deter some young ladies from getting up and having a twirl around the floor with me. On my first visit I spotted the girl I wanted to spend my leave with. After a couple of circles around the dance floor I found out she told lies as well, she said I was a good dancer. The offer to walk her out and to see the latest attraction at the Electric cinema was duly accepted. I knew then that the leave was going to be a success, and it was.

All too soon it was time to return to Shotley and reality. My newly found girlfriend fondly kissed me goodbye at the station, in return I proclaimed undying love and a promise to write soon and often. With hindsight I should have memorised her address because in the hustle and bustle of settling back I misplaced her details.

Groups of returning boys displayed a definite lack of enthusiasm as they scurried back before the deadline. First we went through the showers and then a medical check before getting the all clear to go to our messes. There was no room for false modesty as we lined up stark naked to be inspected. Particularly when the doctor lifted our 'private' parts with his pencil and looked at them as if it was something the dog had left on the pavement. Misery was written all over a number of faces, their stay at home made the return journey an ordeal. Most of us were too preoccupied exaggerating tales of our exploits at home to feel homesick. Stories seemed to get better and better with the telling but no one bothered to contradict or question as the revelations reached a degree of impossibility, particularly about the female conquests.

6 Farewell to Shotley

My time at Shotley was nearing its end, and there was a general feeling of anxiety in the Mess as we prepared for, amongst other things, the dreaded final kit inspection. Evenings were spent 'pointing' and 'grafting' the clews and lashings of our hammocks as well as swotting hard for the final exams in seamanship, gunnery and school. To fail any one of the subjects would mean being held back from going to sea. It was a thought that put the fear of death into every boy. Happily everything went well and the course was finally over. During the last week at Shotley the time was spent working 'part of ship'. The boys were given various jobs inside the barracks as they waited for the finalising of their draft papers. I suspect the work schedule was conceived to keep us out of mischief rather than what we contributed to the well being of the 'ship'. I was employed on a hand operated spirit duplicator in the General Office. Although I liked doing it, the last few days dragged on agonisingly slow.

After one year and seventeen days the time finally came for me to leave for sea with the rest of my class. My Official Number was to be D/JX158438. The D was for Devonport and the JX meant I was on continuous long service. It was an exciting time for everyone as we eagerly prepared to be drafted to our first real ship. It was also a very nostalgic time, knowing that we were to be split up between the three depots of Devonport, Chatham and Portsmouth. Most boys had formed solid friendships that would in many cases stand the test of time, even though they were going to different ships. The non-stop talking after 'lights out' the night before leaving made sleep impossible. It was astonishing there was so much to say after so long in each others company. Equally amazing was to see all the class, even the normally late sleepers, up, washed, dressed and packed, long before 'Charlie' sounded. Everyone seemed to be shaking hands with everyone else and making promises to keep in touch. There was an atmosphere of celebration with just a touch of genuine sadness. It was a moving occasion and I suspect several had lumps in their throats as they said their farewells. Any lingering bad feelings that might have existed between boys were forgotten. For me personally it meant saying goodbye to those I had been friendly with, knowing that I might never meet them again. Wonderful lads, like O'Grady, Harrison, Butler, Dredge, Jones, Gregory, and Pirie to name but a few. When Petty Officers Cardew and Rook came to the Mess to say farewell and wish each of us Bon Voyage, they got an almighty cheer. The class began to sing one of the famous 'Ganges' songs but it sounded more like a dirge.

To me H.M.S.Ganges was an enigma, a contradiction in terms. On one hand the authorities were over considerate, they spared nothing for the physical and mental development of the trainees. The professionalism of care and attention in the hospital, classrooms, and especially the sporting facilities, contrasted to the cuffing, kicking, verbal abuse and discipline more in keeping with a pre-war Borstal Institute. Paradoxically the hardships had a converse effect. In spite of the severity the boys remembered Shotley with immense pride and affection. It was always the 'best' rather than an infamous place to decry. Hoisting our kit bags and hammocks on to our shoulders we 'fell in' outside the mess for the last time. Petty Officer Cardew paced up and down in front of the ranks eyeing us with care to make sure we didn't drop our standards on this last parade. Suddenly his voice barked out in that old familiar tone. "Class. Classsss Shunnn!". Boots cracked on the paving stones as we came rigidly to attention. Then seconds later. "Classeee, Righttt turn, Quick March". The P.O.s' didn't follow us as we stepped smartly through the main gates. Outside transport was waiting to take us to the railway station for the journey south. Our Ganges days were over but the imprint remained, we were and would always be 'Ganges Boys'.

I never saw P.O.Rook again but I did see P.O.Cardew a couple of times. Once during the war when a destroyer he was serving on came alongside H.M.S.Dorsetshire off the West Coast of Africa to take on fuel oil. The next time was nearly fifty years later when he contacted me, after seeing my photograph in a local newspaper. My Wife and I visited him and had an enjoyable time on his small farm near Liskeard in Cornwall. Not long afterwards he died, his illness a legacy of the terrible suffering he endured in a Japanese prison camp.

7   My first Draft

Plymouth was first and foremost a naval town with all the benefits and the usual disadvantages of a garrison town. The local economy relied heavily on the ships and men of the Royal Navy. The Fleet required the dockyard at Devonport that provided employment to a vast number of people. It also provided apprenticeships in a variety of trades and skills for school leavers who would otherwise be unemployed.

I travelled there to join H.M.S. Diomede, but the ship was in dock for repairs so I went to H.M.S. Ceres instead. The three light cruisers, Ceres, Caradoc and Diomede moored together in the river Tamar, were used for the sea training of boys. They were not very big ships, the next step up from a destroyer, but I felt good to be actually afloat even if the atmosphere smacked a little of 'Ganges'. I remember one boy being put on a charge for whistling. Although he was let off with a warning, it seemed a frivolous indictment in the interests of an old fashioned tradition that banned whistling on ships of the Royal Navy.

'Ceres' was kept scrupulously clean with sparkling fresh paintwork. The decks were unblemished from energetic scouring with sand and canvas, and every rope end was neatly 'cheesed' down. Nothing was out of place, above or below deck. "Cleanliness is next to Godliness" and "A place for everything, and everything in it's place" was the constant chant of the Petty Officers in charge. Messing was the old 'Broadside' system, a style not used in the navy of today. Each mess was furnished with a long table and two wooden bench seats. A metal racking secured to the ships' side held the cutlery, cups, plates and other utensils. Another fixture held our ditty boxes and black-japanned hatboxes. There was the luxury of a locker to keep our clothing in and stowing space for our hammocks and kit bags. With so many boys on board, the mess area seemed a little cramped. When this was mentioned to the Petty Officer in charge he roared laughing and told us to "Stow thick and get lousy". It was a common expression when space was a little tight. Getting into a hammock for the first time was a cause for light-hearted banter. Bodies swung backwards and forwards from the overhead bars trying to get into the canvas bed. At first, getting in and out required a cautious approach to avoid injury and embarrassment, but with a little perseverance everyone quickly acquired the knack.

Local leave for the boys was fairly restricted and we were not allowed to stay out late. In some ways this was a blessing in disguise because parts of Plymouth were disreputable places after dark. The bright lights of the city, with haunts like the notorious Long Bar on Union Street, acted like a magnet to Jolly Jacks with money in their pockets and hell bent on a good run ashore. The naval hospital at Stonehouse kept an allocation of wards empty, on standby for the flood of casualties that never failed to fill the beds every Saturday night from the fighting in the pubs.

The use of colloquialisms and nicknames was an amusing age-old custom still practised in the navy. The origins of some were vague, lost in the passage of time but faithfully passed down to be preserved for future generations. It was an indication of the Navy's wish to hold on to one more of it's quaint traditions. We had used nicknames at 'Ganges' but never to the extent they were used on ship. Surnames were given a strange collection of forenames like Pedlar Palmer, Pony Moore, Bungy Williams, Sharkey Ward, Jimmy Green, Pincher Martin and Knocker White. There was less complementary jargon, like referring to officers as 'pigs', and midshipmen as 'snotties', 'warts', 'crabs' and 'wonks'.

Timekeeping was different to what I had been used to. Although I was conversant and accustomed to the twenty-four hour clock system, the ringing of a bell marked now the passing of time. When the bell was rung at 'Ganges' it was ignored, having little relevance to our routine. From now on it was the important part of timekeeping, linked to the watches. Each twenty-four hours was divided up into watches. The cycle started at 0000 midnight.

    0001 – 0400. Middle Watch.
    0400 – 0800. Morning Watch
    0800 – 1200. Forenoon Watch
    1200 – 1600 Afternoon Watch
    1600 – 1800. First Dog Watch
    1800 – 2000. Last Dog Watch
    2000 – 0000. First Watch.

The reason for the two Dog Watches was to provide an odd number of watches so that the times men were on watch changed daily. The bells were a little complicated at first, but like everything else it became easier with use. Every half hour after the start of a watch a bell was struck. For example a half hour after 0800, the start of the Forenoon Watch, one bell was rung at 0830, then two at 0900 and three at 0930, up to eight bells at the end of the watch at noon. Then the sequence was repeated with one bell at 1230 up to eight bells at 1600. Only one bell was rung at 1830, two at 1900 and three at 1930 followed by eight at 2000. This was the period of the last Dog Watch.

Bells were not struck between 2200 and 0830, known as the silent hours. The exception was midnight on New Years Eve when sixteen bells were rung to welcome in the New Year.

We 'sprogs' enjoyed our newfound freedom on board 'Ceres'. For the first few days we smoked like factory chimneys, making up for lost time and the last vestige of defiance against the restrictions of 'Ganges'. The 'Ships Only' cigarettes were duty free making them extremely cheap to buy. Cheaper still was the loose tobacco known as 'Ticklers' for hand rolled smokes that everyone could afford. With the money the Paymaster had put aside on my behalf at Shotley I bought a pair of shoes for going ashore, they were a delightful change from my 'pusser' boots. Next I splashed out on a best suit from C.H.Bernards, the naval tailors at Keyham. It cost me the princely sum of sixteen shillings [about 80p], a pittance today but a lot to a boy then. It was well worth the outlay, no self-respecting matelot would buy his No.1's from the Slops to be easily recognised as 'Pusser Rigged'. Naval uniform was long associated with legends about it's origins with no evidence to support the popular theories. The black silk supposedly commemorating the death of Lord Nelson in 1805, or the three white tapes on the collar representing the three great victories of the Nile, Copenhagen and Trafalgar, were good examples. In fact seamen gunners (18th.Cen.) to wipe the sweat from their eyes in the heat of battle, originally in the form of a cloth, wore the black silk, many years before Nelson's death. The number of white tapes on the collar was a compromise by members of the Admiralty Committee deciding on the standard uniform to be worn by seamen. Some wanted four others two, they were equally divided so they settled on three.

I never regarded myself as a part of 'Ceres', it was a brief transitional period to familiarise me with ship practises. There were a million and one things to learn and only a very short time to do it in. Talk was again about war and the possibility that it would come sooner than later. Boys of my age were not particularly concerned with political affairs we preferred to leave that to the politicians. Nevertheless there was a sense of urgency that could not be ignored, especially with our training now that the dark clouds of war were gathering over Europe and expected to soon roll over Britain. A Captain Beckett RN was given the unenviable task of sorting out the naval dockyard. His single-minded dedication as he struggled to convert an untidy sprawl into an efficient work place took a heavy toll on his health. He did earn the undying gratitude of the C in C Admiral Kelly, for his remarkable achievements and hard work. Sailors had little respect for the pre-war civilian dockyard workers they considered an idle, shiftless, bunch of scroungers. The working practises of the dockyard could never be accused of encouraging a hernia from the strain of hard work before Captain Beckett took over.

When the country's leaders finally accepted the full realisation of Germany's objectives, the lifestyle of ships in the Royal Navy changed dramatically from their traditional peacetime role. Previously His Majesty's ships were preoccupied with paying goodwill visits, 'showing the flag', and entertaining local dignitaries in ports around the world. Awnings spread, bands playing and cocktail parties with visiting ladies adorning the Quarter Deck was very much part of the scene. Regattas and a few cricket matches against the natives in far away places, was another important role the Fleet had to play to support the Empire. At the time the Royal Navy was universally acclaimed as one of the world's dominant sea powers, with nothing to fear from a potential enemy. Combat and aggression involving the navy was confined to their own ships' during Regatta Weeks. Friendly rivalry to prove who was the best at sailing and rowing to achieve the coveted title 'Cock of the Fleet', or the prestigious Yokohamo Bowl, was about the extent of real conflict. There was an occasional skirmish with pirates in the far away China Sea, cross words with the Japanese Imperial Navy, and Italians dropping bombs on ships like H.M.S. Gallant in Spanish waters, but nothing to seriously disturb the tranquillity of the naval social events calendar.

On 'Ceres' I teamed up with Fred Ball, a lad of my own age. We were opposites, distinctly different in many ways. I was dark haired and he was very fair. I had a quick temper that got me into trouble but he had a calm approach to most situations including getting me out of trouble. He was methodical and precise whereas I made snap judgements and decisions that did not always pay off. When we were posted along with another good friend called Charlie Lear, our draft chits were for H.M.S.Courageous. Charlie was a 'townie' of mine from Torquay; unfortunately he was killed in action as a teenager.

8   HMS Courageous

On the June 27th.1939, with twenty-seven other boys, I stood on the Devonport dockside and stared up at the 22000ton H.M.S. Courageous, my new home. Originally laid down as a battlecruiser in May 1915, but later along with H.M.S. Furious and H.M.S .Glorious she was converted into an aircraft carrier. In the navy they were jokingly referred to as 'Outrageous', 'Spurious' and 'Uproarious'. As a battle cruiser, Courageous was famous for holding the 'blue riband' for an Atlantic crossing in 32-33 knots, a record that remained unbroken for 30 years. The rebuilding of 'Courageous' to carry 48 Fairy Swordfish planes was completed on May 5th 1928, at a cost of over two million pounds. But when I joined her, she had been relegated to the Reserve Fleet. Now, with the increasing uncertainty and threats of danger from across the Channel, she was being prepared as quickly as possible for a positive wartime role. The motto of the gunnery school 'Si vis pacem para bellum' [If you desire peace, prepare for war] was to be the Government's policy in these troubled times. Anxious to get on board I struggled and grunted up the sloping gangway with my hammock and kit bag. After giving my name and number to the Quartermaster I was shown the way to the Regulating Office to get a Station Card. The formalities completed I set off with the others to find the Boy's Mess.

The first few days were pleasantly chaotic, there was so much to discover. Between decks the carrier was a labyrinth of endless steel passageways and compartments, some running fore and aft and others going athwartships. The smell of warm paint, the constant hum of electric motors and the noise of the air-conditioning was to be an integral part of my new environment. There was a non-stop flow of people busily going about their business with a sense of urgency. Commanders, Lieutenants, Chief Petty Officers, Artificers, Shipwrights, Supply Officers, Gunners, Torpedomen, Engineering Officers, Surgeons, Signalmen, and many more who contributed to the working of the ship. A large number of naval reservists and pensioners joined the ship at the same time. They were a happy chattering bunch, most of them pleased to be going to sea again for what they assumed was a temporary escape from their civilian routine. Their ribald remarks and general cheerfulness made their expectations clear as they went about their work, unsuspecting that sooner rather than later they would be enmeshed in a bloody conflict. Hundreds of them were never to return home to their families, they were destined for a watery grave in the Atlantic Ocean.

During my time at 'Ganges' I won the Class Seamanship prize and the Class School prize and came second in the Gunnery examinations as well as being a Leading Boy. My previous good record might have been instrumental to me getting a 'perk' job on the Captain's staff, albeit in the very minor role as his messenger. The most important part of the work was to accurately convey his verbal messages to other officers. It was also essential to know where things were, like his telescope, when he wanted them in a hurry. In my own interest I learnt to forget any comments and snippets of conversation I overheard, especially on the bridge. When rumours were 'buzzing' around the ship, I was an obvious target to be waylaid in the mess and quizzed if I had heard anything. It was assumed that I eavesdropped on the Captain's smalltalk, which I did whenever possible but never admitted it.

'Working up' a newly commissioned ship is a difficult thing to do at the best of times, with a carrier there is the added problems relating to aircraft. Although 'Courageous' was presently without planes there was still a lot of preparation to be done before the ship could head for the open sea. When the ammunition and other highly inflammable substances were embarked it was a good sign that we were getting ready to cast off. One day a timetable appeared on the notice board that finally set our minds at rest; we were to leave port the next day. Right on schedule, the Bosun's Call [Pipe] shrilled for 'Special Sea Dutymen' to close up. Next came the order for "Both Watches of the Hands" to muster. Divisional Officers and their Petty Officers scuttled around like scalded cocks barking orders, making sure their part of the ship was above reproach and fully prepared for sea. All moveable gear and boats were made fast, watertight doors, hatches and scuttles closed and secured. Main engines, communications and electrical circuits were tested and reported ready. It was an anxious time with so much that could go wrong with a newly commissioned crew. The ultimate responsibility rested with the Captain but to me he seemed the calmest on the bridge. As 'Courageous' burst into life the big propellers churned up the oily seawater into boiling foam. It was the cue for an endless stream of orders. "Cast off", "Let go" Springs, Braces, Head Rope, Stern Rope, Breast Rope, "Look lively with that Manila, Grass, Sisal and Hemp". Standing at the rear of the Compass Platform I wondered if everyone really knew what they were supposed to do. Then, "All gone Forrard", "All gone Aft", "Very well No.1", slow ahead starboard, slow ahead port, slow ahead together. Signal halyards ran up flags to flutter in the breeze conveying a message to someone.

The big ship eased her way out into the Hamoaze to be conned down the river Tamar. Passing Plymouth Hoe I could see groups of interested spectators watching and waving as the ship slowly turned inside the Breakwater. With all navigational checks completed, 'Courageous' put out to sea. It was a milestone in my young life, at long last I was a seagoing sailor, although at sixteen years of age a very junior one. As the coastline disappeared astern the Duty Watch took over and the rest of the crew stood down. It was time for me to get my 'sea-legs'. The wind off shore created a sizeable swell causing the carrier to pitch and wallow in a drunken roll. Dipping down lazily into a trough, she stayed for what seemed an eternity before easing herself out again like a giant whale. Walking through the long corridors between decks took some getting used to. One minute it was an uphill plod, before changing to a downhill gallop. The long drawn out seesawing effect was something I never experienced again on another ship, not even in a typhoon. It had the effect of bringing my stomach up into my mouth. 'Courageous' still needed aircraft and for these she sailed to Portsmouth, first to have a minor defect attended to and then to take on planes from the Gosport air base. During the time at sea the hands were kept busy. There is not much to tell about my short stay in Portsmouth, except to say it was the only time I was ever thoroughly searched by dockyard police on my way ashore. Presumably they were looking for anyone taking out excess 'duty free' tobacco. They found nothing and I joined my oppos outside the dockyard gate, where they were loudly voicing their opinions of M.O.D. policemen in a most uncomplimentary manner.

Boys never had any money to spare, and we were no exception with very little to spend on this run ashore. To conserve every penny we decided to visit the seamen's mission to see what could be scrounged. We were in luck and after singing a few hymns we were rewarded with a couple of big buns and a mug of tea. It provided enough sustenance to keep us going for the short time we were allowed ashore. Leaving the mission we made our way to the fairground on Southsea Common, knowing we would be spectators as far the rides were concerned. We didn't have much money in our pockets but we did have exuberant youth on our side. It proved our biggest asset and we had very little difficulty finding suitable female company to have a bellyful of laughs. Young and carefree we could make our own fun and amusement with the girls, using a sense of humour for collateral. One day I went ashore with the captain's wife and a young pretty girl I took to be her daughter. The Coxswain drove us in the car to the Commodore's house where Mrs. Makeig-Jones did a lot of measuring up for curtains and such like. My job was to carry several parcels to the house for her. I asked the Coxswain what it was all about and he said that the Captain was soon to take up residence there on his promotion to Commodore. He also told me to keep it to myself because it was not common knowledge as yet. Anyway I enjoyed the day out away from the ship as much as the 'eats' the ladies provided.

When the Swordfish aircraft were due to join the carrier, Courageous made ready for sea to take them on board. As she eased her way tentatively towards the Channel those of us on deck were treated to the impressive spectacle of the two world famous liners, Queen Mary and Normandie, moored one behind the other. Bosun's Calls piped the Still and ensigns on all three ships were dipped in the traditional manner. For once it seemed worthwhile to go through the pointless exercise in maritime diplomacy. As the ship passed the gaunt looking blockhouses that rose up out of the water like giant sentinels, the roar of aircraft engines could be heard approaching in the distance. It was exciting for me to see the first of our planes sweeping in towards the carrier. The pilots undoubtedly felt just as apprehensive about their first landing as the deck crews felt about receiving them. After an initial pass over the ship the leading flight broke formation and took up position to land, arrester hooks trailing under the bellies of the planes. Everyone on deck seemed to be 'on pins' as the first 'Stringbag' came down very precariously towards the steel surface. It skidded along the deck, before coming to an abrupt stop as the hook caught in the wire hawser, then the pilot switched off his engine and all on the Bridge sighed with relief. With more planes coming in nobody had the time to watch the formations 'buzzing' around overhead. Touching down the planes wings were folded back and the 'kites' quickly lowered by lift to the hangers, clearing the deck for the next incoming Swordfish. H.M.S. Courageous was allocated a reduced compliment of aircraft but it was sufficient to make the carrier a significant force to reckon with.

There was always 'perks' attached to being a special 'dutyman' and more so on the Captain's staff. For me personally it meant being excused general ships' duties, many of which were considered obnoxious chores. One I was particularly pleased to be excused was acting as human ballast for the aircraft. This came about mainly when the fresh young pilots rehearsed landings and take-offs to improve their skills. It was considered an unnecessary waste of Fleet Air Arm Observers and Wireless Operators valuable time to sit in the planes during these practise sessions. The ships' hierarchy considered boy seaman the ideal substitute to fill the role of makeweight. When needed, the duty Petty Officers had the responsibility to supply the necessary ballast. They moved swiftly through the messdecks like the 'press gangs' of old, rounding up sufficient bodies. Protesting all kinds of ailments and phobia the reluctant 'volunteers' were herded to the planes already 'ticking over'. The old fashioned 'Stringbags' were reputed to have a mind of their own. In inexperienced hands they barely got airborne before running out of flight deck. On approach they had a habit of weaving badly from side to side prior to leapfrogging to an unsteady stop. Crashes, when they happened, were not always the fault of the pilots. A heaving deck, a sudden strong gust of wind, or poor visibility could make it difficult for the most skilled of the flyers. Finding the carrier was difficult in bad weather and the Swordfish were constantly grounded, radar having not been introduced at this time.

From a vantage position at the side of the bridge I enjoyed the spectacle of my faint-hearted messmates peering uneasily over the rim of the rear cockpits waiting for take-off. It was a source of great amusement for the other boys who had escaped capture this time, they were totally unconcerned that tomorrow it might be their turn to change their underpants after a free flight. Less nerve racking but avoidable if possible was 'chock boys'. Two boys were detailed to lie flat on their stomachs, one under each of the planes wings holding two large wooden chocks against the wheels. When the pilot signalled 'ready', the flight deck officer lowered his flag and the boys pulled the front blocks away to let the plane move forward. After the tail wheel had passed between the boys they stood up and dragged the blocks to the side of the flight deck by the rope lanyards. If they stood up too quickly the slipstream from the aircraft on full throttle hit them square on, strong enough to bowl them over. It was not a very pleasant job but it was necessary

9   The Royal Visit

In August 1939, His Majesty King George VI was scheduled to visit H.M.S. Courageous during his review of the Reserve Fleet. H.M.S. Effingham was the flagship, flying the flag of Vice-Admiral Sir Max Kennedy Horton KCB. DSO, but H.M.S. Courageous was best suited to accommodate the large contingents representing all the other warships for inspection. For days the ships' company was kept busy scrubbing, painting and polishing every inch of the big ship. It was the normally accepted procedure for welcoming high-ranking visitors. This being a Royal visit the preparation went much further including black-leading the enormous steel flight deck. It brought back memories of Captain's Rounds at H.M.S. Ganges. Due to the uncertainty of the weather I was detailed off to attend to His Majesty's raincoat. At first I could not understand why he would be concerned about a few drops of rain as nobody else had a coat. Later when I saw the amount of gold braid and decorations he was carrying I realised the need to keep him dry. I had plenty of instruction beforehand by the Coxswain, and the captain's valet, on how to deal with my moment of glory. Doing my normal duties for the captain I had to be meticulous in my dress. Not to be would have merited a swift 'rocket' from the Coxswain. For this occasion I was especially well turned out, having taken great care with every small detail of my uniform.

The King travelled down from Balmoral on the Royal train and arrived at Weymouth station at 1000 hrs on August 9th. in the uniform of an Admiral of the Fleet. He drove through the cheering crowds to Bincleave pier to disembark for the Royal Yacht,' Victoria and Albert'. She was lying just inside Portland harbour breakwater next to the Admiralty yacht 'Enchantress'. Waiting to greet His Majesty on arrival were several distinguished high ranking officers including the First Lord of the Admiralty, Lord Stanhope, Vice-Admiral Sir Dudley North and Admiral Francois Darlan the Chief of the French Naval Staff. After the usual formalities of being presented to the King they joined him on the Royal barge to start the review. The day of the visit turned out grey and wet, with a choppy sea running. On board H.M.S. Courageous, ratings from the different ships had been formed up on the flight deck for some considerable time getting cold and fidgety. Bemoaning what they described as a "bloody waste of time "they were quickly losing any feelings of loyalty to the Monarch. Aft on the Quarter Deck there were signs of nervousness as officers scanned the bay, waiting impatiently for the Royal entourage to make a move. When it did, word was swiftly passed around the ship to "Stand-by". The Guard of Honour realigned itself, the Quartermasters prepared to pipe and the officers readjusted their caps. Escorted by two Motor Torpedo Boats the Royal barge first went to HMS Courageous to inspect 1500 servicemen representing the 12000 men of the fleet.

It came smoothly alongside the after gangway and the King stepped sprightly on to the platform. As he came up the steps, followed by the other top brass, the Guard presented arms, the 'pipes' shrilled the 'Side' and everyone saluted. I was a little taken aback at how small he was, expecting him to be taller. His lack of height was emphasised more so when he stood alongside Captain Makeig-Jones who was a well built powerful man. The King decided to discard his raincoat and I anticipated his intention. With a well-rehearsed dignity and forced casualness I took it off him and folded it over my arm. Later when it started to rain he half turned and I opened his coat and put it over his shoulders. I walked immediately behind him and the captain and in front of Admiral Darlan. The last time I was as close to the French navy was at Shotley when I visited two French warships anchored off Harwich. The ships were dirty and untidy by our standards and left me with a poor impression of their navy for all time.

On such visits it was important that the Monarch was treated with every respect and consideration. Anticipating he might take some refreshment before leaving, a mouth-watering spread had been prepared. The captain's cook, his steward and the best of the ships' catering staff had toiled assiduously to demonstrate their culinary skills. The Wardroom tables were beautifully laid out with delicacies not normally associated with naval cuisine. To everyone's disappointment King George declined the invitation to eat but thanked the captain and congratulated him on the excellent condition of his ship. As a final gesture, which ingratiated him to the ships' company, he told Makeig-Jones to 'splice the main brace'. This traditionally meant an extra tot of rum for the men and limejuice for the boys for work well done. The delicious displays of food in the Wardroom were left to the officers to demolish it was some consolation for the King's absence. The Coxswain came into the pantry with what should have been the table centrepiece, a replica of Windsor Castle made of ice cream. I assumed he was acting on the Captain's instructions, but I always knew he could pull rabbits out of a hat when he wanted to. "Do you like ice cream"? It was a daft question to ask a boy. "Yes Coxswain, I love it" "Well go and get two of your oppos and see this off. And bring your own bloody spoons. Do you hear?"

"Yes Swain" I dashed to the boy's messdeck, fearful that someone else might eat it before I got back. Convincing two pals that free ice cream was in the offing was the hardest part, but they followed me in disbelief. Back in the pantry we made the intricately designed masterpiece disappear at a disgusting rate. To be asked to eat the King's ice cream was a treat never to be repeated during my time in the navy.

The King spent forty minutes on 'Courageous' before leaving for the Flagship H.M.S. Effingham. Next he went on board H.M.S. Cardiff and then H.M.S. Exmouth later returning to the Royal Yacht for lunch. In the afternoon His Majesty made a two-hour cruise in the Victoria and Albert to review the rest of the ships that had been 'dressed overall' that morning. Before he left at 1700 hrs to be driven to Weymouth station accompanied by his Aide Louis Mountbatten, he sent a general signal to all the fleet to 'splice the main brace'. Prior to the war, the Reserve Fleet was regarded as a backwater for officers and men who had been passed over for promotion to eke out their time before pension. That was until Vice-Admiral Horton took command in July 1937 and gave it some pride in itself and standing in the navy. Max Horton's efforts could be appreciated this day as the 132 proud ships of the Reserve Fleet assembled in Weymouth Bay.

Shore leave was allowed which resulted in me 'blotting' my copybook. Unfamiliar with Weymouth, my friends and I chose the wrong place to get the boat back and returned late. With hindsight it was understandable, with so many ships disgorging thousands of men ashore, and then collecting them again, there was bound to be confusion. We were in plenty of time to get the picket boat but waited in vain at the wrong place. Others came and went full of returning seamen but nobody seemed to know where the boat for 'Courageous' came in. We was finally taken back by another ships' liberty boat and immediately put in the 'rattle'. When the Coxswain heard about it he came to the rescue and argued my case persuasively to get the charge dropped and save me from Commander's Report. It meant there wouldn't be a black mark on my record sheet. I didn't get off scot-free, the coxswain found every dirty job he could for me to do in my leisure time for the next couple of weeks. The extra work didn't worry me but his abusive language got on my nerves. With hindsight it would have been better to do the proper punishment.

10 "The Admiralty Regrets"

The territorial conquests of the Third Reich, and the events leading up to the Second World War have been well documented by countless historians and biographers. I leave it to them to argue on the pros' and cons' of the decisions made by our illustrious politicians in the diplomatic minefield of appeasement. Suffice to say that Britain had an agreement to act in the defence of Poland. When Hitler invaded that country on September 1st. 1939 the British government had no alternative but to issue an ultimatum. Germany was given until 1100 on September 3rd. to withdraw their forces or face the inevitable consequences.

The ship left Weymouth at 0530hrs on September 2nd.1939 ready for war. The next day Sunday, September 3rd. 1939 was a truly memorable day for me, and the rest of the ships' company of H.M.S.Courageous. We had been told that an important wireless announcement would be relayed through the ships loudspeakers at 1115hrs. I met Fred Ball going 'forrard' and we decided to listen to the news in the boys' messdeck. Right on time the tannoy clicked on and the voice of the Prime Minister, Arthur Neville Chamberlain, came mournfully across the air waves. He told the nation that Adolf Hitler had not responded to the British ultimatum and that we were now in a state of war with Germany.

H.M.S. Courageous joined the Channel Force as part of the fleet protecting the route of the Expeditionary Force to France. Later on Saturday

16th.September, we sailed on a search and destroy mission against U-boats operating in the Atlantic Ocean. Their menacing presence would be a constant threat to the Allied ships bringing vital supplies for the country. The Fleet Air Arm crews had been spending more and more time in the air, with additional mock bombing and torpedo attack exercises. Night flying had also been stepped up but not without loss of aircraft, possibly due to the inexperience of the pilots. Everyone was involved in 'dummy runs' especially the gun crews, familiarizing themselves with their Action Stations. Practise was the only way to ensure the best of teamwork. Strangely enough, 'Abandon Ship' procedure was overlooked, which proved a fatal mistake. With all the brashness of a sixteen year old, and the self-confidence from a disciplined training, I didn't feel unduly alarmed about the declaration of war. I would have been if I could have foreseen that in two weeks I would be a survivor from the first British warship to be sunk by the enemy. Many of the reservists had seen action at sea during the First World War and needed no reminders of it's horrors. It could be said that the number of pensioners that made up the crew was a contributing factor in the tragic loss of life when H.M.S. Courageous was torpedoed and sunk.

When the war started I found myself doing two conflicting sets of duties, watch-keeping with a gun crew and captain's messenger. When he was on duty I was on standby in case needed. I ended up leaving one spell of duty to immediately start another on the gun, and for the first three days at sea I had little or no sleep. On the third day I collapsed into a sleep-inducing stupor. The captain, wanting something fetching noted my absence, and his coxswain came to find me asleep on the steel deck below the charthouse. After a very brusque wakening from an irate 'cox', I explained the circumstances and got a few grunts acknowledging my predicament. He soon sorted the matter out and after that my watch-keeping duties were confined to the bridge and the wheelhouse. It was an arrangement that I enjoyed very much. Exactly two weeks after the Prime Minister's fateful broadcast H.M.S.Courageous, with an escort of four 'I' class destroyers, was patrolling off the South-west coast of Ireland. To all intents and purposes the flotilla was more than capable of dealing with any marauding 'wolf packs'. It was a misconception which, with hindsight, the Admiralty was to regret and hastily rectify. Aircraft carriers were quickly withdrawn from submarine sweeps and returned to their proper place in the Fleet. The powerful unit made a pleasing sight as it majestically cut a swathe through the water. There was no thought of danger as men went about their normal duties. Then a distress signal came in, implying that a merchant ship in our area, SS. Kafiristan, was being attacked by a U-boat. Captain Makeig-Jones ordered two of the escort to break formation and investigate. It was reassuring to see the graceful lines of the destroyers as they altered course and sped away to deal with the matter. Disappearing in the distance at high speed, it was easy to see why they were called the 'greyhounds of the sea'.

About 1800hrs the German submarine U29 was cruising at periscope depth when her captain Lieutenant Otto Schuhart sighted the carrier and the two escorting destroyers. Aircraft were still in the air scouting a wide area ahead of the ships. Their presence gave a feeling of security, no U-boat commander would dare risk his boat with aircraft buzzing around overhead; or so we thought. Lt. Schuhart had other ideas as he stalked his prey. A skilful and daring seaman, he knew the risks but was prepared to take them for the valuable prize on offer. The distress signal turned out to be false, probably sent to lure the destroyers away from the aircraft carrier, which it did. The two 'I' boats that left us earlier had still not returned as daylight faded. Dawn and dusk are notoriously dangerous times at sea and ships are at their most vulnerable. The disappearing light plays tricks with the eyes, and lookouts have difficulty spotting the low superstructure of a U-boat or it's periscope.

As the daytime patrols finished, the remaining airborne planes started to return to the ship. To assist the aircraft to land, the normal procedure of turning the carrier into the wind was carried out. The 'Stringbags', landing on one at a time, had their wings folded back before being quickly lowered by lift to the hanger. Captain Makeig-Jones could not have suspected that the manoeuvre presented the ships' port side to the U-boat, offering a huge target to fire at. Shortly after the last Swordfish touched down, and before the ship had resumed course, U29 attacked. I clearly remember someone asking me the time and as I was replying that it was four minutes to eight, there was a terrific explosion and I was knocked off my feet. It was the first torpedo hitting the ship, seconds later there was another almighty bang as the second one struck home.

I was down below when the lights went out and the carrier began to list to port. As it lurched further over, everything that was not securely fastened down went crashing to one side. Groping my way through the darkened passages towards the upper deck I could hear the screams and cries of men trapped in the vastness of the big ship. I didn't know what to expect but when I finally made my way into the open I was bemused to see men jumping into the sea.

Nobody seemed to have a ships' lifebelt, which was the old-fashioned cork type. They were stored in metal lockers in various parts of the ship but had not been issued to individuals. In the confusion nobody appeared to have found them in time. I asked what was going on and someone said 'Abandon ship' had been sounded, which was obvious from the number taking to the water. It felt cold but I hurriedly stripped down to my underpants and picked a suitable spot in the grey looking sea. Then taking, a deep breath, and without a lifebelt, I dived into the Atlantic Ocean. I struck out to get as far away as possible from the doomed ship before her final plunge sucked me under. Turning on my back I saw men struggling to release the lifesaving Carley Floats. They were plentiful but during the dockyard refit the painters had not bothered to remove them, they just painted over the lot, ropes and all. The hard dried paint on the ropework made it impossible to launch the floats in time. The slipshod work was indefensible and another contributing factor to the huge loss of life. Only one boat and one Carley Float got into the water, a mere token lifesaver for a crew of 1200.

As I watched, the huge steel mass of H.M.S. Courageous disappeared beneath the waves the sea closed over her like a shroud.
I decided to try turning my back to the oncoming waves but they crashed over my head and left me spluttering for breath. I soon found it easier to swim into the 'rollers' and take air as I was lifted up on a crest.

Darkness began to close in and it got much colder with a worsening sea. Those of us who had been fortunate enough to dive or belly-flop into the inhospitable water would have to call on all our reserves of stamina, plus a generous helping of good luck to survive. The two escort destroyers were chasing around trying to pinpoint the U-boat, frustrated that they couldn't depth charge the area for fear of killing the men in the water. It must have been agonizing for their captains to see so many helpless swimmers and not able to pick them up. To do so would run the risk of making themselves sitting targets for the U-boat. Earlier in the day the flotilla swept past a small tramp ship, the Dido, steaming on a parallel course. Her captain later said he had increased speed to follow the warships, assuming that our presence in the vicinity was cast iron security for his own ship. Now as darkness fell the little vessel came upon the tragic scene. With some disbelief, all they found was a wide area of oil covered ocean dotted with bobbing heads and waving arms, accompanied by desperate cries for help. H.M.S. Courageous had gone down in less than twenty minutes after being hit. 518 men and boys died that evening, including Captain Makeig-Jones, who was last seen on the bridge saluting the White Ensign.

It was an impossible task to rescue everyone, but bravely her captain disregarded any possible danger and stopped his engines to pick up those men strong enough to swim to his ship. Surprisingly there was a lack of flotsam immediately after the sinking, I would have expected lots of wood to come shooting to the surface for us to hang on to.

When the ship first sank, men started singing 'Roll out the Barrel' to keep up their spirits. They turned to hymns when they realised there was an odds on chance of meeting their Maker before the night was out. Eventually the singing ceased and there was just a lot of shouting in the dark, mostly from men threshing about struggling to stay alive.

In the dim light I made out the dark shape of the coaster and swam towards it. It wasn't easy because my arms and legs felt like lead weights. Swimming and treading water for about two hours was taking it's toll and I was feeling every one of my sixteen years. The action of the choppy sea and the cold was sapping my strength, making me very weary. At times my senses left me and I wondered if I was about to drown. Strangely I had lost the fear of dying, and resigned myself to going under.

A Fleet Air Arm Observer, I recognised, was swimming close by and saw I was getting weaker. He had enough to do to look after himself but he shouted to me "Keep going son, your Mother and Father will be expecting you to come home. Come on lad, keep at it". It encouraged me to try harder and keep swimming towards the 'Dido'.

He stayed near, urging me on until we reached the little tramp steamer. I was far too exhausted to climb the rope ladder but an alert seaman on board saw my plight and scrambled down to pull me to safety. With great relief I was unceremoniously bundled on to the deck. Inside the ships' cabin I joined several other scantily clad survivors, huddled together trying to keep warm but rejoicing to be out of the cold sea.

Word was passed that a destroyer would come alongside some time during the night to take us on board. We were warned to carry out the transfer as swiftly as possible because the U-boat might still be about. When the flotilla leader H.M.S.Inglefield arrived, we needed no encouragement to 'look lively', some brave souls took a gamble and jumped precariously across from one ship to the other. Once on board the 'Inglefield' I got rid of my oil soaked underpants which seemed to be the 'rig of the day' for all the survivors. The first job was to remove as much of the foul smelling fuel oil as possible, especially from around mouth and eyes. I was given a blanket by one of the destroyer's crew and taken to join a queue for an issue of neat rum.

When a mug with an over generous measure was thrust into my hand by the Quartermaster I sheepishly confessed "I don't draw, I'm only sixteen", meaning that I was too young to be issued with spirits. His reply was typical of most Quartermasters. "Bloody-well get it down you son, and then get another bloody cupful". I didn't argue, it had been a long night and I was very tired.

Forrard in the seamen's mess I downed endless mugs of hot tea before the soothing effects of the rum, and the warmth of the blanket, sent me into a deep sleep. I was oblivious to the fact that H.M.S.Inglefield, now on her own, was still sweeping, desperately trying to find the submarine.
Circling at speed throughout the night the destroyer's crew kept a constant watch while the ASDIC operators sent a constant 'ping' from their detectors to probe the depths of the ocean for the U-Boat.

The captain of 'Inglefield', hoping to find more survivors, decided to carry out a final search in daylight. As dawn came up I joined the others on deck. Wrapped in my blanket to cover my nakedness and to keep warm, I looked out on a scene of chilling desolation cloaked in a mantle of eerie silence. Nobody spoke, we just stared at the melancholy spectacle that was a harsh lesson in the realities of war and the consequences of getting caught off guard.

Floating debris and bloated corpses could be seen everywhere but not a living soul. The now abundant flotsam would have been welcome the previous evening. Now it only reminded us of the tragic loss of life in a war that was just two weeks old.

The trawl proved hopeless and the search was reluctantly abandoned. 'Inglefield' set course for Plymouth, at least she was bringing some survivors home. After tying up at Devonport we handed the blankets back to their owners. In return we got small squares of cloth to hold over our 'private' parts for the walk to the barracks. A truck was waiting at the jetty with plimsolls of mixed sizes to save us walking in bare feet. Earlier survivors had been lucky enough to get blankets to cover themselves with Men and women working in the dockyard and barracks turned out to see us. It was embarrassing at first because of the groups of women lining the roadway.
Tightly holding the piece of cloth over my 'you know what' I kept my head down and eyes fixed on the ground. I was quickly put at ease when one of the women shouted "Don't you worry lad, you're home and you're safe that's what matters". Others joined in with similar shouts of comfort, easing the embarrassment. The contingency plans drawn up by the Navy for such an emergency were excellent. Hot showers and plenty of soap removed the last traces of oil before we were kitted out. Then everyone was ushered into a dining hall for a good hot meal. Afterwards, we were asked some very basic questions such as name and rank, and then issued with train tickets, money and leave passes. Getting us on our way home as soon as possible was

obviously the main priority for the authorities. The treatment I received after the sinking of H.M.S. Courageous contrasted dramatically with the disgusting reception I went through in 1942, when I survived the sinking of H.M.S. Dorsetshire. This I will cover in detail later in the book.

News that another batch of survivors had arrived in port spread like wildfire, and crowds gathered outside the barrack gates. Women desperate for news of their menfolk wept as they scrutinised everyone leaving the depot. Emotions were running high, people knew that if their loved ones were not with our party they would not be coming home. As the police forced a passage to let me through the crowd, I was bombarded with questions about missing men, and had I seen them. Sadly I had to shake my head at the names I heard, I just wished I could have said something to ease the pain on the faces around me. The Quartermaster of the 'Courageous', who had often given me instruction on the ships' helm as part of my training, was amongst the crowd. He lived locally and had arrived home with an earlier party of survivors, now he had come to see who else had been saved. When he spotted me he pushed forward and grabbed my hand, shaking it furiously with joy. A newsreel cameraman witnessed the incident and asked us to repeat the handshake for the camera team doing a news item. When it appeared on the screen at the old Electric Cinema in Torquay, several of our neighbours rushed around to tell my Mum that I had been on the 'pictures'. Dad and Mum were very proud of me, the first dramatic naval incident of the war at sea and their son had been part of it.

My standing with my civilian chums was very much enhanced, sad to say some of them joined later but did not survive the war.

On the 5th.September 1939 the Admiralty sent a message to the C in C Home Fleet stating that a general issue of lifebelts had not been anticipated but arrangements were being made to obtain supplies as soon as possible. The death of someone so respected and with the seafaring experience Captain Makeig-Jones must have been a great loss to the Admiralty. Captain William Tofield Makeig-Jones was born in Yorkshire the son of a doctor. One of six children, 3 boys and 3 girls, he entered the Royal Navy by the normal pre-war channels for officer cadets at the Royal Navy College H.M.S. Britannia at Dartmouth. Specialising in torpedoes and communications he was promoted Lt. Commander in 1921, Commander in 1923, Captain in 1930. He and was to be elevated to the Flag Rank of Commodore in October 1939 but was killed just weeks beforehand.

11 H.M.S.Dorsetshire

On June 5th. Naval transport took the draft to join the heavy cruiser H.M.S.Dorsetshire. When I first set eyes on her I knew in my heart that this ship was a thoroughbred. I still held the same opinion two years later when Japanese dive-bombers blew her apart. 'Dorsetshire' belonged to that special breed of cruiser known as the County Class. Their capacity to stay at sea for long periods, 12500 nautical miles when the speed was kept at 12 knots, coupled with an exceptional firepower from 8 x 8" guns, made them a workhorse for the Navy. With a maximum speed of 32.25 knots, every conceivable task seemed to be within their scope. Land bombardment, surface to surface, engagements, convoying, rescue missions, capturing enemy ships, and oiling submarines and destroyers in far away places was all part and parcel of a days work. The famous German sea raiders 'Thor', 'Kormoran', 'Pinguin' and 'Atlantis' were all sent to their doom by this class of 10,000 ton cruiser. H.M.S.Dorsetshire was a very happy ship, members of the crew retained a special affinity for her. Of course the men had their grumbles and grouses about one thing or another but this should be seen in it's proper context. Sailors enjoyed a 'drip', it was a form of letting off steam after long periods at sea. Sometimes the 'moaning' appeared to be justified. This time 'Dorsetshire' was in port for fifteen days after an overseas commission of two years, eight months and eleven days. There was just enough time to give those who had been abroad, one week of home leave before returning to foreign parts on another commission.

Accommodation was never plentiful on warships. They were constructed for warfare not as luxury liners. Fighting equipment took priority when space was available. County Class cruisers fared far better than most ships for creature comforts. When Sir William Berry designed them as all-purpose, all climate vessels, his specifications were generous particularly with headroom. Their main weakness was the lack of heavy protective armour, brought about by the restrictions on weight under the Washington Treaty of 1922. Another vital weakness was the inadequacy of the anti-aircraft weapons. The updating of this important part of the ships' defence had not kept pace with the rapid advance in naval aircraft development, most especially that of the Imperial Japanese Navy. All this was far from my mind as I followed the others up the gangway. Getting on board caused a bit of commotion before we lined up with our cumbersome hammocks and kit bags to answer our names and get our station cards. While this was going on the Boy's Instructor appeared, casting a critical eye over us. He was obviously taking note of the 'cut of our jib' for future reference. He looked a tough no-nonsense individual that would need handling with care. As he lifted his cap to run his fingers through his close-cropped fair hair it accentuated the granite like features sitting on broad shoulders. This was Petty Officer James Schollet the man entrusted with our welfare and discipline. He lived in a curtained off section of our mess where he could keep a 'weather' eye on his precocious charges. In the coming months we felt the speed and force of his hand for misbehaving, skulking, or acting 'green'. He preferred his own brand of chastisement to putting a boy on an official charge that would blot his record sheet. We were happy with the arrangement, knowing that when Big Jim dished out punishment we deserved it. We soon came to appreciate that under the hard exterior lay an honest, fair-minded, considerate man with a high level of moral conscience and a genuine interest in our welfare. Everyone came to respect him, and acknowledge his help and guidance long after we had left his care on the boy's messdeck.

Once again when duties were allocated I landed a 'perk' job, this time as the commander's messenger. Captain's messenger went to sixteen-year-old 'Dinger' Bell who came on board with a personal recommendation from the captain of his training ship. 'Dinger' deserved it, having been an Instructor Boy during his time at H.M.S. Ganges. We became very good pals and shared the many little confidences our big ears picked up when working in close proximity to the senior officers. The Captain and Commander were completely different in temperament, personality and social background. Commander John Westmacott was a tall elegant figure, immaculately dressed at all times with a ready smile and charming manners. Although credit for his well kept wardrobe must go to his Royal Marine 'flunkey', it needed the charismatic presence of the Commander to carry it off. Signed photographs in his cabin, from such as the Duke of Kent and his wife Princess Marina, were evidence of the social circles he moved in. I always had the feeling he was a little piqued to be subordinate to a former Lower-Decker like Martin. At times he must have felt intimidated by the down to earth brusqueness of the captain, who was never noted for his diplomacy. Whenever 'Dinger' Bell came to say the captain wished to speak to him in his quarters, John Westmacott always asked the same question. "Did he say he wanted to speak to the Commander, or did he say he wanted to speak to John". It was the yardstick to judge the mood of the meeting. Whatever the Commander's feelings it never influenced his dedication to making 'Dorsetshire' a happy and a well run ship in every way.

Captain Benjamin Charles Stanley 'Pincher' Martin was something different, his origins were from the other side of the track to the Commanders. He was a very special man in the eyes of all those who served under him, epitomising the archetypical English seadog, subscribing to the old adage ' A bloody war and quick promotion'. He left nobody in doubt what mattered most to him, his ship and achieving high position in the navy. Educated at the Royal Naval Orphanage School, Greenwich, he joined the navy at 'Ganges' in 1907 as a Boy Seaman 2nd.Class. He served in the Persian Gulf and Somalia Campaigns as a boy but distinguished himself at the Battle of Jutland in 1916 and was awarded a commission after the battle. He was a dedicated careerist who achieved the seemingly impossible by graduating from the lowest rank in the navy to the exalted position of a Post Captain. At the time it was an unusual accomplishment; the gulf between the Lower Deck and senior rank was considered insurmountable. He crossed the divide with a deceptive ease born from confidence in his own ability, brilliant mariner's acumen and the commitment to reach the upper echelons of the Royal Navy. He was the first Lower Decker to be knighted in the 20th.Century, and finally retired from the navy in 1948 as Rear-Admiral Martin KBE. CBE. DSO. Suffice to say the ships' company held the captain in the highest esteem and unquestionable trust. He earned respect from all on board who acknowledged him as their peer in matters of seamanship, gunnery and navigation. Captain Martin and Captain Blyth had one thing in common, a profound dislike for Midshipmen. He voiced his resentment quite openly for the 'snotties' privileged start when he was struggling to get on the first few rungs of the promotion ladder.

This then is a brief synopsis of three important people on board that controlled my destiny, the Captain, the Commander and the Boy's Instructor. They were people I could look up to and respect knowing they were men with special qualities of their own.

When I first came aboard I was surprised to see Chinese civilians, mainly stewards and cooks. They were a legacy of the time 'Dorsetshire' spent on the China Station up to the outbreak of war. An opportunity was lost to put them off in Hong Kong, Amoy or Wei Hai Wei, before the ship left the Far East station for the Indian Ocean then the South Atlantic and eventually Plymouth. Before 'Dorsetshire' sailed this time they were put ashore to work in the officers quarters until they could be safely sent home. Although the ship was being re-commissioned a large number of the crew were staying with the ship. Most of them had spent several years in the Orient and used a lot of Chinese words and phrases, which had crept into their vocabulary. Like Mynah birds we youngsters picked up much of it although sometimes we were not too sure of the true meaning of the expressions we used. The most popular messdeck pastime was the Chinese game of Mah-Jong, and each mess had it's own school. Men reading or writing seemed oblivious to the constant clattering of the 144 ivory blocks, as they were shuffled and slapped down accompanied by unusual cries like Rickshaw, Bams, Street, Wickets. They were not the authentic Chinese descriptions for the characters on the tiles, more the adapted version that was standard in the navy.

It was fascinating to listen to the inexhaustible repertoire of tales the older hands told about their travels in China, Japan, Australia, and other faraway places. These were men who had come crashing out through more windows than doors in Shanghai's Blood Alley, wallowed in the hot mud springs of Japan's Beppu in Kyushu, and were privileged to see what is described as the most beautiful sight in Japan the snow-capped summit of Mount Fujiyama. They had explored Australia's Great Barrier Reef and the islands of the Pacific, visited the most picturesque places in the East and were better acquainted with places like Miyajima, Tsingtao, Hong Kong and Shanghai than they were with their home county. The authenticity of the travel stories could be corroborated from the bulging photograph albums showing the sailors ashore at the places. Simple anecdotes about people, amusingly related by their oppos', were my favourites. Like the tale of Stoker Pitts in Shanghai. At that time Shanghai was shared by different fleets including, American French, Italian and British. Nightlife in the notorious Blood Alley displayed the tougher side of the city. A fight between the different navies had a snowballing effect throughout the clubs, with breaking windows showering glass into the street as a normal event. When the weary matelots mustered on the Bund to be taken back to their ships, feeling 'browned off', all animosity was forgotten. Black eyes and bloody noses were evident but any ill feeling was reserved for the next run ashore.

'Zassu' Pitts a young sailor from Devon could vouch for the common bond between the seafaring community. He missed his liberty boat and was standing disconsolately on the Bund looking across at 'Dorsetshire', wishing he was back on board. Reflecting on the amount of 'jankers' he would get, he watched the Admiral's barge from the USS Augusta pull alongside the steps and put the Admiral ashore. As the pinnace started to push off, the American coxswain noticed the lonely dejected 'Zassu' and called out to him. "What's the matter Limey" "I've missed the liberty back to Dorsetshire". "Come on, we'll drop you off on our way back" offered the Yank. "Thanks mate, you're a pal" and Pitts meant every word of it. He would still be adrift but the shorter the time of absence the better, so he quickly jumped into the stern. The barge set off across the Whangpoo still displaying the Flag Officer's insignia on a large circular board, which should have been taken down when he went ashore. A vigilant Officer of the Day on 'Dorsetshire' spotted the approach of the boat with the rank of Admiral clearly visible and quickly alerted the commander. Puzzled that a high ranking American naval officer should be arriving without prior notice, he immediately sent for the captain and ordered the guard on deck with a Side Party to pipe him on board. The captain was equally anxious about the visit assuming it must be something very important. He cast a quick look around to make sure nothing was amiss to disgrace the welcome and stood by to receive the Admiral. As the barge came alongside the Bosun's 'calls' shrilled in a manner befitting the officer's status. Everyone on deck stood rigidly to attention and put on their best smiles. Out of the stern sheets and up the steps came the very lowly rating. As the Americans bore off with a flurry of boat hooks, Pitts was confronted by a bewildering group of officers and a dumbfounded captain. "I missed the liberty boat Sir and the Yanks gave me a lift back" he stammered. The 'skipper' at the time was Captain Barry, known as a kindly man, he stared at Pitts for a full minute as he struggled to regain his thoughts and composure, then he spoke. "I've bloody well heard of this type of thing happening but I never expected it to happen to me. Master at Arms, see to him". "Yes Sir. You, Fall in outside the Regulating Office now, now, now" snapped the very irate Master. Fortunately the captain was spared a similar incident a couple of days later, but that is enough for now.

12 Leaving Plymouth

HMS Dorsetshire finally sailed from Plymouth at 1500hrs on June 9th.1940 to carry out a series of sea trials, including the testing of the newly fitted degaussing gear. The most noticeable part of this equipment was a large hawser that lay right around the ship on the upper deck. It carried the electric current to demagnetise the German acoustic mines that had become the scourge of allied shipping. Martin was only too aware that many of his ships' company were freshmen that needed knitting together as a team. Starting from now and continuing for many months, the men practised dealing with every type of emergency. This included explosions, mechanical and electrical breakdowns, internal fires, collisions and gun misfires. Fortunately the drill of stuffing hammocks into a holed ships' side only needed to be done in theory. I often wondered just how efficient this remedy would be.

At 2000hrs the same day we returned to Plymouth for reasons I don't know, but at 2300hrs 'Dorsetshire' cast off her moorings and eased out through the breakwater-heading south. I was to travel many nautical miles and see many interesting things before this good ship brought me back home. It was to be a wondrous experience that was all part of the process of my growing up. We encountered foul weather in the Bay of Biscay and a few faces turned pea green. As she rolled and pitched it was the opportunity to test our sea legs and the ability to withstand that most nauseating of ills, seasickness. For some it was their first taste of sea sailing and they still had to master the art of swaying gently with the roll of the deck. I preferred the quick movement of 'Dorsetshire' to the lingeringly slow dip and dive of Courageous. It was pleasing to see the squeamish expressions of misery on the faces of some young officers whom, when possible, discreetly disappeared to be sick in the privacy of their cabin or Gunroom. At least they were spared the facetious remarks of the ratings who never missed a chance to poke fun at them.

At 1000hrs on June 12th, we joined up with H.M.S. Cumberland and H.M.S. Shropshire escorting an impressive convoy of world famous ships. My post on board invariably meant I was with the commander on the after conning position to run his errands and man the headphones to the Bridge. It was an excellent vantage point to view all that was going on, today was a bonus, I could clearly see the Queen Mary, Empress of Canada, Empress of Britain, Andes and Acquatania amongst others. The ships, with a total tonnage of 251,425 tons, were carrying a large contingent of Australians to England for the war in Europe. The three heavy cruisers swept around and around the giant liners like collies tending sheep. Every precaution was to be taken to protect the ships against U-boat attack. The consequences of losing one vessel, packed with servicemen and women were too traumatic to contemplate. ASDIC probed for lurking submarines, lookouts scanned their overlapping arcs with extra vigilance. The guns traversed and elevated to reassure the Bridge that everyone was on their toes.

On June 14th, at 0900hrs the mighty H.M.S. Hood hove into sight with three destroyers and the aircraft carrier H.M.S. Argus. It was the first time I had seen the Hood and her size certainly impressed me, she looked so formidable. Argus was a funny looking carrier with a box like appearance, it accounted for her being known as the floating ditty box. Within the hour

'Hood' and her escorting warships took over the convoy and we left for Gibraltar. The watch stood down to Cruising Stations and the hands on deck went about their normal work programme. 'Bows down and bilge free' the cruiser sliced through the water, with the sun glistening on her newly painted superstructure to accentuate the lines of this graceful ship. The dark uniforms of the Home Fleet were gladly stowed away and replaced with the clinical 'whites' of the tropics. Wearing shorts made it obvious who were the newcomers. There was no disguising our lily white knees. It was also the time when several of the crew were suffering painfully swollen arms as a result of the inoculations that were compulsory going overseas. The peaceful routine came to an abrupt end just before noon when a U-boat was sighted. The alarm sent everyone scurrying to their action stations in a quick but orderly manner. Decks vibrated as the speed increased and the ship accelerated through the water to attack.

Gun crews were loaded and ready to fire by the time I got to the after bridge, but the swiftness of the aircrew really took the biscuit. The Supermarine Walrus was catapulted into the air while the alarm bells were still ringing. It made direct towards the target and dropped four bombs accurately on the U-boat. As it disappeared under water, the pilot reported hits and a 'kill' was registered. It was over as quickly as it started. "Check, check, check, revert to normal" came over the headphones and the incident was closed. It was a small contribution to the war at sea but every submarine destroyed was potentially an allied ship saved, more especially during the month of June 1940. This was a black month for the Allies. France, our close ally, capitulated to the Germans and signed an Armistice during the evening of June 22nd, which could have serious repercussions for the Allies. After the fall of Paris and the disintegration of the land forces, only the French fleet remained intact as an efficient fighting force. The fleet was amongst the largest in the world and the Germans would not allow it to remain outside of France. Under the terms of the cease-fire agreement the warships must return to French ports to be neutralised. The British government had little faith that this would be carried out, convinced that after a cooling off period the massive French fleet would be taken over by the German Kriegsmarine and deployed against the Allies.

This would be catastrophic and tip the scales in favour of the Axis winning the war. Churchill was determined to forestall the French warships from returning home. Operation 'Catapult', was put into action and a British naval squadron, Force H, arrived off the North African naval base at Oran, near Mers-el-Kebir, on July 3rd, 1940. Vice-Admiral Sir James Somerville commanding the squadron presented a clear ultimatum to the French Admiral in charge. The ships must join the Allies, dismantle and disarm, or scuttle in port. Admiral Gensoul agreed to speak with Captain Holland the British liaison officer but, on Admiral Darlan's orders, refused to cooperate. A time limit was given for the French to make a positive reply and in the meantime Admiral Somerville tried hard to convince his French counterpart that it would be insane to refuse the options. At 1745 hrs the deadline passed and the British Admiral reluctantly carried out his orders to open fire on the French ships. It was an unprecedented bloody and brutal attack which sent shock waves around the world. Over 1200 French sailors were killed and several warships sunk or damaged, including the battleships and battle-cruisers Bretagne, Dunkerque, Provence and Strasbourg. The French people were dumbfounded and extremely bitter that a former ally could do this.

Vice-Admiral Sir Andrew Cunningham fared better with Admiral Rene Godfroy in Alexandria. To prevent another occurrence like Mers-el-Kebir the French Admiral agreed to neutralise his ships if the British promised not to attempt to take them over. The fleet, including the battleship Lorraine and a squadron of cruisers, was de-fuelled and disarmed without loss of life. Now it was Dorsetshire's turn to become involved. The most modern and possibly the most powerful battleship at sea was the new 30.000 ton French battleship 'Richelieu', as yet unaccounted for. It was inconceivable that such a colossal warship should fall into enemy hands where it could do incalculable damage.

Dorsetshire's amphibious Walrus could not be remotely considered an attractive aircraft, ugly would be the best description, but for reconnaissance purposes it was an invaluable asset and never more so than on the 26th.July 1940. At 0500hrs it took off on an early morning patrol and could hardly believe it's good luck when it sighted the 'Richelieu'. The battleship was on a course that suggested she was complying with the German conditions and returning to a homeport. The Walrus made wireless contact with Dorsetshire but then total silence, causing fears for it's safety. The captain immediately ordered a sweeping search to be carried out, unaware that the plane had been forced down due to engine trouble but was still intact and riding the waves. Extra look-outs were posted as Martin impatiently paced up and down wanting to find his plane but also wanting to chase the battleship. To everyone's relief the plane was found at 1000hrs on the 27th and hoisted inboard, twenty-four hours after 'ditching'. What the aircrew had to tell Martin sent him speeding after the French warship, with his men closing up at action stations.

I nearly wet my pants when I saw the 'Richelieu', she was big and we were so small in comparison. Commander Westmacott never uttered a word or took his eyes from his binoculars and I wondered what was in his mind, nobody doubted what the Captain was thinking. With guns loaded 'Dorsetshire' steamed straight towards 'Richelieu' committed to opening fire or withdrawing in an undignified retreat. There was a suggestion put about on the Lower Deck that Martin was really a reincarnation of the famous English sea dog Sir Richard Grenville. This could be worrying in situations like the one we were in now, it might be far more prudent to flee on this occasion and fight at a more convenient moment in time considering the overwhelming odds. The tension was electric as the two ships got closer, we were within range of the battleships guns but she was out of range of ours, fortunately she was still holding her fire. In my headphones I heard someone say "I think the stupid bastard is going to get us all killed" but I didn't relay this to the Commander, I assumed he had the same thought himself. I am convinced to this day that the perspiration running down my legs was not entirely due to the tropical heat.

The massive 15" guns of the battleship were pointing at Dorsetshire. A confrontation between her and the 8" guns of the cruiser was a truly David and Goliath encounter. When he was in range Captain Martin, signalled, in plain language, ordering the captain of the battleship to proceed to the French West African port of Dakar. If he refused the British cruiser would have no alternative but to open fire. Minutes seemed like hours as I watched and wondered what the outcome would be. I felt more concern about this encounter than I did when Martin steamed straight at the German battleship 'Bismarck' and torpedoed her. After what seemed an eternity, and when it appeared as if nothing would prevent an unequal exchange of gunfire, the big guns of the Frenchman swung 'fore and aft'. The neutral position indicated that her captain was willing to co-operate with the British request, a decision that saved many lives on Dorsetshire and possibly a few on the French ship as well. Word was passed that the crisis had been avoided for the time being and it put the smiles back on our faces. The topic of conversation on the messdecks was about Martin. Some thought he was displeased at the outcome because he wanted a fight but I didn't agree with that. He had achieved what he wanted and that was to have Richelieu where it could be monitored.

The following day the battleship passed through the boom defence outside Dakar and made her way around a small headland bluff to tie up. The boom gate opened to let her in was quickly closed again to stop Dorsetshire following. Our Engineer Commander reported a low level of fuel oil and the captain reluctantly decided to slip away during the night and make full speed for Sierra Leone to replenish his tanks. Arriving at Freetown the ship quickly took on oil and immediately returned on station outside Dakar

13 The 'Richelieu'

Monotonously patrolling outside the French port, the boredom was occasionally relieved by Vichy French bombers carrying out high level strikes against us. Every time they approached we went to 'repel aircraft' stations and our gunners put up a deafening barrage with the 4" A/A and multiple pom-poms to keep the planes as high as possible. The clatter of the guns and the clanging of the empty cartridge cases as they ejected on to the steel deck was reassuring, it gave me a feeling that we were hitting back. The bombs rained down to send fountains of salt water cascading around the ship as it twisted and turned at speed to avoid being hit. It provoked a dry comment from someone nearby.
"Bloody Frogs. They couldn't hit a barn door with their finger in the lock". A biased remark considering we didn't hit any of their aircraft either. Whatever our feelings about the unsuccessful air attacks it was a pleasure to be joined by H.M.A.S. Australia and the aircraft carrier H.M.S.Hermes on July 5th. The presence of the carrier made it plain that the Admiralty meant business.

The negotiations going on between the two sides broke down so our 'powers that be' decided 'Richelieu' must be rendered unseaworthy. Sheltered behind the headland it would be difficult to damage her with gunfire and an air attack was ruled out. The British captains hatched a more devious plan. Subsequently on July 8th a crash boat set off from 'Hermes' on the pretext of further discussions and it was allowed through the boom gate. Unknown to the French it was carrying depth charges in it's stern covered by a tarpaulin.

Drawing alongside the after gangway, with the French watching from their Quarter Deck, the crew of the power boat whipped off the cover and rolled the depth charges under the battleship's stern to damage the steering and propellers. The boat then took off at full speed before the charges detonated and the French realised what was happening. The explosion alerted an armed cutter in the harbour and it came to investigate. Travelling as fast as he could the crash boat's coxswain raced towards the boom only to find the entrance was closed. Trapped, and with the armed cutter closing at speed, it was time for desperate measures. The ships 'laying off' couldn't give covering fire without risking hitting their own boat, they could only wait and watch as the chase continued. The coxswain decided to crash the boom and take the consequences. Anything was better than being taken prisoner of war. Knowing he only had one chance he fully opened the throttles and approached with every ounce of speed.

Just behind me I could hear a couple of 'worthies' laying a bet. "My tot he won't make it". "Make it Gulpers and you're on". Another joined in. "I'll take three sippers he does". All bets were on; it was like watching a horse race. Rum was a popular unit of gambling currency on the Lower Deck. The tot was expertly divided into 'gulpers' and 'sippers' according to the stake. Etiquette demanded that anyone winning a tot never drained the full measure, it was inexcusable bad manners not to leave a 'sippers' for the loser. "Here she comes" shouted the commander, he was as excited as the rest of us. Our binoculars picked up the Hermes boat in full flight still chased by the cutter. With its bows nearly out of the water it hit the top of the boom hawser before rearing up and crashing over the wire. Unbelievably it carried on towards Hermes and the French cutter decided to abandon the chase, knowing the British guns would open fire at the first opportunity. The success of the mission had a stimulating effect on everyone, with loud cheering the boat was safely hoisted on board the carrier. Knowing that the 'Richelieu' was put out of commission for a while the British warships left Dakar, with 'Dorsetshire' and Hermes making for Freetown. The next night, with time to relax, I decided to sling my hammock on the upper deck. Tropical nights could be very hot and sticky and I preferred to sleep in the open air rather than in the Mess.

At 0330hrs on July 10th, I was suddenly awakened by shouting, just in time to see a large black shape pass within yards of our ships' side. In the darkness, 'Dorsetshire' and Hermes had sailed right into a northbound Allied convoy and we had narrowly missed colliding with the armed merchant cruiser 'Corfu'. Putting her helm hard over to avoid hitting 'Dorsetshire' the AMC ran straight into H.M.S. Hermes, cutting a hole in the carrier's bows and killing a sailor. The 'Corfu' was also damaged in the collision and needed urgent repairs. Makeshift patching made it possible for the two ships to get under way and make for port. Later Hermes sailed to the Cape stern first, because her damage was more extensive she needed specialist dockyard attention, 'Corfu' could only steam at 20knots, but with 'Dorsetshire' escorting she sailed for Freetown. There was an air of expectation in the messdecks as the 'shellbacks' who had done time around Africa narrated a variety of interesting stories based on personal experiences. Easily available girls, from the ebony black and dusky maidens of the West Coast to the leggy blondes of the Cape, cheap beer and mouth watering food, it was heady wine for youngsters with vivid imaginations. That was before the killjoy Surgeon Commander rendered the boy seamen celibate for the foreseeable future. 'Bones' was a genius at instilling a terrifying fear into the hearts and minds of fledging mariners. Healthy bodies and free giving women did not mix, and he forcibly explained why. He left us with serious misgivings about relationships with the opposite sex and an assumption that they all suffered from some advanced form of unsociable disease.

At 1700hrs, on July 12th, we dropped anchor long enough to take on oil before sailing again. Freetown, capital of Sierra Leone (Mountain of Lions) was to be a frequent watering hole for us. There is no truth in the story that it is possible to smell the place before you see it. I could always make out the buildings on the waterfront before the rancid hot smelly odours got up my nose. Halts in Freetown were disparagingly referred to as Oil, Toil, Yam and Bloody Scram stops. The main engines had hardly stopped turning before fuel oil was pumped into the tanks. Paint brushes and chipping hammers appeared by the hundred to remove signs of wear and tear. Provisions invariably included the infamous Yam, a poor substitute for the humble potato. The root vegetable defied every known ploy by our cooks to transform it into an acceptable replacement but it still finished up hard and indigestible. The 'Scram' came as soon as oil and provisions were on board and Captain Martin impatiently made ready for sea to search for that elusive German raider. The long, seemingly endless, patrols made it apparent that finding an enemy ship in the vastness of the Atlantic Ocean was as difficult as the proverbial needle in a haystack. Stepping off the liberty boat for my first run ashore I experienced the mobs of touting children, some very young, who wanted to know if anyone would like to have a 'jiggie' 'jiggie' with a nice English school teacher. I don't suppose many on board would have refused the offer in the right place at the right time, but here the commodity was as rare as an English three-pound note and just as suspect. Why they picked on that particular profession was something I could never understand, or why they added that she had red hair.

Polite refusal was like water off a duck's back to the juvenile salesmen. It took a swift kick and a verbal 'sod off' to impress on them that their wares were not wanted. Market stalls provided the real fun places for us boys to spend an hour haggling with the traders. They assumed we had money to spare but what we had we intended keeping for later in the Sugar Bowl or the King Tom bars, the drinking places for sailors and marines. Bartering was an art with the persistent stallholders, most of which were Syrian or Indian. With our limited resources we had no intention of buying anything, irrespective of how low the price dropped. It was great fun to have the traders throwing their arms up to the sky and shouting in exasperation at our ridiculous counter offer to their original price. If they asked for the equivalent to five pounds we parried with the comparable sixpence to bring a bewildering look to their faces, not being sure what to make of us. Fred Ball and I preferred to save our money for a drink and a snack in the Sugar Bowl. It was noted for three specific things. The warm but welcome beer, the little roasted chickens (Shanghai Runners) about the size of a clenched fist, and witnessing the inevitable brawls that was a feature of a good run ashore. All three had some therapeutic value for releasing anxieties and tensions built up over, long hours of watchkeeping, lack of news from the family, and the slim chance of getting home in the near future. Youngsters were the least effected by the stresses, but they had few family responsibilities and were enjoying the new adventure abroad. Sailors fighting in the bars felt no bitterness towards their fellow antagonists, any aggression was generated by a fleeting desire to let off steam.

The natives in Freetown had an uncanny instinct when a ship was arriving. Long before it anchored the 'Bum' boats were ready to greet the incoming vessels with a very limited variety of goods. The main items for sale were plantains, bananas and green oranges. Occasionally they brought out a couple of monkeys hoping to fetch a good price, not knowing that Navy ships would not allow anyone to have a monkey as a pet. Bartering for fruit was a simple ritual, but monkeys presented a more exacting challenge. To get the animal on deck and release it without paying was a difficult task that needed a devious approach. Has your monkey got fleas, it looks sick Johnny". "No Boss it not, it clean". "Send it up in the basket Johnny, if him clean you get plenty money". "No Boss. You send Johnny money just for him to hold" The negotiations usually continued on the same lines for some time with no one giving ground. If in desperation the native sent the monkey up in a basket for inspection it was his undoing. The frightened animal was released to disappear up the ships' rigging and the boys responsible disappeared just as fast below deck. Officers on watch kept a constant lookout for our high jinks but it was difficult to find the guilty ones and put them on a charge. A bigger headache was getting the monkey down before it was seen by one of the senior officers or worse still the captain. Retrieving it, once it had found it's freedom, was no easy task and often involved the use of fire hoses to dislodge the creature. A more acceptable pastime was tossing coins into the water for the natives to dive for. It was amazing the length of time they stayed under water. One noteworthy fellow would dive from his shallow canoe and swim completely under the ship for the princely sum of a shilling. It was a tremendous feat and he was invariably paid more by an appreciative audience. Having watched him leave his dugout we raced to the other side of the ship to see him surface and get his money and a cheer. It must have sapped his strength because he seldom repeated the dive again the same day.

On this particular visit, after taking on oil and seen the 'Corfu' in safe hands, 'Dorsetshire' left harbour at speed to follow up a report of enemy activity five hundred miles west of the Cape Verde Islands. It was a fruitless chase with nothing to show for hurrying to the area expecting action. That was until July 24th, when Captain Martin stopped a Portuguese merchant ship and decided to search her. Although her captain argued his neutrality he was powerless to resist and hove to. A boarding party scrambled on board just in time to stop an Italian Consul from destroying his official papers. He was asleep in his bunk when Dorsetshire stopped the ship, unaware of the boarding party until it was too late. I heard later that the papers contained reports on Axis supply vessels operating in the South Atlantic and provided our naval intelligence with vital information. The Consul was returning from South America aboard the neutral ship expecting to slip safely through our blockade and get back to Europe. He was closely watched as he dressed into something suitable for getting into the waiting cutter. Four days later we were back in Sierra Leone to disembark our prisoner, his war was over. The following day it was back to sea on search and destroy patrol although a 'buzz' was circulating that the captain was extending the next patrol before taking the ship to Simonstown.

14 DURBAN S.A.

Expectations were shattered when we returned instead to Freetown to replenish the oil supply. Both watches got a couple of hours ashore before we left again to continue the chase for the phantom German raider reported in the South Atlantic. The lower deck sages were busy with their crystal balls, adamant, that this time we would end up in Capetown or neighbouring Simonstown when the patrol finished. At 1700hrs on August 5th.1940 we dropped anchor at St.Helena. I wasn't especially interested in its claim to fame as the last resting-place of Napoleon Bonaparte. For me it was best remembered for being surrounded with the bluest water I had ever seen. The islanders were obviously pleased to see the warship, knowing we carried several items of merchandise they had requested from the Crown authorities. The following day we carried out a full main armament shoot at a smoke target as well as a whole series of day and night exercises to test our fighting efficiency. Night time 'Action Stations' was never appreciated by men off duty, called out of their hammocks to find their way along the darkened upper deck half asleep, without colliding into fixtures. Except for the odd curse, conversation was non-existent as the ghostly figures moved silently and quickly, observing the rights of way to get speedily to their stations. We were never warned beforehand if the alarm was a practise so every call was treated as the real thing if we valued our lives. At 0500hrs on August 24th, we weighed anchor and set off to make contact with the SS Orian bound for Capetown. We found her on the 28th, escorted by a Netherlands cruiser. 'Dorsetshire' was happy to relieve the Dutchman of his charge and more than willing to accompany the merchantman to the Cape. The consensus of opinion decided that the captain was the only one not overjoyed at the prospects of some shore leave, suggesting he would prefer to be at sea hunting elusive Germans.

The threatened passage through the Mediterranean Sea and the Suez Canal to the Far East increased the importance of the route around the Cape as a safer alternative for Allied shipping. Simonstown with its new dockyard and victualling facilities was invaluable to the convoys and their escorts. South Africa, with two capitals and two official languages was a self-governing dominion that could have understandably remained neutral, the only tie with the Empire was recognising George VI as its King. In the predominantly Dutch speaking areas there was still a ground swell of bitterness towards the British. The root cause of the grievances went back hundreds of years when the Cape was a staging post for the Dutch and English trading between Europe and the Indies. At the outbreak of war it was touch and go whether South Africa would remain non-partisan and deny the Allies the use of the all-important bases. A vociferous Dutch (Afrikaner) lobby campaigned to stay out of the conflict but fortunately, under the persuasion of Field Marshal Jan Smuts the Union decided to support England. Afrikaner ill-feeling never included the British servicemen. Thousands have recorded their grateful thanks to the Dutch and English speaking people of South Africa for the generous welcome they received when ships called there. The only armed forces I can remember being made unwelcome were the Australians, and from my personal recollections the South Africans had cause to dislike them for their abusive behaviour to the local people.

On the 29th.August 'Dorsetshire' passed Robbin Island and entered Table Bay, with it's backdrop of the famous flat-topped Table Mountain, to see the 'Orian' safely inside the Capetown breakwater. For days the boy's messdeck had been a model of good behaviour, everyone taking care not to get up to any mischief that might jeopardise the exciting prospect of visiting Capetown. Unfortunately shore leave was denied us this time. We carried on around the Cape Peninsular into False Bay and anchored off Simonstown for a very brief pause before leaving for Durban. A short distance along the coast from False Bay, 'Dorsetshire' took care to steer well south of Danger Point and the notorious submerged rock two miles off the point. This infamous spot was the scene of a tragic sinking when the troopship 'Birkenhead' foundered in 1860. Two hundred soldiers and sailors drowned or were eaten by sharks before they could reach land. In true maritime tradition the ships' boats were given up to the women and children who thankfully all reached shore safely. A memorial was unveiled on the point in 1938 to commemorate the tragedy.

Remembering that a large part of the crew, after two years and eight months abroad had only one week at home before sailing again, it was understandable why the cities of the Cape appealed. Durban, Capetown and Simonstown were idyllic ports of call, not only for refurbishing and provisioning ship but equally important for the men's welfare. As Durban was sighted the ship prepared for entering harbour. Special Sea Dutymen were already at their stations with rope and wire hawsers at the ready for tying up to the jetty. I preferred this to shackling to a buoy, it was easier to just walk down a gangway instead of using a crowded liberty boat. At last civilisation: As we eased our way past the whaling station on one side and the town on the other we were greeted by the beautiful singing of a lady standing on Maydon Wharf. Dressed all in white, her powerful rich operatic voice came across the water, welcoming us to a safe anchorage. Ships that made frequent visits expected her to be waiting on the jetty, and they were seldom disappointed. It was estimated that she sang to approximately 3,000,000 servicemen, arriving and leaving port, during the war years. They knew her as 'The Lady in White' because few knew her real name was Mrs. Perla Siedle Gibson. When ships left she sang a sad farewell as if knowing that many of those waving from the packed decks of the troopships would never be returning. With great pleasure the H.M.S. Dorsetshire Association welcomed her as the guest of honour to their reunion at Plymouth in 1970. It was a small 'thank you' for the many voluntary hours she spent working in the service canteens.

The hospitality of the South African people was legendary and especially by H.M.S. Dorsetshire. The people seemed to have a special affinity for our ship, possibly because of the ships' long association with the Cape Station. During the 1933-35 commission 'Dorsetshire' was the flagship of the Commander in Chief of the Cape. Bonds of friendship were made that lasted throughout the life of the cruiser. South Africans made up an appreciable part of 'Dorsetshire's' crew, unfortunately several who volunteered their services died when the ship was sunk in 1942. Now as heaving lines snaked through the air from ship to jetty to carry the heavier securing ropes, the perils of the sea were forgotten. Shore leave was 'piped' for the off duty watch and the lucky ones hurriedly changed from shorts into full white No6 uniforms, the girls ashore were not going to be disappointed today. A new word was now added to our everyday vocabulary, 'Up-homers'. It was the term used to express the homely comforts and generosity extended to the sailors and especially to boy seamen. It not only revived and refreshed, it also prepared us for our next stint at sea. 'Dorsetshire' was scheduled to stay in port for two weeks with the prospects of all night shore leave for adults, the first since leaving England. As soon as the ship made fast Fred and I could hardly contain us in our eagerness to get on dry land and enjoy the fruits of this African Utopia.

We had been assigned, a more appropriate word would be 'adopted', by a Mr. and Mrs. Dixon for our 'Up-homers'. They met us when we stepped on to the jetty and drove us to their home. Mr.Dixon was a tall man who, as I was told, was the managing director of Lever Brothers S.A. Mrs.Dixon was a small gentle woman with an abundant reserve of motherly affection to bestow on the new additions to her family. The Dixon's children, I understood, were away at school in Switzerland where they would be staying for some time. Every possible luxury was provided to make our visits to the Dixon mansion an annexe to heaven. A chauffeur driven car was always available to transport Fred and myself to the house when we were ashore. We were taken to the best restaurants and shows, often joined by two very pretty girls of our own age. Mr.Dixon unfortunately had a tendency to get bright ideas for our enjoyment and he was prone to "I'll telephone your captain and arrange it". It was a statement that sent shivers down our backs. That anyone should mention our names in the presence of Captain Benjamin Martin to ask a 'favour' was an awesome thought. It took a lot of pleading to convince the Dixons that boy seamen must at all times adopt a very low profile in the propinquity of their captain. On one occasion Mr.Dixon found out the number of our messmates and two days later a lorry arrived at the ship to unload a large cardboard box for each boy on the messdeck. They contained every type of soap product the boys would need for some considerable time.

On another occasion when we had been talking about ships' entertainment he phoned 'Dorsetshire' to ask if the crew would like a dance at his company's works canteen. The offer was accepted and Captain Martin ordered the Marine band to attend as well to act as backup for the dance band provided by Lever Brothers. When Fred and I arrived, we found the canteen transformed. Colourful bunting, balloons, streamers and flowers, gave the place a carnival appearance that put everyone into a jolly mood. The dance band was already in full swing with dozens of potential 'Fred Astaires' twirling their 'Ginger Rodgers' around the floor to a lively quickstep. There was plenty of unattached girls so we found two who were willing and courageous enough to 'have a go', even after we warned them that we were terrible dancers. Tables at one end of the room bulged with a cornucopia of delicacies for the evening buffet, plus a plentiful supply of wine and beer to wash it down. The Royal Marine band did an excellent supporting job as well as joining in the festivities and 'letting their hair down'. The Last Waltz came all too soon with everyone remarking how well they had enjoyed themselves. Needless to say when it was known that our 'Up-homers' had been responsible for the bash, Fred and I collected a few pats on the back from our shipmates. Pleased by the success of the social evening, Mrs. Dixon asked us to bring a few friends to the house for dinner. We agreed, providing the ship was still in port. The difficulty was finding another four boys not already committed, but we managed to muster Tom Murtagh, 'Eddie' Edmunds, Oscar Parkes and 'B'. The identity of 'B' must remain undisclosed to protect his stupidity and veneer of table manners. After a couple of aperitifs we all sat down to a beautifully laid table, with Mr. Dixon sitting at one end and Mrs.Dixon the other. The centrepiece was a mountain of strawberries and cream, which she thought would appeal to us for dessert. Black servants stood attentively waiting to serve. After 'Grace' was said the servants filled the green glass finger bowls and waited for Mrs. Dixon's nod to start serving the first course. There was a short pause and it was at that precise moment 'B' lifted his finger bowl and drank the water, much to the astonishment of the servants.

One of them refilled the bowl only to prompt 'B' to take another swig, sending the servants eyes rolling in disbelief. Noticing Mr.Dixon's mouth twitching in a suppressed smile I felt embarrassed. I knew about finger bowls because my Mother had been the housekeeper to a very prominent Lawyer and his family where the use of such things was commonplace. She had a set in her china cabinet at home, possibly 'acquired' during her days in service. In our working class environment there was little call for them but we were brought up to appreciate their purpose. Likewise, it appeared everyone else at Dixon's knew what they should be used for except that prat 'B'. Mrs.Dixon rescued the situation by starting the meal that carried on without incident, until coffee time. As it was being served the servants placed boxes of cigarettes on the table for those wanting to smoke. Mr.Dixon, who enjoyed a cigar himself, asked out of courtesy if anyone else would also like one. Five of us confessed we preferred cigarettes but 'B', the plonker, said he preferred a cigar. Unfortunately he didn't know, or forgot, that the end had to be snipped. That was why a servant was offering him a cutter. His lung punishing efforts to light up allowed the blacks to enjoy a few stifled sniggers until one servant intervened and pierced the end for him.

In addition to the hospitality of the 'up-homers', local charities added their contribution by organising a number of popular sightseeing tours. A strikingly colourful sight in Durban was the rickshaws and their owners. The rickshaws were quite a sight but the 'boys' pulling them were spectacular. The ever-smiling black faces under massive brightly coloured headdresses, with equally impressive costumes of stunning hues and shades, had a special appeal to the sailors. Rickshaw riding was harmless fun and an agreeable way to add to the pleasures of a few hours ashore. What usually started off as a sedate sightseeing jaunt often developed into a wild chariot race when a few carriages met up on Marine Parade. It was not uncommon to see them, three and four abreast, speeding along the seafront to the amusement of onlooking South Africans. Urged on by their passengers the Zulus jostled for front position knowing that the first rickshaw to reach the end of the promenade would get a winner's bonus. Invariably after a race, the tired drivers were put into their own carriages and the sailors got between the shafts to pull them back to the other end of the esplanade. Riding and getting paid for it, the Zulus must have thought that the sailors were a mad lot. White South Africans in the street just smiled and shook their heads at the spectacle of a grinning Zulu sitting back in his rickshaw while two immaculately dressed sailors sweated to pull him along the prom.

In Capetown a trip to the top of Table Mountain with the panoramic views was a favoured venue. Solitude Valley [The Valley of a Thousand Hills] outside Durban was another. On my first visit to this spectacular place with two South African families, that included a couple of girls about my age, I displayed a naivety unbecoming a sailor-boy. As soon as our party arrived and parked the vehicles, the adults busied themselves choosing a suitable spot on a slope near the river to have a picnic. The two girls produced a ball and started tossing it from one to the other so Fred and I joined in. Suddenly one of them gave it a mighty throw, sending it right over my head and flying down the slope into the river. I immediately turned and chased after it but came to an abrupt stop at the edge of the water when I was confronted by a group of bare breasted young black women displaying very proud nipples, and a lot more, as they splashed about in the river. They must have been crouching down in the water when we first arrived but got up as I approached. The unexpected sight of their glistening nakedness confused me for a moment and I lost my composure. My immediate reaction was to enjoy a long lingering look, but conscious of our hosts' presence I overcame my natural curiosity and beat a hasty retreat. Scrambling back up the riverbank I felt piqued to hear everyone laughing at my awkwardness.

The South Africans assured me that native girls exposing their bare breasts was a normal feature in this part of the world and that I would soon get used to it. I then realised that the ball had been thrown deliberately as a joke to embarrass me but I got my own back later. Canteens manned exclusively by voluntary workers were another attraction for sailors. Most of the volunteers came from better off Springbok families, but it didn't deter them from doing all the menial chores associated with dispensing stomach filling meals to satisfy voracious naval appetites. One canteen in Durban, known as the Victoria League Club, provided an extensive mouth-watering menu for a mere pittance. An abundant supply of foodstuff, donated by the local people, free of charge to keep the price of meals extremely low. The less pleasant side of a stay in dock was carrying out repair and maintenance to make the ship ready for sea. One job that always caused a considerable amount of moaning and groaning was 'chipping off' before repainting. Dozens and dozens of chipping hammers banged away all day on the steel of the ships' side to remove the layers of old paint. The work was tedious, noisy, dusty, and dirty and went on for days before the metal surface was ready to be wire brushed in preparation for the coats of red lead and grey paint. Fortunately for me on my first visit to Durban I was still the Commander's messenger and considered part of his staff, which excused me the filthy chores. My turn was still to come when I became an Ordinary Seaman and relinquished the post traditionally reserved for Boy Seamen.

15 Sea raiders in the Atlantic

The necessary work on the ship was finally completed and at 0700hrs on the 18th.September 'Dorsetshire' cast off her mooring lines and prepared to stream paravanes once clear of the harbour. It was an ongoing procedure when entering and leaving port as a precaution against enemy mines laid in the approaches. Later the P.V.s were winched in and we settled down to Cruising Stations. It was announced that we were to make a delivery stop at Simonstown but not long enough for men to be allowed ashore. A lot of catching-up had to be done after the time in dock. Engineers, Shipwrights, Electricians and a host of other trades needed to ensure their equipment was functioning at its best. Gunners and Torpedo-men for their part needed realistic drills to test their efficiency. Contact with the easy-going style of life ashore, even for such a brief time, had a nasty habit of dulling the instant reflexes required in action. On the way south the barometer dropped dramatically, a warning that had to be heeded. Both watches were piped on deck to batten down the hatches and stow everything moveable before the rapidly freshening breeze increased to gale force. The mountainous seas of the 'Roaring Forties' were soon pounding the ship, spilling tons of grey-green foam-crested water over the bows. It caused a lot of damage on deck, as well as smashing most of the ship's boats, even though they had been swung inboard and made fast on their davits. The big guns were muzzled and swung broadside on to prevent water penetration, but the fury of the howling wind was not to be denied. Instead, water got in through the ventilators and flooded several of the messes. Damage Control parties worked non-stop pumping out to contain the effects of the maelstrom weather. Decks were awash with rushing water as the ship rolled and pitched making walking precarious on the slippery surfaces. The unfortunates exposed to the elements were drenched with salt laden spray as the roaring waves crashed over the ship. Lashed by the driving rain and the wind and buffeted by the pounding seas, 'Dorsetshire' lurched from one deep trough to another in a series of sickening plunges that did little for the stomach. With noticeable relief we anchored at Simonstown long enough to drop the despatches and let our insides resume a state of normality, then we were under way again.

Rounding the Cape the weather became warmer, and the seas calmer. As we moved briskly northward before the Trade Winds, it was a good time to repair some of the damage inflicted by the heavy seas. There was plenty of drying-out to be done to keep the ships' company busy, but the replacement of the boats would have to wait until arrangements could be made to pick them up later. As we approached the area between the North-East and South-East winds, known as the Doldrums, the heat became intense. With not a breath of wind to ease the sultry stickiness, I could understand the feelings of the men in old time sailing ships becalmed here for long periods. Above and below deck it was stifling, oppressive and uncomfortable, more so at night when a strict blackout was observed. As we 'crossed the line' I remembered the first time I did it and some of the shellbacks felt cheated out of the good-humoured discomfort King Neptune and Queen Amphitrite should have inflicted on us newcomers. The 'old timers' took a dim view of the ceremony being put into cold storage for the duration of the war. The most they could expect was the Quartermaster announcing over the tannoy to 'stand-by' to cross and then shouting 'bump' as the ship passed over the imaginary line. Eventually even that became sporadic, on one occasion I crossed the Equator six times in one day as 'Dorsetshire' steamed a zig-zag course along it. Having never taken part in the frolicsome ritual I didn't receive a 'Crossing of the Line' certificate. Clocks were frequently changed backwards and forwards as the ship passed between the different time zones. There were winners and losers, depending on the watch you were keeping at the time of the change over, but the process was regarded as an irritation that happened too often. We arrived at Freetown long enough to oil before resuming patrol off the West Coast of Africa.

The next day the Captain ordered a full shoot for the 8" guns. In addition to the general duties of running the ship everyone was involved in what seemed a continuous programme of exercises. It included simulated attacks on surface vessels, hostile aircraft and enemy submarines. Most days, when weather permitted, the Walrus plane was launched to carry out reconnaissance flights. Before the installation of the radio location system it was the only source of finding ships on the other side of the horizon. Action Stations was frequently sounded without warning, day or night. It was the way to assess the competence of the men to bring the ship to First Degree readiness in the shortest possible time. Drills were carried out regardless of need for sleep or food, those just coming off a long watch had something to justifiably moan about. There were little spare leisure spells for the men during the long periods at sea. When time did permit, men washed, ironed and repaired their clothes. Afterwards it was a game of Mahjong or cards before 'crashing down' to catch some sleep, not knowing what the next hours might bring. It has to be said that 'Pincher' Martin was a hard task master when it came to making H.M.S.Dorsetshire a good fighting machine. One thing was for sure, he was determined that our ship should not become a wallflower tied up in port for the least excuse.

On this patrol we stopped and boarded a merchant ship that turned out to be packed with Vichy French sympathisers openly hostile to the British. 'Dorsetshire' escorted the Frenchman, first to Takaradi in the Gold Coast and then to Keta in Ghana where it was interred. During the handing over, a signal was received that a German raider had been reported in our area. It was all Captain Martin needed to have his ship racing out into the Atlantic to find it. He was unlucky because the German had slipped away into the wide expanse of ocean, and 'Dorsetshire' went back to Sierra Leone, on the 18th.October 1940 to collect a convoy. The large number of ships including the Monarch of Bermuda, Orantes, Duchess of York, Capetown Castle, and Sterling Castle, set the grapevine buzzing with all kinds of rumours. The Lower Deck lawyers had a field day with their predictions based on facts from an impeccable source high up. Word had it that we were going straight into the Med through the Suez Canal, more commonly referred to as the Sewage Canal. Instead we sailed back around the Cape and into the Indian Ocean to be joined by another seven merchantmen, making it a sizeable convoy.

For once the messdeck prophets were partly right, we were heading towards the Suez Canal but only as far as Aden. Martin was never happy playing nursemaid to merchant ships, it restricted his obsessive longing to find and sink a German sea raider. He wanted that prize like a big game hunter wanted a lion's head, but he would have to wait a little longer before he got it. Nine days later as we approached our destination, four warships joined the convoy to give extra protection, signifying the importance of Convoy W.S.3. The additional escort was more than welcome as we rounded the 'horn' of Africa between Cape Guardafui in Italian Somaliland and the island of Socotra. The close proximity of the enemy coastline to the west made Allied convoys vulnerable to attack, especially from the numerically strong Italian air force. As a precaution, the ships' company went to 2nd.Degree Readiness, with additional lookouts posted and told to be extra vigilant. Captain Martin was taking no chances with such a large convoy, even against the Italians, he made all haste across the Gulf of Aden to the safety of the other side. Thankfully this run was trouble free and at 1400 hrs on the 15th.November 1940 I got my first sight of Aden as 'Dorsetshire' steamed past Pinnacle Rock and entered the port. The presence of the oil refinery at Little Aden, and the endless pipes and terminals, made it obvious why this barren place was so important to the Allies. It's safe anchorage and facilities had the capability of refuelling several large ships at the same time

Having handed the convoy over to others, the captain took the opportunity of topping up with oil before turning the ship around and setting a southerly course back the way we came. It didn't matter that I was unable to go ashore at Aden, the chance to enjoy the delights of the few palm groves and salt pans on the bleak landscape could wait. During the daytime the heat was intense and strict attention was paid to make sure everyone dressed in the 'rig of the day'. Men on deck had to be properly covered, especially with the appropriate headwear at all times until 1630 hrs. Failure to do so meant ending up in the Commander's report. Older hands recalled an unfortunate incident on a previous visit to these parts by 'Dorsetshire'. Off Perim Island, Boy Seaman Quinn was taken ill with sunstroke and died as the ship put into

Aden where he was buried. It was sad that this avoidable death should happen to a young lad setting out to see the world for the first time. The relating of the tragedy was a warning to us all not to take liberties with the tropical sun before late afternoon.

Early on the morning of November 18th the captain spoke over the tannoy, informing us that later in the day we were going to attack the city of Dante (now Hafun), capital of Italian Somaliland. Dorsetshire was to cause the maximum amount of damage to the Italian port as well as sinking any ships sheltering there. Boys coming off the bridge remarked how pleasant Martin appeared to everyone, not a good sign. They were quickly reminded that this was his normal pattern of behaviour when there was a good chance of ordering his guns to fire in anger. The coastal city came into view at 1600hrs and shortly afterwards within range of Dorsetshire's main armament. The 8" guns of County Class cruisers had a phenomenal range and striking power out of all proportion to their size. The Italians were to find this out as soon as the range-takers selected their targets. On my headphones I could hear the checks being made and finally the Gunnery Officer in the Director Control reporting that all guns were ready to fire. In turn I repeated everything to the Commander to keep him informed what was happening on the bridge. Martin had issued instructions to the Gunnery Officer to pay particular attention to targets that appeared to be oil storage tanks and warehouses. What looked like the residential area was to be avoided for humane reasons. Much to the disappointment of the Captain and the crew, all Italian surface ships had dispersed, possibly word had got out that a British cruiser was on the prowl.

As soon as I heard "Standby to Fire" I braced myself knowing what to expect. "Fire". The flash and bang of the guns as they obeyed, was like music to my ears. It sent the adrenaline pumping with total disregard for the poor souls on the receiving end. The long steel barrels firing and recoiling fascinated me. Standing just forward of 'X' and 'Y' turrets I got the heat and black smoke every time they belched out, but in my excitement I was oblivious to any discomfort. With each thunderous roar the guns sent high explosive shells speeding towards the city to do more destruction. 'Dorsetshire', cruising backwards and forwards in front of Dante, kept outside the range of the shore batteries but close enough to hit everything at will. Through my glasses I watched buildings collapse as salvo after salvo found their mark. After firing over 200 hundred shells and demolishing the bigger buildings, the order came to "Cease Fire", then "Check, Check, Check, Revert to Normal". On reflection I felt a twinge of sympathy for the Italians. Operation 'Rope' as it was code-named was too one-sided, particularly as nobody took the Italians seriously as a fighting force, The Walrus had been catapulted off to 'spot' and report on the damage being done. It was a relief to see the Old Duck returning having miraculously survived being hit by the gunners ashore. On this occasion no one on board the plane was injured but unfortunately the same aircrew died later in tragic circumstances.

The frustration of the Torpedo Department was openly voiced by a disgruntled Torpedo Officer, Lieutenant Carver. The lack of shipping deprived his men the chance of taking any part in the operation. Captain Martin must have thought the gunnery department had already received their share and gave the last remaining target to the Lieutenant. With the charitable gesture of a benevolent uncle he told Carver to destroy it. 'It' was an extremely long loading jetty that protruded far out from the shore and obviously used for the lading of deep-water ships. The explosion from a direct hit by a single torpedo on the seaward end of the jetty produced a spectacular domino effect, destroying the entire structure. As it tumbled like a pack of cards there was a spontaneous cheer from the torpedo section, sufficient to bring a wry smile to Martin's lips; he was never a man to show undue emotion. Having completed what he had come to do, the captain gave orders that set the ship on course for the open sea heading south, leaving the enemy city a smouldering mass. For me it was enough excitement for one day, going off watch I got my head down and slept like a lamb on new straw.

Some time later at sea, we got the good news that 'Dorsetshire' was bound for Simonstown. This was especially pleasing for the Springboks with family in the Cape. I was overjoyed that the ship was expected to be staying for a few days. At long last I was going to get the opportunity of seeing for myself the place I had heard so much about. At 0800hrs on December 4th.1940 we came alongside and tied up inside the harbour for an unbelievably long stay of six days. The ships' company only got restricted shore leave, even the South Africans who lived locally were not allowed overnight passes to be with their families. This did not go down too well with them or their relatives. We were told we had to be on constant alert and ready for sea at short notice, whilst at the same time carrying out much needed maintenance work. Regarding leave, this was hard to believe, considering the ship was scheduled to be in dry dock for three days to have her bottom scraped of barnacles and the whole ship repainted.

16 Simonstown

Serendipity is possibly the most appropriate word to use for Simonstown, or as it was more popularly known as 'Snoekie'. Named after Simon van der Stel a one-time governor of the Cape, it could produce unexpected surprises for newcomers. Not the least was an extremely large Great Dane dog known to everyone as 'Just Nuisance'. This canine celebrity came to fame for it's ability to round up tipsy sailors in Capetown and herding them to the railway station for the return journey to 'Snoekie'; a kind of sheep dog for humans. Strange tales about 'Just Nuisance' have been told by the multitude of sailors who visited the Cape during the war years, some of them similar to experiences I personally witnessed. The dog was always waiting at Simonstown station to catch the train with the first libertymen going up to Capetown. After spending the day there he never failed to turn up for the last train back in the evening, usually towing four or five well 'oiled' but peaceful matelots. Any sailor unsure and unsteady could rely on Nuisance making his rounds to provide support and guidance to the station. Nobody knew if the dog had an owner but his adopted residence became HMS Afrikander, a shore establishment on the outskirts of Capetown. He first started hanging around the ships when he was still a puppy. Even then it was plain he would be a massive hound when fully grown. His determined begging and pestering for tasty morsels to satisfy his ravenous appetite meant he was often referred to as just a nuisance, and the name stuck. When Just Nuisance was in Capetown his usual habitat was the naval canteen, here he was assured of a hearty meal followed by uninterrupted sleep. Just as important he was in the company of the people he liked best, the men in square rig. The only flaw in an otherwise amiable nature was his open hostility towards women, in or out of uniform. The presence of Nuisance became such an intrinsic part of the Royal Navy and the authorities arranged payment for a seasonal pass on the railway to avoid any trouble with ticket collectors.

For the men not going into Simonstown or up to Capetown, the dockyard provided an excellent canteen selling Lion and Castle lager at very low prices. It was essentially a place for serious drinkers to consume vast quantities in an atmosphere of masculine egotism. As the evening wore on and the vocal chords got well lubricated, so the tempo mellowed. Singing usually started with solo efforts of mournful ballads about 'dear old England' and homeless orphans. This was guaranteed to be followed by 'Roll out the Barrel' and 'Hearts of Oak'. At some time during the evening it was a certainty that HMS Dorsetshire's 'national anthem' would get an airing. The opening verse it was a signal for everyone to join in with gusto, an enthusiasm that belied the fact that 'Dorsetshire' was a much-loved ship.

> "This is my story, this is my song.
> We've been in commission too bloody long.
> Roll out the Rodney, Nelson, Renown.
> This three funnelled bastard is getting me down".

I went there a few times with Fred Ball but found it boring listening to repetitive recollections of waterfront brawls and slurred confessions of female conquests. It was not the best way of spending time away from the ship. Thankfully the canteen was well inside the dockyard precinct and far away from the ears of the civilian population. Astonishingly, I never saw or heard of anyone fighting, even when most of the regulars had supped enough to sink a battleship. I think I speak, not only for H.M.S. Dorsetshire, but for all naval ships that visited South Africa when I say that the general good behaviour of sailors ashore showed the respect they had for the South African people. For their part the Springboks always treated us well, never referring to visiting British servicemen as Uitlanders (foreigners).

The daily routine in harbour continued with the usual cleaning, painting and general maintenance, but work seemed easier to carry out in the environment of this lovely place. Then like that old saying 'all good things must come to an end' it was time to leave. Everyone busied themselves making ready for sea to do the job we were being paid for. The only person with a noticeable smile on his face as we 'cast off' was Captain Benjamin Martin. He was never happier then when heading out into the vastness of the ocean with prospects of an enemy encounter. Once again I could look forward to adding many more sea miles to my tally before enjoying the pleasures of another run ashore. Most ports of the world leave some lasting impression on those that have visited them. Sydney its harbour bridge, Rio the famous statue and Yokohama has Mount Fujiyama. For me the sight of flat topped Table Mountain, especially when the clouds settled over it giving the impression that the table cloth was being laid, was a sight I would always remember.

On the 18th.December 1940 H.M.S Neptune joined H.M.S. Dorsetshire. Admiral Raikes ordered the two cruisers to search about 500 miles out into the Atlantic west of the African coast because a positive sighting of a German raider had been reported. Christmas Day arrived just like any other at sea except for one small incident during the afternoon. HMS. Neptune, away to our starboard, accidentally fired one of her torpedoes narrowly missing 'Dorsetshire's' stern. It was the topic of much light-hearted banter in the Mess, nobody seemed to take the possible consequences seriously. I never did get to know the outcome of the enquiry. There must have been quizzical questions asked in high places why one Allied ship fired a torpedo at another, especially during the day of goodwill.

During the Christmas Day there was one or two half-hearted renderings of well-known carols from the men as they went about their work, but no provision had been made to mark the occasion. The remote possibility of a bottle of beer or some extra rations was too much to expect in the circumstances, which was just as well because we never got them. Unnecessary fire hazards, such as paper trimming, to decorate the Messdeck, was forbidden. As I stood my 'watch', the nearest I got to a Merry Christmas was thinking of the folks at home. Almost certainly the family would be enjoying the once a year event of having a chicken for dinner, the 'bird' it was always referred to. Mum would have cashed in her Christmas Club money all of three pounds she had saved throughout the year, half at Lipton's and half at the Home and Colonial Stores. There would be the bottle of Sandemans port that was a special treat to be slowly sipped and relished by the adults, and especially there would be the nuts and oranges.

One thing we always had plenty of was Christmas pudding. Mum started making them early in the year to allow time for the mixture to properly mature. For nine months of the year, the cloth-covered basins around the shelf of the kitchen were a constant reminder of Advent. This was the second Christmas of the war, and both of them like all the others I had in the

Navy, would be spent away from home. My eldest brother must have also been missing Christmas. He was somewhere in the Pacific, later to be captured by the Japanese.

On New Years Day H.MS Dorsetshire joined up with the aircraft carrier HMS Furious and the light cruiser HMS Dunedin. A week later we changed company and linked up with the carrier Formidable and our sister ship HMS Norfolk for exercises that included an 8" Full Calibre shoot. January 11th.1941. My eighteenth birthday and I was elevated to Ordinary Seaman. It was time to say goodbye to the Boy's Mess and move to the Fo'c'sle Messdeck. It meant the end of my time as Commander's messenger and the start of new duties. I had matured enough not to get excited about birthdays and all the things like cards and congratulations that went with them; not that I was about to get either. My new Cruising Station was in the main director control for the big guns, high above the Bridge. After instruction, I operated the range and deflection dials conveying information to the Transmitting Station deep in the bowels of the ship. The T.S. was the nerve centre where all information such as range, speed, wind, fall of shot, enemy course, was fed into the mechanical computer of the day to be analysed and fed back to the guns.

Action Stations was in 'A' turret magazine where I later shared the discomforts with another long time friend George Bell and two other youngsters. It was an uncomfortable place packed with highly explosive material. Cordite wrapped in long shalloon bags gave off an obnoxious odour that seemed to give everyone a headache by the end of a 'watch'. I would have felt sorry for anyone suffering from claustrophobia working in the confined space of the magazine. After entering the Shellroom through a thick steel hatch, the magazine crew then had to go through another small metal door. When this door was closed and clipped, an additional steel door was closed over the top as an extra precaution. A very long key was inserted through the two doors from the outside to secure them. Once inside we were totally reliant on someone in the Shellroom letting us out in an emergency. It was a necessary safeguard if the magazine had to be flooded in the case of fire. The decision to unlock the doors to save their own lives, at the risk of blowing up the ship, could not be left to the magazine crew themselves.

On the 15th.January the other ships left for the south and 'Dorsetshire' resumed her role in the Atlantic. Time at sea was now made up of seemingly endless patrols and fruitless searches. Coupled with the monotony of constant watch-keeping in the oppressive heat of the tropics, often watch and watch about day and night, it started to have an effect on the ships' company. On one particular patrol Martin kept the ship, already severely short of food and water, at sea for three days short of four months because he suspected a German ship was prowling about. He only returned to port when the main part of our diet was beetroot and rice and with very little drinking water. On that occasion when the ship got to Capetown, he made it known that we were not stopping, he intended to put to sea again the same day as soon as sufficient provisions had been taken on board. There was to be no shore leave, not even for a few hours. News of his intentions caused the nearest thing to a mutiny I was ever to experience. Men muttered amongst them about refusing to obey orders and what measures they would take to prevent the ship sailing. The men's feelings of discontent were quickly made known to Captain Martin who was only too well aware of the harm it could do to his career prospects if the good name of his ship was tarnished. He would have been mindful of the brusque treatment meted out to ships' captains after the Invergordon mutiny. Through no fault of their own they were unsympathetically relieved of their commands, and made the scapegoats for the Government's ill-conceived and badly implemented policy to reduce the pay of naval ratings in the Fleet. Incidentally, I think I am right in saying that the captain of HMS Dorsetshire at the time, Captain Power, was the only one not relieved of his command on that occasion. Now as the men moaned and groaned as they provisioned ship, good sense on the part of the captain prevailed and shore leave was granted. We were allowed an afternoon ashore, it was sufficient to restore goodwill whilst doing nothing for the captain's impatience to sail.

An absence of mail from the family on how they were coping, long spells at sea and the frequent lack of proper sleep because of the constant emergency call outs, was a receipt for overstretched nerves and friction. The close confines of broadside messing in the sweaty heat did little to help the situation. Everyone was intimately aware of each other's habits and faults. There was no scope for privacy or solitude. At work, washing, sleeping, eating, and off duty periods, 'Jack' lived cheek by jowl with his messmates. Conditions below deck worsened at night when scuttles were closed and covered by deadlights to enforce a strict blackout. The air blowers were never adequate enough to freshen air that got heavy and unpleasant with sleeping bodies. Every space was taken up with hammocks swinging from the steel bars, even over the tops of the Mess tables. Whenever possible I preferred to sling my hammock on deck, either in the port or starboard waist if I was lucky. Regrettably, spaces in the open were limited and more often than not oversubscribed to. Not surprisingly, there were times when tempers flared and fists flew for what seemed minor disagreements. It would have required a limitless sense of humour and the tolerance of a saint to live peacefully all the time without some cross words being exchanged. I once came off the morning watch longing for a cup of tea while it was still hot. When I got to the Mess, a lad named Edmunds was drinking from one of the few unbroken cups and he appeared to be deliberately lingering over his drink. I told him to hurry up and he told me to wait my turn. It was enough cause for me to challenge him to a fight in the locker flat away from the prying eyes of the Boy's Instructor. I had fought him before but he must have improved considerably because this time he quickly knocked me unconscious. I came around to find him holding my head and apologising for knocking me out. We shook hands and remained the best of friends until he was later killed in action. Whatever the daily differences 'Dorsetshire' was still considered a happy ship by any standards although there were a couple of tragic incidents.

As part of my ongoing training as a young seaman, I was assigned to the Sailmaker's workshop for instruction on sewing canvas, under the supervision of Petty Officer Sailmaker Goss. I really enjoyed the work, it was a lot better than most other 'part of ship' duties. Under the PO's watchful eye I learnt to sew neatly with a 'palm' and needle to the regulation number of stitches per inch. I liked working with PO Goss because he took such a genuine interest teaching me the craft he was an expert at. I had a feeling he wanted me to follow in his footsteps and become a sailmaker. There was another reason why he showed so much interest in me, he and his wife were good friends of my parents. The gardens of their houses backed on to one another at home in Torquay. I often suspected that my father had asked PO Goss to keep a weather eye on me to ensure I behaved myself in foreign places. Early on the morning of the 16th.January he came into the sailmaker's store to tell me that Petty Officer Gunner's Mate Aspen, had committed suicide during the night. All the gory details were described to me by PO Goss, who had been called out to sew it into it's canvas coffin for burial at sea. According to PO Goss, PO Aspen withdrew a Service 45 revolver from the small arms cabinet and shot himself up through the head, making a terrible mess. The news of the tragic event went around the ship like wildfire. A Gunner's Mate is a key man on any warship. His expertise on gunnery matters was invaluable. Many theories were expressed as to why this level headed and much thought of man should decide to end his life when he had so much to look forward to in the service.

That morning the body was brought out on deck and placed on a board at the guardrail. At 1030hrs the ship paused momentarily, the Last Post was sounded and the board under the body tilted. There was a swishing sound as the weighted canvas covered body slid downward into the ocean. With a farewell splash, Petty Officer Aspen was committed to the deep. It was all over quickly and the ship picked up speed again to resume the patrol. A couple of days later the ritual of auctioning the dead mans effects took place with shipmates bidding far in excess of what the items of clothing were worth. It was a time-honoured tradition to raise as much money as possible for the man's widow and children.

17 Patrolling the Atlantic.

On January 21st.1941 'Dorsetshire' intercepted the Vichy French merchant ship 'Mendoza' trying to run the British blockade. The ships' company still, feeling a little sad after the tragedy of P.O. Aspen's suicide, perked up at the prospect of a little belated Christmas excitement. Once the ships' Vichy identity was established a boarding party was swiftly despatched to take over the ship and declare it a 'prize' of war. The officer in charge had strict instructions to keep in touch with the cruiser during the journey back to Freetown. On an earlier occasion when 'Dorsetshire' had chased and caught the German ship 'Wakama', her captain scuttled before being boarded. Captain Martin was now taking every precaution to ensure this 'prize' got back intact and 'Dorsetshire' claiming the credit.

During the night the unthinkable happened when contact was lost between the two ships, to the extreme annoyance of Captain Martin. When I met George Bell he told me he had just learned several new nautical expletives listening to the captain's conversation about 'Mendoza'. An extensive trawl, including a search by our plane, failed to find the 'Frenchy'. Despondent, the captain called off the hunt and set course for St.Helena hoping that the wayward vessel had put in there, but when we dropped anchor off Jamestown at 0800hrs on January 25th it was obvious the news was not good. 'Dorsetshire' waited until 0930hrs the following day and then left for Freetown calling at Ascension Island on the way. It turned out to be a providential decision because 'Mendoza' was anchored there as if waiting for us to arrive. A rigorous interrogation took place, but the happenings on board the Frenchman remained a matter of conjecture. The boarding party reported how they had been overpowered in their sleep and taken captive. Later, according to them, they managed to escape and fought back to retake the ship against great odds. Capt. Martin's findings remained sub judice but the Lower Deck felt they were better acquainted with the true facts than the investigating officers. When closely questioned by their messmates the ratings gave a different story. Apparently the prize crew was liberally supplied with wine and spirits by the cunning French some of which were women. By nightfall the British inebriated matelots were too far-gone to resist being locked up in a cabin before the captain of the 'Mendoza' altered course and disappeared into the dark. The next day our lads, although still suffering the after effects of drink, were sufficiently sober to exert enough force to break out of their cabin and regain control of the ship. To be more precise they knocked hell out of the 'Froggy' crew before sailing to Ascension Island. As soon as we got the troublesome vessel to Freetown it was handed over to the authorities, then we took on oil and put to sea again.

The next day 'Dorsetshire' rendezvoused with three merchant ships needing an escort to Capetown and on February 19th. Table Mountain came into view. It was a heart-warming sight for those of us anticipating an afternoon ashore. The day after arriving tragedy struck when a young seaman committed suicide. Early in the morning, on the 20th., Leading Seaman Rennie hanged himself outside the telephone exchange. The reason for his tragic death was puzzling to his friends and close associates, they put it down to stress and strain. Shrouded in gloom at another unnecessary death of one of our own, we left with the convoy on the 21st., heading up the

Mozambique Channel. News had been received that the German pocket battleship Von Scheer was possibly operating off the East African coast. Apparently the aircraft from H.M.S. Glasgow had sighted it before it made off. This seemed to be confirmed just after midnight on the 24th when action stations sounded and the ship speed increased to 25 knots. Word was quickly passed that a raider was ahead of the convoy and that we were investigating. The search continued over a wide area until the afternoon of the following day but without success. Captain Martin fearing that the report was false to lure the cruiser away from the merchant ships returned to the convoy but we remained on alert. H.M.S. Glasgow took charge of the convoy on the 28th.February and we parted company to search the waters around the Seychelles Islands.

There was excitement on board when we were told that H.M.S. Cornwall had taken a German raider, it was the kind of good tidings everyone wanted to hear and it put smiles on faces. Later it was verified that the raider was in fact a Vichy French passenger ship but we still felt pleased for our sister ship. Dorsetshire's search came to nothing and needing fuel oil she made towards Mahe the main island to replenish her tanks. When the masthead lookout called 'Land ahead' it was the start of a lasting love affair I had with this, then totally unspoilt, exquisite place. As 'Dorsetshire' eased her way through the smaller islands and coral reefs to drop anchor off Port Victoria, the sight of the beautiful white sandy beaches with palm trees growing right down to the water edge was a breathtaking spectacle. Unfortunately shore leave was rarely granted to big ships visiting island communities and on this occasion I could only view through binoculars, the only ones to go ashore was a limited few on official business. Happily I did return at a not too later date, on the tiny boom-defence vessel H.M.S. Barrymore, to get to know the islands more intimately. A quarter of a century before tourists realised the paradise existed. A terrible calamity beset 'Dorsetshire' on the first day of her 24hour stay. The ships Walrus aircraft on a courtesy reconnaissance flight over the islands crashed, killing all on board. It included the pilot and his aircrew, a civilian said to be the Governor of the islands, and an Army officer. A funeral party attended the service ashore the next morning before we weighed anchor and sailed for Simonstown. The journey was uneventful and we arrived at 0700 hrs on the 12th.March 1941 for a ten days stay. The sight of our second home could not have been more welcome, it gave the ships' company a chance to carry out much needed maintenance work while waiting for another convoy.

For us ratings 'Paint Ship Overall' was the first priority and we were soon busy with pots and brushes. Before work started the Petty Officers ('captains') responsible for parts of the ship, organised the rigging of staging around the hull. Two men to a plank that was held by a lowering rope at each end. We operated without safety lines unless painting in dry dock, a fall into water was not considered dangerous. When an area was painted the men asked for their plank to be lowered from above so that the next section down could be reached. This went on until the complete run (a fleet) down to the waterline was finished, and then an attendant boat took the men off to paint another run somewhere else. 'Responsible' Leading Seamen and three badge ABs were in charge of lowering planks, often displaying a warped sense of humour to wile away their time. The standard prank was to hold a bight of the lowering rope in their hands and when asked to lowers, releasing the bight in one go causing the stage to drop suddenly. It scared the wits out of the inexperienced and timid to realise they had nothing to hold on to until the rope went taut again. I learned that it was best to show no fear even if I felt terrified. It frustrated the perverted pleasures of the 'killicks' and 'strippies' who soon reserved their tricks for more nervous victims. The timid inexperienced gave themselves away when asking to be lowered. "Hooks, can you please let me down just a little please". Being polite was a dead give-away and caused others to stop painting and watch for a guaranteed 'drop'. The best way to avoid attention was to feign disregard for their capers by shouting out loud and clear " Jan. Wake up you dopey bastard and drop us, and don't forget the bloody pot".

It was a mark of indifference to their capers to call them a bastard and add instructions about the paint pot. The Chief Bosun's Mate was mainly responsible for the overall supervision of maintenance operations. He was open to a swift 'rocket' from the Commander if work fell behind schedule and he kept his wits about him to make sure it didn't happen. Time wasting was an obvious target for his attention to keep everyone hard at it. It was customary in the tropics for a couple of 'chancers' to 'accidentally' fall off the planking into the water to enjoy a cooling off. Chief 'Buffer' Archibald Yeoman, was wise to all the tricks, he had served too long in the Navy not to be able to tell the difference between a genuine accident and a 'cooler'. A repeated mishap by a 'dab dab' was sufficient for a trip aft to the Officer of the Day, followed by Commander's Report. Not having paper money to get wet or leaving your hat with your mate when you fell into the water were the kind of things the 'Chief' could spot at a ships' length.

Painting aloft required the agility of a monkey and no fear of heights. It was an accepted fact that ex-training ship boys were the quickest and best with a paintbrush high above the deck. Lads formerly from the 'Ganges', 'St.Vincent' and 'Impregnable' retained the skills they developed during their time up the mast at the training establishments. Acrophobia was a word not in their vocabulary. They were always in great demand for painting the upper parts of the mast and 'blackening down' the rigging. When a mention of chipping and scraping was heard, the sick, lame and lazy brigade increased dramatically. 'Sawbones' was well aware of this and so were the Sick Berth Attendants. An acute appendicitis could be guaranteed to receive every consideration and careful nursing. Anything of a less serious nature meant joining the scabs, crabs and dhobi-itch queue for a liberal coating of a purple solution normally reserved for Impetigo. All recipients of the 'purple' were also advised in solemn tones by the Sick Bay 'tiffy' to "Watch it carefully son, just in case it comes to nothing". The cure all for obvious malingerers internal complaints was a dirty brown looking mixture called Cascara. Mixed with a quantity of liquid paraffin it earned the 'patient' a reserved seat in the first cubicle inside the Heads door and a few extra sheets of stronger than lino toilet paper. It was never profitable to 'swing the lead' on 'Dorsetshire', careful nursing was only intended for the genuinely sick. Surgeon-Commander Bamford was a capable doctor and so were his assistants, Surgeon-Lieutenants Wood, Pratt and Concannon. Lieut Concannon was the man to curry most favour with if possible; he was the ships' dentist. A choice of his chair to the electric chair was only marginally preferred. It was sad that this young RNVR officer and the Surgeon-Commander were to both die in action the following year.

Steaming northwards again on the 27th.March with ten merchant ships, 'Dorsetshire' joined up with H.M.S. Cornwall escorting nineteen ships. Although the cruisers were the same County Class they were not identical. 'Cornwall' had an aircraft hanger on deck and carried two planes, only H.M.S. Norfolk and H.M.S. Dorsetshire were true 'sisters', right down to an Admiral's stern walk. The two convoys combined and carried on into the Indian Ocean. For a time we were involved in a hazard very much of Mother Nature's making. It was a part of the ocean that contained very large amounts of phosphorescence that lit the whole area up when the ships disturbed the water. Shoals of surface fish created picturesque illuminations that needed constant investigation. Regrettably the light created by this phenomenon meant the convoy could also be seen from a considerable distance and this meant constant vigilance by the warships. Extra look-outs were posted and both parts of the watches closed up as an added precaution against attack. Captain Martin received orders on the 7th.April 1941 to turn his ship around and return to Durban, an important convoy was waiting for an escort. Three days later 'Dorsetshire' eased her way to Maydon Wharf and tied up close to the pitiful sight of H.M.S. Illustrious. I was amazed to see the large areas covered with shrapnel holes and burnt paintwork, evidence of the aircraft carrier's recent encounter with the German Lufwaffe in the Mediterranean. She was first attacked on Friday 10th.January escorting a convoy to Malta but managed to limp into Valetta where she was the target for an all out assault by enemy aircraft on the 16th and 19th January. After being taken to Alexandria for some repairs, the carrier made it through the Suez Canal and down to the safety of Durban. From here 'Illustrious' was destined for the U.S.A. naval base in Norfolk, Virginia, for an extensive overhaul.

Our next convoy was waiting for us, it included the Empress of Japan and the Monarch of Bermuda. In general, matelots felt sorry for the people herded like cattle on the troopships, not all of them were allowed shore leave in the Cape because of the vast numbers. Those who were lucky enough to get on dry land, not knowing the 'ropes', seemed to wander about aimlessly looking for enthusiastic ladies. 'Jack' became a sort of unofficial guide to direct the lonely 'pongos' to more desirable haunts, like the Victoria League Club. We took the ships as far as Capetown and left them there while we went back to Durban to collect H.M.S. Illustrious. Having rejoined the convoy on the 23rd., we all set off again heading out into the Atlantic, first to St.Helena and then to rendezvous with H.M.S. Dunedin on April 29th to give the troopships into her care. At 45 degrees west and 7 degrees north on the 4th.May 1941 we met H.M.S. Caradoc and handed over the carrier for the rest of her journey to the States. The sight of the old C Class light cruiser brought back memories of my training on the river Tamar, I was grateful not to be serving on her in the tropics. After wishing them bon voyage Martin set sail for Freetown, where we could expect more oil, toil, yam and scram.

Two days later, just before 0500hrs, as we made our way to the West African port, an 'object' was sighted and the alarm sounded. Everything was hostile until proven otherwise and this was no exception. 'Action Stations' sent us scurrying to our positions, self preservation could make even the slowest matelot move at an alarming rate of knots. For battle stations I was once again back on the after conning station with the Commander, the exposed position did have it's drawbacks but it was the place to be to see all that was going on. We closed at speed with guns and torpedoes at the ready.

At a distance the shape in the water could be said to vaguely resemble a U-boat so a pattern of depth charges was on standby to destroy it if it submerged. Abruptly the order came to 'check, check, check, revert to normal', it was non-hostile. The cause of the flap was two rowing boats containing thirty-five survivors from the British merchant ship SS Oakdene. The vessel had been torpedoed at 1010hrs that morning by a German submarine on a bearing 6 degrees 19 minutes N and 27 degrees 55 minutes W. It was a forceful reminder that U-boats were active in the area. The survivors perked up when we got them inboard, today the Gods had smiled on them and they were grateful. Our medical staff was well equipped for such emergencies and in no time the survivors were fully recovered from their experience. As we continued on our way to Freetown the wreckage from another ship was sighted but although 'Dorsetshire' made a thorough search across a wide span of water no survivors were found. Later we found out that a Sunderland Flying Boat had picked up survivors from another torpedoed British merchant ship just before we arrived on the scene. Cleaned, fed, and adequately clothed the survivors of the SS Oakdene were disembarked at Freetown for repatriation to the United Kingdom. Their warm thanks for our hospitality and rescue was appreciated and we joined them on the upper deck to wish a safe journey home.

As we waited for our next assignment the resident Admiral decided to carry out an inspection. This created an atmosphere of frantic activity cleaning and polishing in readiness for his visit. It was inconceivable that the 'top brass' would find anything untoward that would merit an adverse comment. From the masthead down to the bilges ever man jack, officer and rating, made sure their responsibility was beyond reproach. I was in the immaculately turned out party lined up on the Quarter Deck waiting to be inspected after the Admiral had been piped on board. There was the usual amount of saluting, 'bull and 'flannel', before he started to poke around. I thought he resorted to nit picking when I saw him looking down one of the QD scuppers as if expecting it to be dirty. Naturally he found nothing to complain about, but when he was heard to compliment the captain on the excellent state of the ship before leaving, everyone sighed with relief. His barge didn't leave soon enough for us, to get him off our back.

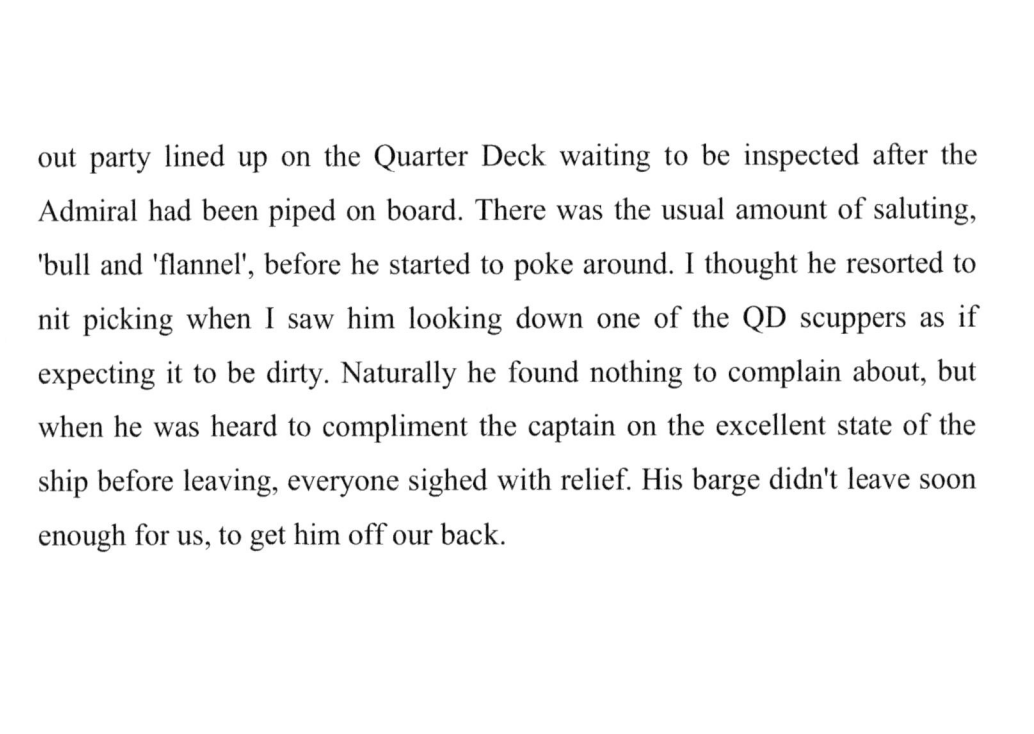

18 Sink the Bismarck

On May 11th.1941 at 0530hrs H.M.S. Dorsetshire left Freetown on what we assumed was to be another routine assignment. As usual 'buzzes' were flying around the messdecks like flakes in a snowstorm. The harmless gossip oiled the wheels of the ships' monotonous routine and made it palatable. We could not have envisaged that we were destined to go into naval history as the ship that finally sank the pride of the German navy. Clear of the land the captain spoke over the tannoy putting the rumours and guesswork to rest. He gave us the best news we had heard for some time, the ship was going home. The married men were elated at the prospect of seeing their families. So were the unmarried ones, with a chance of indulging in their fascination for girls, females, women and the opposite sex.

Next day Dorsetshire took charge of the forty-three ships in convoy SL74 bound for England. Helped by the Armed Merchant Cruiser 'Bulolo', Captain Martin was responsible for getting the ships safely through the notorious U-boat hunting grounds without loss. The convoy was slow with an overall speed of 7 knots, and 'Pincher' showed his annoyance by continually chasing up the stragglers who found it hard to keep up at times. A Royal Air Force Sunderland Flying Boat based in Gambia gave added protection by over-flying the ships for a period and it's presence was greatly appreciated. Steaming slowly northwards, we got the shattering news that the German battleship 'Bismarck' had sunk H.M.S Hood. In company with the 44500ton battleship Prince of Wales, she had the misfortune to get within range of the German guns. 'Hood' blew up and sank, the Prince of Wales was damaged and forced to make for port. The combined efforts of 'Bismarck' (Capt. Lindeman) and her escort the heavy cruiser 'Prinz Eugen' (Capt. Brinkmann) had destroyed one of the largest fighting ships in the world, and a myth. For many years H.M.S. Hood had been portrayed as the all-powerful warship, a view not shared by everyone who had served on her. My first thoughts went back to the stories told to me by boys who had worked in her turrets about worn out guns. Although of immense size she was an elderly lady, twenty years older and no match for the modern 'Bismark', except in propaganda films. Only three men survived from the ships' complement of over 1400 picked up by H.M.S. Electra. The destroyer had raced to the scene expecting to save hundreds. Little did we realise as we discussed the appalling loss of life, that within three days we would be the ones to rescue the greatest number of survivors from a stricken 'Bismark'.

There was a general feeling of excitement on the 26th as 'Dorsetshire' steadily increased speed towards 25 knots. The thrust from the Cammell Lairds engines sent a pulsating sensation through the ship from stem to stern, a warning that something was happening. The frantic liveliness in the wireless room, with messengers rushing backwards and forwards between the Bridge and the Cypher Officer, had all the telltale signs there was a 'flap' on. Surprisingly, action stations had not been sounded, implying we were not in any immediate danger. When the Bosun's call (pipe) shrilled over the tannoy it got everyone's attention. The Quartermaster announced that the captain would speak to the ships' company in ten minutes time, and he repeated the message to stress its importance. When Capt. Martin addressed us it was to say that we were proceeding in all haste to find the German battleship Bismarck and as always he expected only the very best from us. Many of us listening jokingly expressed reservations about fighting 'Bismarck', especially after what it had done to the 'Hood' and Prince of Wales. We thought the 'old man' should look around for something more of 'Dorsetshire's' size, but whatever our misgivings they were soon forgotten when we closed up at battle stations and made ready for combat. We knew that if the occasion did arise 'Pincher' Martin would point his cruiser at the enemy battleship, as he had done with the mighty 'Richelieu', and engage no matter what the consequences might be. George Bell told me later that he had overheard the captain telling officers that if he couldn't sink the German with gunfire or torpedoes then he would ram her. Eyebrows were raised when Captain Martin first left the large convoy behind in sole charge of the merchant cruiser. It was a decision he made on his own initiative without bothering to seek authorization from a higher authority. A signal to the Admiralty informed them of the convoy's position with 'Bulolo' and his intention to leave to intercept the enemy. He knew he would have to accept full responsibility for any loss to the convoy but it was a calculated risk he was prepared to take. 'Pincher' Martin had no intention of missing the chance of a confrontation with the enemy and enhancing his promotion prospects.

He mercilessly punished the ship and it's engines driving 'Dorsetshire' on in heavy seas and foul weather. He demanded, and got, every ounce of speed to ensure his ship would play an important part in the destruction of 'Bismark'. Giant waves and howling winds caused the cruiser to pitch and roll like an old scow. A mist that reduced visibility although not the ships' speed made conditions worse. Each time 'Dorsetshire' crashed through a wall of water, she shook herself like a dog shaking off water to get rid of the glistening spray before ploughing onward again. Below decks it was like riding a roller coaster, but without the screams of delight. Many justifiably reasoned that 'hard layer' allowances should be extended to all cruisers with captains like Martin in command. At mealtime the 'cooks of the mess' had great difficulty getting from the Galley to the messdeck. It was not easy to hold a hot tin dish with two hands and find another limb to grasp a fixture when the ship rolled. One unfortunate from No.5 Mess, carrying a tray of dinner steadied himself at the top of the steep sloping ladder. Putting his leg over the hatch coaming he waited for the opportune moment to start his descent. Suddenly the ship lurched and he slithered down the steel steps, upending the sloppy concoction over himself and the mess space. The poor fellow had to be taken to the Sick Bay. No words of patriotic zeal could console him, fighting the 'Bismark' did not feature on his list of priorities. He put the blame for his misfortune squarely on the shoulders of the Captain for speeding in such harsh conditions.

At 0900hrs on the 27th.May 1941, H.M.S. Dorsetshire came out of the mist, proudly streaming her battle ensign from the foremast, and sighted the 'Bismarck'. I suspect we were nearer to her than had been expected but it was the moment Captain Benjamin Martin had been impatiently waiting for. The weather was still bad with a heavy sea running but it was of no consequence, looking through my binoculars I could only gasp at the sight of the powerful German battleship. Her elegant lines were truly beautiful but frightening. An ambient grace belied the destructive capability of this vessel, deservedly called the pride of the Kriegsmarine. Built by Blohm and Voss in Hamburg, Bismark was laid down in 1936, launched on the 14th.February 1939 and finally commissioned in August 1940. She was a floating fortress with every modern aid that German technology could provide. With a displacement of 45,900 tons, this was increased to 50,960 tons when fully loaded, 'Bismark' had an overall speed in excess of 30 knots produced from banks of turbines. It made her one of the fastest battleships afloat. The main armament consisted of eight 15" (380mm) guns, twin mounted in four turrets. The secondary weaponry was made up of twelve 5.9" (150mm) and sixteen 4" (105mm) guns. The secondary armament could support the sixteen 1.5mm and eighteen quick firing guns against enemy air attack. For reconnaissance and spotting, 'Bismark' carried four single engined 196 Arado aircraft. The ships' compliment of 2200 men enjoyed the up to date living accommodation that this vessel 823ft (251metres) long, with a beam of 118ft. (36 metres) could provide.

'Dorsetshire' with her 8" guns must have looked a very puny adversary from the bridge of a ship that was aptly named after the famous Iron Chancellor who united the peoples of Germany. Prince Otto von Bismark would have been proud of the ship that carried his name, as it stood alone fighting overwhelming odds. It surprised the other ships in the vicinity when 'Dorsetshire' came into view making straight for Bismarck. That our arrival was unexpected was soon made evident with a sudden and very unwelcome greeting from one of our own capital ships. Like the sound of a thousand 'banshees' shells whistled overhead and erupted in the sea off our port quarter. The direction of the salvos caused fears that one of the British battleships had mistaken Dorsetshire for the 'Prinz Eugen'. The German battle cruiser had been accompanying Bismarck earlier but had slipped through the net to Brest. Frantic signals made 'Dorsetshire's' identity clear to everyone, it was one thing to be fired at by the Germans but not what was expected from friends. H.M.S. Rodney and H.M.S. King George V were already engaging 'Bismark' but showing cautious respect by firing from a great distance. It was recorded that although damage was extensively done to the upper part of the enemy ship, no shells from 'Rodney' or King George V had penetrated the armoured deck of 'Bismark'. The booming of the big guns rumbled like thunder as the British battleships kept up their barrage in reply to the enemy's fire. On the 26/27th Captain Vian, of 'Altmark' fame, led his destroyer flotilla of 'Cossack', 'Maori', 'Sikh' and 'Zulu' in repeated attacks on Bismarck. The daring attempts to torpedo the battleship were repulsed with fierce gunfire, forcing them to withdraw.

At 0910 hrs Bismarck came within range of our guns and Captain Martin gave the order to open fire. The response was immediate with the turrets sending deadly missiles towards their target. The procedures for reloading were instantaneous and efficiently carried out as the gun crews sweated to save every second. The big shells and the cordite moved smoothly in a continuous stream, from deep below in the Shell Rooms, up through the hoists and into the gun Turrets. Hydraulic rams finished the job of pushing the long steel cylinders and the charges into the breeches of the hot guns. The language from the Turret 'captains' was as powerful as the recoiling guns with seasoned gunners like, Petty Officer Braden and Petty Officer Cottrell driving their men to greater effort. The Gunhouse crews were oblivious to the heat and the intensified smell of sweat, oil and cordite. They were far too busy with the important task of loading and firing the guns in the shortest time possible. A, B, and Y Turrets are traditionally manned by the seaman branch but X Turret was the domain of the Royal Marines, now the 'bootnecks' were showing the Gunnery Officer why they were recognised the world over for their gunnery skills. With every crash and crack of the main armament Dorsetshire was wreathed in bellowing smoke and flashes of orange flame. As the guns recoiled the ship was pushed beam down into the water which was a natural shock absorber to take the aftermath of the broadsides. As the guns settled back the breech-blocks swung open for reloading. Above the noise the cry 'Interceptor closed' indicated that the whole procedure for reloading had been completed and the guns were ready to be fired again.

The morale on board the cruiser was very high, born from the confidence the men had in their captain and their respect for his ability. After the action, Captain Martin was told by a German from Bismarck's gunnery department that the second salvo from 'Dorsetshire' had put the fire control out of use, it was a comment that established our accurate firepower. As our ship veered slightly it was possible to bring all guns to bear at the same time and fire broadsides. Hits were soon recorded on Bismarck's Control Top, encouraging our Rangetakers, their sights were properly set to produce results. 'Dorsetshire' was now firing at the reported rate of a broadside every fourteen to twenty seconds which was exceptional. Survivors from the 'Bismark' remarked afterwards that 'Dorsetshire's' rate of fire and its destructive effect had been grossly underestimated until it was too late. The Germans gave the ship far more credit for her role in the sinking of the 'Bismark' than was acknowledged by the British senior staff. Loud gunfire continued to thunder as both sides exchanged shots with the greater volume coming from the British ships. The rumbling of the guns sounded continuously as broadside after broadside from the Allied ships sent the ear-splitting missiles raining down on the doomed German ship. It was a one sided fight with the Bismarck battling on against impossible odds although the two big ships of the Royal Navy, Rodney and King George V, were still keeping a discreet distance.

Admiral Somerville commanding Force H, flying his flag on the 32000 ton battle-cruiser Repulse, was unable to arrive in time for his surface ships to take part in the final action. Although he had used the aircraft from the carrier Ark Royal with some success Bismarck was still afloat and hitting back. Finally, Admiral Jack Tovey commanding the British Fleet was forced to admit that gunfire alone could not sink the enemy battleship in the immediate future. Time was of the essence with fuel oil running low and the ever-present threat from U-boats plus possible air attack from the German occupied air bases in France. Admiral Tovey made the position clear to Somerville in an exchange of signals. At 1025 hrs Admiral Somerville signalled Tovey asking " Have you disposed of the enemy" and got the reply "Have to discontinue action for fuel" adding a short time later "She is still afloat". The Prime Minister, Winston Churchill, had addressed the House of Commons about the action. He told members of Parliament that it appeared Bismarck would not be sunk by gunfire, it would have to be done with torpedoes. It was obvious he was being briefed on the situation, with the very latest information coming straight from the flagship.

At 1044hrs the C in C sent a general signal to the Fleet "Any ships with torpedoes are to use them on Bismarck". I can only assume he meant H.M.S.Norfolk, the destroyers or H.M.S.Dorsetshire. A few minutes later he sent a message to Force H "Cannot sink Bismarck with gunfire". Before receiving the first message Captain Martin had pre-empted the order, anticipating the need for such an attack he was already closing to get within 3000 yards to launch torpedoes. Once in range 'Torps' released two 'tin-fish' and like everyone else on deck I anxiously watched them running towards their target. To our elation both 'tin-fish' were hits. Circling at speed, Martin manoeuvred around the German's bows and attacked the port side firing one more torpedo, which struck home. Three hits out of three were the best possible result. The Torpedomen on the cruiser were ecstatic and Jack Tovey must have felt the same way, particularly as 'Rodney' and 'Norfolk' had between them fired off fourteen torpedoes previously without scoring a hit. At 1045hrs Capt. Martin signalled. "Enemy is sunk, am picking up survivors - Too rough to lower boats - Hundreds of men in the water". The next signal from 'Dorsetshire' read "I torpedoed Bismarck on both sides before she sank - her colours were still flying". At 1120hrs C in C to Fleet "I should like to pay tribute to the most gallant fight Bismarck put up against impossible odds". This justified compliment must have ruffled some feathers at the Admiralty because at 1610hrs Admiral Tovey received a brusque message. "For political reasons it is essential that nothing of the nature of sentiments expressed in your 1119/27 should be given publicly however much you admire a gallant fight".

Bismarck sank at approximately 1045 hrs, accompanied by loud bangs and hissing steam, taking Admiral Gunthur Lutjens, and Captain Ernst Lindemann, with her. Going down stern first the bow section remained sticking straight up out of the water for a short time. Just as it was disappearing under the surface the drone of aircraft engines could be heard and our A/A gunners prepared to repel enemy aircraft, they had been silent while the main armament was doing it's destructive work. The constant threat of an air attack from the French coast was always a consideration, but in this instance the planes were quickly identified as belonging to the aircraft carrier HMS. Victorious. They arrived just as the last piece of 'Bismark' slipped under the waves. The prolonged pounding of the British guns had crippled the 'Bismark' albeit not enough to finish her off. The devastating destruction was mainly to the upper sections of the ship, some areas were a twisted mass of steel. Doors and hatches became distorted, trapping some of the German seamen below decks, who consequently they drowned. Now hundreds of oil covered Germans littered the sea as 'Dorsetshire' edged towards them to rescue as many as possible. Lines were thrown out to be grabbed by the desperate swimmers who were in a sorry state.

Except for us and the destroyer 'Maori' all the other ships had quickly left the scene without attempting to rescue survivors. It was up to 'Dorsetshire' and 'Maori' to do the best they could in the shortest possible time. Many Germans were wearing life jackets but the heavy swell made it difficult for them to reach the lifelines. Oil fuel on the surface covered the men blackening their faces. Having been in the same predicament myself I had a rough idea what the poor devils were going through. Our lads worked frantically to pull the Germans inboard, they realised that time was running out. The Germans congregated in groups, holding on to the ropes. There was a definite language barrier because we shouted at them not to get too many holding on each line, especially as some ropes had nobody on them. Unfortunately the appeals seemed to be ignored. They appeared to be oblivious to the fact that half a dozen men on one rope made it impossible for the rescuers to haul so much weight to safety. It could have been that they were afraid to gamble the little they had for a better chance of salvation.

Commander Bias told me to follow him and we went to help with the rescue, that was until an officer was hauled on board who turned out to be a senior gunnery officer. Commander Bias accorded him the privilege of rank and took him to a cabin to be cleaned up and given a dry change of clothes. His uniform was sodden with salt water and stained with oil so the Commander asked me if I knew a 'dhobi wallah' who could wash and press it. I took it for'ard and found a 'strippy', renowned for his laundering skills, who was willing to do it knowing he would get well paid by the Commander. When the uniform was returned it looked good but it was minus the eagle insignia. The German officer gave no indication that he noticed the loss, perhaps as a prisoner of war he opted for diplomacy. Isolated cases of survivors giving the Nazi salute when they were pulled up on deck was accepted as nervous reactions by the British seamen although when one also shouted 'Heil Hitler' he got something he had not bargained for. Suddenly I could feel the deck vibrating as 'Dorsetshire' started to gently ease forward through the mass of bobbing heads. Everyone, on the ship and in the water, realised that we were under way which meant leaving the rest of the swimmers to certain death. The anxiety and torment was plain to see on the faces of the men in the water now they knew they were being left to die, their cries and screams were pitiful to hear. It spurred our chaps to work even faster and some started throwing anything that came to hand into the sea, that might provide a lifesaver for the poor wretches to cling on to.
Earlier, Midshipman Joe Brooks had jumped overboard into the heavy swell to help tie the lines on some who were too tired to help themselves. As he

struggled to secure ropes around exhausted Germans he was unaware of what was happening on board until he heard the repeated shouts of warning from his close friend Sub-Lieutenant Allon Smith, and was pulled to safety in the nick of time. Captain Martin later reprimanded him for putting his life at risk under such circumstances. The son of a naval officer Brooks was unaffected by the ticking off he got from the captain. It had been a natural reaction for him to jump overboard and attempt the dangerous rescue, disregarding his own safety. When he lost both of his legs at a later date, the disability did not prevent him leading a full and active life.

Critics condemned Captain Martin for his seemingly heartless termination of the rescue operation. His decision was influenced by two indisputable facts. Firstly, German bombers based in France had the range to attack the ship and they would have been alerted. Secondly, U-Boats in the area would be converging on the scene to assist 'Bismark'. A U-Boat alarm, when an officer on the Bridge sighted a periscope, finally decided the Captain to leave. Later it was confirmed that Admiral Luetjens had signalled for a U-Boat to rendezvous with 'Bismark' to collect his war diaries. U74 was in the area when the German battleship sank and took up a position to attack but was unable to due to bad weather although it has been suggested the submarine was out of torpedoes from an earlier attack while on patrol. Captain Martin could not be expected to have known this and it would be unreasonable to expect him to endanger his ship and crew in such precarious circumstances. The preservation of H.M.S. Dorsetshire took precedence over the survival of enemy sailors. A U-Boat captain might not pass up the chance of sinking a British heavy cruiser, even if it was on a rescue mission. 'Dorsetshire' and the destroyer 'Maori' remained behind after the other warships had sailed for their homeports. To his credit, Captain Martin delayed long enough to rescue 82 of the total number of 112 'Bismark' survivors. The 'Maori' accounted for 25, a further 2 were picked up by the German weather ship 'Sachsenwald'. Three more survivors, Georg Herzog, Otto Hontzsch, and Herbert Manthey, were saved by the German submarine U-74, captained by Krvkpt Eitel-Friendrtch Kentrat. She surfaced after we left. U-Boats searching the area later reported seeing a considerable amount of debris and floating corpses. It must have been agonising for the submarine captains to witness the scene, where approximately 2000 of their fellow countrymen had died in a matter of hours. Once the survivors, including four officers, were on board 'Dorsetshire' they were given every possible care and attention that our resources could provide. Little luxuries like chocolate bars, cigarettes and playing cards appeared from nowhere and were given freely. The kindred spirit of the seafaring fraternity was evident, even between the victor and the vanquished. That feeling between the 'Bismarck' Germans and us remains as true today and is openly expressed when we meet. On Easter Sunday 1992 the remaining survivors sent a representative from Germany to Dorchester to lay a wreath commemorating the 50th anniversary of the sinking of 'Dorsetshire', honouring her dead.

The Spanish cruiser 'Canarias' also got to the spot as soon as possible after the sinking. Although it searched every piece of wreckage for survivors it could not find any. H.M.S.Hood had been avenged but there was no great demonstration of victory on board H.M.S.Dorsetshire. The British public were fed a lot of politically motivated pap, describing the sinking as an outstanding victory. Relief, that 'Bismark' could no longer threaten the shipping lanes with her mighty guns, was a much better assessment of our feelings. Sixty-four Allied warships had been deployed to destroy 'Bismark' and her cruiser escort 'Prinz Eugen'. This array of naval strength included five battleships, three battlecruisers and two aircraft carriers. Only a few made contact with the German ships before 'Dorsetshire' delivered the coup de grace to bring the chase to an end. On the 28th.May speed was reduced when we ran into dense fog. Soon after we parted company with 'Maori' because her oil supplies were getting very low and she decided to make for the nearest Scottish port.

Meanwhile, below in 'Dorsetshire's' Sick Bay, surgeons were fighting a losing battle to save the life of Gerhard Luttich. He was one of the badly injured German sailors rescued earlier. Minus a leg and suffering the after effects of severe burning his chances of staying alive were slim. It was amazing how he had been able to get to 'Dorsetshire' to be rescued in the first place. Sadly he died and the following day, May 29th, he was sewn into the traditional canvas bag. The 'coffin' was positioned in the centre of the Quarter Deck draped in the flag of Imperial Germany with British sailors lined along one side and Germans the other. Permission had been sought from the senior German officer to use the flag because 'Dorsetshire' did not carry a Nazi one; permission was readily granted. Full burial honours were accorded the dead German and a guard of honour fired three volleys over the body. At 0920 hrs the ships' engines stopped, the chaplain gave a short service, and the body splashed into the sea. Facing each other across the Quarter Deck there was no animosity on the faces of the men from opposing sides, just sorrow that this man had to die.

Captain Martin sent a message to the German gunnery officer von Mullenheim, asking him if he would like to visit the other survivors housed in the recreation space. The Captain wanted to know if there was anything the prisoners required for their immediate needs, which they could have if it was available on board. The German officer willingly agreed and after visiting his men he joined Captain Martin on the Bridge. During their talk von Mullenheim made clear his disapproval of the aborted rescue of the men in the water. He was quickly put in his place by the more experienced captain who made it plain that the issue was not open for discussion. The presence of U-Boats left him no choice but to consider his men and his ship as the first priority. With hindsight he acted wisely and correctly, a fact begrudgingly acknowledged by the Germans.

19 HEBBURN on TYNE

We carried on alone, sailing into some foul weather. The change of climate from the heat of the tropics to the chilly wet off the northern coast of Scotland was a shivering experience. The bitter harshness of the North Sea to the blue of the South Atlantic could not have been a more disagreeable contrast while our blood was still thin. A thick fog had silently shrouded the ship in a clammy dampness that was eerie, penetrating, and very unpleasant. The steaming hot cocoa made from the big brown blocks of chocolate-looking substance was all the more welcoming to the frozen lookouts and watch-keepers on the upper deck. My Duffle coat covered layers of woollens to keep my blood circulating, as did an extra pair of socks. After rounding the top of Scotland the ship continued down the eastern side of England and into the mouth of the river Tyne. Finally berthing alongside the wharf across the river from North Shields on the 30th.May. Although the local surroundings were unfamiliar it was wonderful to be home. Once the ship was tied up the German survivors, now prisoners of war, were taken ashore under a strong military guard. Their time on the ship had been made as comfortable as possible with the supply of new bedding, clothing and tobacco. Their food was the same as ours and they were allowed plenty of freedom to exercise.

On the 30th.May the ship was moved across the river to South Shields in preparation for going into dry dock in Palmer's yard at Hebburn upon Tyne.

A river Pilot came on board and took up the usual position on the Compass Platform to get the best vantage point for conning the cruiser up the river to the dock. His orders to the helmsman and the engine room were quickly acknowledged and the ship moved forward. Captain Martin pacing up and down close by became noticeably irritated by something. Those of us near the bridge were soon to find out the reason for his annoyance.

"Pilot, are you going ahead too fast" he curtly enquired. "No Sir", came the terse reply. Silence prevailed for a short time then Martin spoke again.

"Pilot are you sure you're not going ahead too fast". The Pilot replied peevishly, "Sir I have been a pilot on this river for many years without mishap, I know my job". An uneasy silence followed before Captain Martin spoke again. "Pilot, get off my Bridge" he roared.

"It will be your responsibility if I leave this Bridge, Captain." replied the startled Pilot. Those of us within earshot listened and watched, bewildered by the unprecedented confrontation.

"Get off my bloody bridge, now." bawled Martin, pointing to the ladder.

The river pilot, tight lipped, set off below like a scolded schoolboy unaware that the Captain had paid him a compliment by asking him twice to do something.

Captain Martin stepped on to the Compass Platform and snapped out orders. "Slow ahead both"

"Slow ahead both sir, both telegraphs showing slow ahead " came the reply.

"Midships" he called to the Quartermaster. "Midships sir, Wheels amidships". The orders continued in a rapid stream. Leaning over the Bridge he called to the First Lieutenant, who was responsible for securing the ship when berthing and mooring. "You ready Number One" "Aye sir, alls ready"

"I'll need two springs, Number One" he requested… "Sir" Jimmy the One affirmed.

The Captain took the cruiser upstream before warping her broadside on to the fast flowing currents and easing it into the dry dock set at right angles to the run of the river. Not an easy manoeuvre but he carried it out to perfection. As he came off the Bridge with the 'cats got the cream' look on his face all the hands on deck stood to attention, admiration on their faces for this sod of a Captain they rated so highly.

Home leave was given to one watch at a time and shore leave allowed to part of the watch remaining behind. Later the roles would be reversed for everyone to enjoy the comforts of home. Soon the station platforms were filled with chattering bluejackets all eager to be on their way. For those of us living in the South-West it was going to be a long journey due to a disrupted rail service. It took me twenty-four hours to travel from Newcastle to Torquay. For those remaining waiting their turn, local runs ashore was especially pleasing. The bronzed sailors won a lot of female hearts around the Tyne. 'Bell bottoms' and crossed anchors were in great demand at the Saturday night hops at the Power House and Oxford Galleries dances. A lot of rolled pipe tobacco and cigarettes were smuggled ashore to curry favour with girl's parents. It was a time of shortage and the little extras were much appreciated. One lad had trouble supplying his 'prospective' mother-in-law with a most unexpected request for onions. They were unobtainable ashore and difficult to 'half-hitch' on board, fortunately the ways and means philosophy of the Lower Deck provided the answer. True to form the engagement ring Casanova continued the escapades he had perfected in South Africa, I hesitate to name him because he is now happily married. He was soon betrothed to a local girl, the duration being the length of time the ship remained in port and how receptive she was. The incorrigible gigolo seemed to possess an insatiable appetite for amorous affairs, using the ever-ready promise of wedlock to further his ends.

Several of the ships' company were 'paying off' for a variety of reasons but the main part of the crew was to stay for another overseas commission when we sailed. Many of the replacements were 'Ho's', enlisted for the duration of hostilities, 'nozzers' with little or no nautical experience and certainly none on board a warship. The 'cut of their jib', the baggy regulation serge suits, dark blue collars and the bow on the cap tally, made them easy to recognise. As they struggled on board with their kit bags on their shoulders and sausage like hammocks under their arms, the uncertain looks on their faces said it all. They would sooner be back at home instead of being greeted with the good-humoured banter of a few old salts. The hostility only personnel came from all walks of civilian life. Some had volunteered, others were conscripts, and for the most they were raw recruits. The sum total of their naval training was a few brief classroom talks and some 'square bashing' at a shore depot. It was inevitable that for a time their veneer of seamanship made them the butt of messdeck jokes. Night time was the worst part of their first twenty-four hours on board. Having slung their hammocks it only remained for the tired and perplexed newcomers to climb into the swinging canvas sacks and enjoy a good night's sleep. The hilarious spectacle of flying arms and legs, and falling cursing bodies, brought howls of uncontrollable mirth from the seasoned watchers. When the laughter died down, many willing bystanders demonstrated the secrets of successful hammock drill. They explained that the nettles (cords) holding the canvas had to be adjusted in a certain way.

The fitting of a piece of wood called a stretcher would prevent the sides of the hammock snapping closed, making it easier to get into it.

The next morning the slumbering matelots were rudely awakened by the never varying cry of the Duty Petty Officer as he thumped the underside of the hammocks. "Wakey, wakey, wakey! Heave ho, heave ho, lash up and stow"! "Rise and shine, the morning's fine and the suns burning your eyes"! "Come on now, grab your socks and show a leg"! The old sweats tumbled out in their underpants and vests, the newcomers gingerly dismounted in their pyjamas: it was early days yet. Tips on speedily tying up, and stowing, of the hammocks was readily given to those who had difficulty mastering the art. The 'old' hands would soon have the others doing the job without any trouble. Progress with the newcomers was amazingly swift, in a matter of days the basic terms and descriptions were being used with familiarity. The ceiling became the Deckhead, the floor the Deck, the kitchens became known as the Galley and the lavatories were given their proper name of the Heads.

One new arrival was not a raw recruit. He was the replacement Master at Arms, the Chief Petty Officer of the Regulating Branch. Referred to as the 'Jaunty', he was responsible for recording the crimes and punishment of those unfortunates whom, knowingly or unwittingly, breached the King's Rules and Regulations. He also dealt with 'request men' who often had moments of wishful thinking, like compassionate leave. To the 'Master' the ship comprised of two parts, Defaulters and 'Request Men', anything else was 'gash'. This particular Master at Arms brought his nickname and his reputation with him, he was unkindly known as 'Dillinger', public enemy number one. It used to be said that he carried his birth certificate around with him to dispel rumours about his parentage. This was totally untrue and can only be attributed to lower deck frivolity towards a member of this much-maligned branch. It was true strangely enough, that he was never seen ashore by those wishing to question him about supposed victimisation.

The newcomer's first impression of 'Dorsetshire' could not have been inspiring. They admitted it did not match up to the stories they had been told of the cruiser's reputation for order and cleanliness. The ship was in a dirty state with the gun smoke stains still on her turrets from the 'Bismark' action. The decks were covered with a miscellany of welding leads, oxy-acetylene bottles and power cables. It resembled a scrap yard with sheets of metal and an assortment of steel drums cluttering the waist and fo'c'sle.

The hissing and spluttering of the welding torches sent showers of sparks into the air to light up the passageways. Hemp, Manila and Sisal cordage unreeled and spread out to be checked for wear and tear. Long rows of cable ranged the floor of the dry dock to be closely examined for possible damage. The whole scene presented a spectacle of chaotic filth, perpetual pandemonium and confusion. There was very little the crew could do to restore total order while the ship was in 'dockyard hands'. Civilian workmen (Dockyard Mateys), smoking 'H.M. Ships Only' cigarettes seemed to be everywhere except the restricted and sensitive areas like the Transmitting Station. Their endless cadging of 'fags' seemed to take precedence over the more important concern of getting 'Dorsetshire' ready for sea in the shortest possible time.

Shored up on the keel blocks, the cruisers' bottom was scraped free of barnacles before the hull was chipped and repainted. Ridding the ship of the clinging marine crustacean would give it a few extra knots, speed that could be a bonus in an emergency.

Finally Palmer's part of the refit was completed to everyone's satisfaction and control passed back to the captain who quickly started undocking procedures. The penstocks were opened letting the water surge in. Next the dock gates slid open and 'Dorsetshire' eased out of her pen for berthing at a nearby wharf. We were in good company, our near neighbour being the famous H.M.S. 'pepper-pot' Penelope. The light cruiser had earned her nickname as a result of the severe shrapnel damage she received in Malta.

Normality gradually returned on board with the everyday harbour routine. The first call of the day was 'men under punishment' to muster and the last was for Chief and Petty Officers to pipe down. Sandwiched in between, I, like all the other ratings, used an unaccountable amount of Bluebell metal polish and bundles of cotton waste to restore the sparkling shine to brass and copper. Scouring the wooden decking with sand, canvas and salt water restored it's bleached-white appearance. And there was the inevitable painting, with queues forming outside the paint store waiting to be served. Most requests was for a "Pot and two, Crabfat" or in some cases "Pot and one, Crabfat". In return we were issued with battleship grey paint and the required number of brushes, always accompanied by the PO chanting monotonously "And bring the bloody pot and brushes back, I don't want to hunt for them". Knowing his plea was often falling on stony ground he would occasionally add " Roll on my bloody twenty-two ", wistfully thinking of home and his retirement. The call to 'Quarters Clean Guns' was another important muster when every inch of the armament was cleaned and checked. Bill Braden, 'captain' of A turret, often quoted his favourite saying

"I want it as bright as a brand new dollar on a pig's backside" to make his views known. Much the same sentiment was echoed by the other Petty Officers who valued their position of trust. The hydraulic hoists were operated time and time again to ensure that the shells would be readily available for the guns when they were needed. It gave the turret 'rats' a chance to check every moving part before making their report.

For many, the most welcome call of the day was 'up spirits' just after 1100 hrs, it wetted their appetite before the mid-day meal. For ratings it was a mixture of two parts of water to one part of high-grade rum. Chiefs and Petty Officers were issued with it neat and some often bottled a part of their 'neaters' for a variety of reasons. The diluted issue to ratings had to be drunk because it was unsuitable for keeping. Each mess sent their rum bosun for the ration doled out from a large wooden tub bearing the toast 'The King, God Bless Him' in big brass letters. Supervision was strict and the amounts issued were carefully measured. Any diluted rum left in the tub was poured down the scuppers, a seemingly heartless act to those who loved their grog. Being under age I was not allowed rum, those who could but didn't draw their issue were credited with three pence a day in lieu. This didn't often happen because rum-loving ratings willingly bought the tot from them. Bottling 'neaters' or buying another's tot was an offence, but it was a way of life on board, which was difficult to detect and stop. Officers were not issued with a ration, they had access to a plentiful supply of alternative alcoholic beverages. All alcohol, other than the regulation rum ration, was forbidden to ratings. Punishment for anyone trying to smuggle drink on board was harsh, and consequently seldom attempted.

Various tricks were tried at different times by the more courageous to get an extra 'wet'. One rating realising that the scuppers stopped short of the water line came up with an ingenious idea of supplementing his allowance. A loaf of bread was stuffed up the chute so that any rum emptied down the gash chute would soak into the bread. The idea was to retrieve the loaf and squeeze the spirit out. After baiting the trap, the mastermind waited for his foolproof scheme to bear fruition. Unfortunately someone emptied a bucketful of slops down the chute which swept away the bread and any joyful prospects. He tried again on another occasion but the pulp disintegrated when he tried to recover it making any further attempts too risky. A pal of mine from Torquay called Tom Hutton hit on an equally bright idea when we were in West Africa on the previous commission. He brought a couple of coconuts back from ashore and we brought sugar and a bag of raisins. Coconuts were not forbidden fruit, although the Officer of the Watch, Corporal of the gangway and the Duty Petty Officer all eyed him with some suspicion. The P.O. was the only one to pass a remark. "Bloody coconuts. You're either going nutty or fruity or both". Down on the messdeck the plan of action was swiftly put into operation. The soft eyes of the nuts were gouged out and the raisins and sugar, topped up with water, was inserted to start the fermentation process. We watched over the nuts as if they were prize birds' eggs waiting to be hatched. The holes had been plugged after the sugar had been added and it was hoped that an alcoholic drink could be produced. After a couple of weeks the dabbling distillers tested the liquid. It might have been potent but the taste was abominable and the project was abandoned; the liquid was as bitter as the disappointment.

Training for us young ratings was an ongoing feature to develop our skills, and the divisional officers made sure we received the best instruction. Like my colleagues previously from the boy's messdeck it seemed natural to soak up everything between the covers of our seamanship manuals as a prerequisite for advancement. Our time at the training ship had instilled into us the need to learn our calling, although we needed little encouragement to add to the fascinating subject of seamanship. On the 11th.July 1941 and 18 years of age, I was promoted Able Seaman six months before the normally accepted time for Ordinary Seamen. It was the best start I could expect as I prepared for an early further upgrading to Leading Seaman. My sights were set on becoming a 'no-badge' Petty Officer, the hallmark of a highflier.

I enjoyed my turn of leave at home, and the female company of a long-standing girl friend, even though my father had me relating over and over what I did during the Bismarck action. I got the feeling he credited me with sinking the German battleship single-handed. There were no qualms about returning to Hebburn as it was becoming my second home and I liked the people. I knew the time to leave was fast approaching and there would be sad partings not knowing if we would ever return. Living was for the present, the future was uncertain especially in wartime. On my second run ashore I met a nice local girl, we attended the same Catholic church in town. It was a good start and Helen asked me home to meet her folk who welcomed me without reservation, or at least it seemed so. Our friendship quickly blossomed much to the obvious pleasure of her family, including a brother and sister. In several ways she was different to the other young ladies I was associating with at the time. Maureen had lovelier eyes, Kay nicer hair and Joan longer legs but Helen was an intelligent, gentle, warm-hearted person and good fun to be with. Why she agreed to walk out with me on such a short acquaintance remained an unsolved mystery, the old theory of unlike poles attracting must have applied to us.

Her father delighted in taking me for a drink at his 'local' and introducing me around as his daughter's boyfriend. We always made our way back from the pub in time to tuck in to a well-cooked meal prepared by Helen and her mother. I sometimes felt guilty eating part of their wartime rations but the lady of the house insisted I took my meals with them when I was ashore. I suspect she thought I was a suitable beau for her daughter regardless of my modest financial status as a lowly paid sailor. After being well fed, Helen and I usually set off to enjoy ourselves holding hands and visiting places of interest around the Newcastle area. Evenings were more often spent going to one of the many local dances where Helen seemed eager to introduce me to her friends. Revelling in the generous conviviality I began to realise that Helen's family was known and respected in the locality. The mother wanted to do my washing and ironing or any other small chores that might keep me on the ship, it was a homely atmosphere that I was going to regret leaving. I did find one way to repay the family kindness and generosity, albeit a very small contribution. It was to provide Helen's grandfather with something he could not get enough of, tobacco. He loved his pipe but was always short of something good to put in it due to wartime scarcity, and this gave me the opportunity to return a favour. I considered myself as skilled as the best to roll a good 'perique' of leaf tobacco, always removing every bit of stalk before starting the process. I often kept a couple of spare 'periques' maturing, to take home for my father when possible but now they had a new home. Her grandfather was overjoyed with the first lot and the promise of several more to follow. Getting the 'more than official allowance' of tobacco safely ashore could not have been easier. I simply took my gasmask out of it's satchel before going to Sunday church service in Hebburn and replaced it with the contraband. Helen made sure she sat next to me in church, screened by a couple of my oppos', then it was easy to transfer the spunyarn covered rolls into her bag. To solve my Catholic conscience I looked on the proceedings as a commendable act of charity to an elderly man.

On board ship the transformation of Dorsetshire's appearance was amazing and nearly complete. Everything sparkled, and the absence of the 'dockyard mateys' made life much more peaceful. A thousand and one items had to be shipped before we were finally ready for sea. Shells for the 8" and 4" guns and smaller ammunition for the pom-poms, paint, rope, tinned goods, pulses, the list was endless but with sweat and toil it was safely stowed. Amongst the equipment installed at Palmer's was the new R.D.F. The radio direction finding apparatus was to enable our gunners to seek out their targets with greater accuracy in rain and fog, and especially at night. During our stay at Hebburn on Tyne, world events took an unexpected turn. Adolf Hitler rounded on Stalin his one time ally and invaded Russia. The German offensive on June 23rd, code-named 'Operation Barbarossa' was a tactical error the Nazi leader would pay dearly for.

The day of farewell came on the 27th.July 1941. At 1000 hrs it all seemed so final as I watched the 'dockies' struggle to lift the eyes of the big hawsers off the bollards and let go our mooring ropes. As 'Dorsetshire' passed down the Tyne, bound for Scapa Flow, many sad hearts were left behind. The people here had been the most kind-hearted it was possible to find anywhere in the world. Their unpretentious homeliness greatly appealed to the servicemen. Even the men who had joined at Hebburn were overwhelmed by the response of the local people. For them it was a bonus to enjoy basking in the reflected glory of the ship that sank the 'Bismark'. The crew had unquestionably endeared themselves to the 'Geordies' and it was inevitable that a few tears would be shed when we sailed. The sadness would have been greater if the future destruction of the ship and the death toll could have been foreseen. Once clear of the land the captain put the ship through it's paces to make sure everything was in good working order, with special attention to the engines he had punished so hard prior to the Bismarck chase. Arriving in the Orkneys the following evening, Dorsetshire anchored at Scapa Flow safe in the knowledge that it was a protected haven sheltered by the Mainland and outlying islands of Hoy, Flotta, Burray and South Ronaldsay.

Security had been tightened up considerably since the H.M.S. Royal Oak disaster that took place in the early hours of October 14th.1939. The U47 under the command of Gunther Prien successfully penetrated the Scapa Flow anti-submarine defences to inflict a terrible loss on the Royal Navy. Creeping around the numerous obstacles he torpedoed the battleship with the loss of eight hundred lives. After the attack the daring U-Boat commander slipped away to safety without any damage to his boat. The same could not be said for the pride of the Sea Lords at the British Admiralty. The prestige of the Royal Navy was badly bruised. It was unthinkable that an enemy submarine could possibly infiltrate the protected naval base. The Admiralty quickly closed the stable door and made doubly sure that such an audacious feat would not be repeated.

During our stay the new RDF apparatus was tested with a night shoot firing all guns. The results were exceptionally accurate much to the satisfaction of the gunnery officer. A lot of effort was put into the working up period to fully integrate the new members of the crew who had joined on the Tyne. They soon settled in and were efficiently carrying out the duties of the men they had succeeded.

One last replacement arrived on the 7th. August to relieve Captain Martin it was Captain Augustus Agar VC DSO. The next day Captain Martin, now promoted Commodore, left the ship to take up his new post as C in C of the Cape where he was well known and respected. From the moment 'Gussie' Agar was piped aboard it was noticeable he was a different style of captain. His softer approach to command contrasted enormously with the brusqueness of his predecessor. Captain Augustus Willington Shelton Agar VC. DSO. 51 years of age, was two years older than Martin. The son of an expatriate Irish tea planter in Ceylon, he entered the Royal Navy in 1905 at H.M.S. Britannia the officers training college at Dartmouth. He served in the First World War but won his Victoria Cross and Distinguished Service Cross fighting the Bolsheviks in 1919. Early in his career he served on the Royal Yacht Victoria and Albert and liked to relate his close acquaintance with King George V and Queen Mary when they were on board. His upbringing, schooling and family connections made him the ideal candidate for the officer class of the time.

Whatever the dissimilarities between the two excellent captains, I was sure that having served under Capt. Martin I would never again sail with his equal. It is onerous to make comparisons and it is not my intention to make an unmerited comment. Capt. Agar was the most professional of officers and liked, and he did recommend me for accelerated promotion, but 'Pincher' Martin was a one-off. The 'Snotties' in the Gunroom must have breathed a sigh of relief to see the back of their old skipper. If nothing else, it meant the end of the 'knee-knocking' ritual the Midshipmen performed every time the man not best known for his reticence confronted them.

The day after Martin left, a party of us was sent to the aircraft carrier H.M.S. Victorious to be inspected by His Majesty King George VI. Later, Admiral Jack Tovey came on board H.M.S. Dorsetshire to speak to the crew. Standing on the Quarter Deck capstan he gave us a talk that included matters relating to the recent Bismarck action. I thought he was giving us a load of old flannel for some obscure reason and his remarks certainly fell on stony ground with those around me. He did suggest that if a single ship had been lost from the convoy we had been escorting prior to the 'Bismark' action, Martin could have faced court marshal. If the derogatory comments made by the seamen about himself had been heard by Admiral, he might have felt extremely embarrassed. They were not impressed by the top brass 'bull' and showed their disapproval with a few outbursts of coughing.

An amusing tale of an incident at Scapa Flow circulated around the ship that had everyone chuckling. Supposedly a Stoker was brought before the Commander at Defaulters, accused of being drunk when picked up by a shore patrol. He strenuously denied the charge pleading a misunderstanding of his condition. The Commander confidently played his trump card to demolish the defence. "But you were heard talking to a sheep at the side of the road, you must have been blind drunk." "No, no sir" the Stoker replied quickly "It was pitch dark sir, and I thought I was talking to a WREN in a duffle coat". A smiling Commander who appreciated initiative even at that low level duly passed sentence. He concluded the proceeding by adding a word of caution. "Think yourself lucky I didn't refer this to the Captain. And another thing, stop acting 'green' with me".

At Flotta there was little for liberty men to do except drink beer in the canteen. Even when we got there the canteen was a bare joyless place. It was not the most exciting place for a run ashore although it did give us a chance to stretch our legs.

20 THE LAST COMMISSION

I was as happy as everyone else to leave the bleakness of Scapa Flow accompanied by the unavoidable hordes of screeching gulls as they swooped and dived hoping to be thrown a morsel of food. The journey was a short one to the Firth of Clyde where we dropped anchor on August 16th.1941. It seemed hardly worth the trouble because the next day we left with a southbound convoy to once again exchange the North Star for the Southern Cross. As 'Dorsetshire' passed through the Azores and on towards Cape Verde the look-outs were warned to be extra watchful for enemy submarines. During May, an Allied ship had been sunk every day of the month off the West African coast. This gave some indication of the successful attacks made by the predacious Germans. The ship had barely settled into a balanced routine before the inevitable mushrooming of cottage industries started. They played an essential role in our everyday existence by providing a range of services not officially covered in the ships' manifest. Haircutting was one well supported enterprise carried on by a few self taught 'barbers'. Styling was basic, 'all off' or 'short back and sides' with a little or a lot off, was the extent of the coiffure options on offer. Usually the salon consisted of a box or stool in a quiet corner near an electric light bulb. Other venture 'firms' included 'jewing', shoe repairing, dhobing and photo processing, although anything not provided by the 'Andrew' was an opportunity for resourceful sweats to make a few shillings.

As the cruiser swept through the warmer waters, dolphins and porpoise leapt in front of the ship or raced alongside for hours on end. The beautiful mammals were a source of pleasure for the men new to the tropics. It was a completely different world for them and they were delighted with the change of environment. A couple of dysentery attacks and several sleepless nights would dampen the enthusiasm for watching the playful fish. Later they could expect to see large shoals of flying fish, the occasional albatross, and whales. The latter, at first a novelty, became a boring nuisance. At a distance they vaguely resembled submarines and this meant extra time closed up at action stations until the captain was satisfied of their identity and that a crafty U-boat commander was not using the floating monsters as a screen, particularly in fading light.

Soon enough they would start to experience the months of endless patrols with long hours of watchkeeping. They still had to learn that spare time was too precious for such luxuries, priorities were sleep and catching up on personal cleanliness. Dhobing and frequent changing of clothes was essential in the sticky climate to prevent skin complaints. The coarse blue serge uniforms were superseded with the lightweight tropical whites. As always a few of the crew applied for permission to grow a 'set' (beard). Weeks on there would be the usual competition for the best one grown, and a prize for the most abominable display of facial fungus.

The first port of call was inevitably Freetown in Sierra Leone, referred to by Captain Agar as 'that salubrious watering hole'. Here we joined H.M.S. Newcastle and the aircraft carrier H.M.S. Eagle to form Force 'F'. Admiral Algernan Willis the C in C, decided to mount a concentrated attack on the slippery German raiders still sinking Allied merchant ships. The huge loss of

Allied ships was a constantly reminded of the dangers to vessels carrying supplies and personnel via the Cape route to war zones in the East. For the next three months Dorsetshire was set for plenty of sea-time, landfalls at St. Helena and Freetown were made only when essential oil and provisions was urgently needed. During exercises on the 21st.September our Walrus aircraft crashed over the bows of 'Eagle', and we had to wait until October 8th. for a replacement.   Elegance is not the word to use when describing the amphibian plane, valuable though it was. It was said that in a very strong wind the plane was known to stand still in the air and someone said they had seen one move backwards. The pilot, observer, and gunner cum telegraphist, were accredited with nerves of steel and lack of fear. This I must say contrasted with the story put about that Dorsetshire's pilot always took a prayer mat with him to enhance his options during take-offs by catapult. I prefer to believe it was a cushion he was carrying.

H.M.S. Newcastle left Force 'F' and was replaced by the light cruiser H.M.S. Dunedin. Although H.M.S. Dorsetshire was part of this unit we operated on our own most of the time. It was known that six German armed merchant cruisers were operating in the Southern Hemisphere, four in the Pacific and Indian Ocean and two off the West African coast. It was also known that the German cruiser HIPPER and the pocket battleship ADMIRAL SCHEER were separately at sea, this was in addition to the numerous submarines and armed supply vessels. It meant that 'Dorsetshire', with it's long range capability, was ideal to chase out after them if there was a whisper of a sighting. The continued success of the raiders was causing a lot of political concern at home that was passed on to C in Cs, who in turn stepped up their operational patrols. Captain Agar received orders on November 26th.1941 to sweep an area south of St. Helena known to have been popular in the past for refuelling and provisioning enemy ships. It had proved to be an ideal region for transferring supplies because of an all year round phenomenally calm expanse of water. 'Gus' Agar had the professional skills to track down an enemy ship, but in the vastness of the South Atlantic it required a lot of luck and good fortune to catch the elusive Germans with their expertise for avoiding confrontation with warships.

'Dorsetshire' had extensively searched these waters in the past without success, but it was always with a sense of expectation that we searched again. Two of our sister ships had already recorded good fortune and we hoped it would soon be our turn. Off the Seychelles H.M.S. Cornwall sank an armed cruiser after a cat and mouse chase. Captain Kruger of the 'Pinguin' failed to outwit Captain Mainwaring of the 'Cornwall' and the British guns sent the German raider to it's grave on the 8th.May 1941. Kruger tried every trick in the book to get close enough to 'Cornwall' to drop his protective disguise and fire on the British ship. Fortunately Captain Mainwaring suspected the true identity of the German from the beginning and used his speed and range to out-manoeuvre and destroy the enemy vessel. H.M.S. Devonshire added her contribution by chasing the 'Atlantis' and forcing her to scuttle on the 22nd.November 1941. This raider was undoubtedly the most famous German armed cruiser of the Second World War. Under the command of Kapitan zur See Bernard Rogge it had acquired a notorious reputation, sinking twenty-five Allied ships totalling 145,000 tons since leaving it's homeport. It was unfortunate that 'Dorsetshire' narrowly missed this prestigious prize on four separate occasions.

Captain Oliver of H.M.S.Devonshire had a strong suspicion that U-Boats were close by and declined to pick up the crew who had taken to the ships' lifeboats. He was right, when 'Devonshire' first approached the submarine took evasive action and dived to wait for the cruiser to leave. When the coast was clear U126, commanded by Kapitanleutnant Bauer, surfaced to rescue the 'Atlantis' survivors. Two days later the U-Boat supply ship 'Python' arrived and took them on board. Other raiders with the names of 'Thor', 'Komet', 'Orion', 'Kormoran' and 'Pinguin' were all feared and respected by unguarded ships, but 'Atlantis' more so. Converted from the cargo liner 'Goldenfels' she was equipped with very efficient 5.9 guns, which Rogge and his gunners put to good use. The living conditions on board the German ship were exceptionally good with every possible home comfort provided for the men's welfare. It had to be, Rogge kept his ship at sea for nearly two years since setting out to harass the Allied merchant navy. This was a difficult operation when things went wrong with equipment and machinery, all repair work had to be carried out with limited resources in alien waters a long way from a friendly port. As a marauding Sea Wolf, Rogge needed to be alert twenty-four hours a day, putting a constant strain on the watchkeepers. Like his fellow captains he was a master of disguise, capable of changing the overall appearance of his ship with a few false fittings and a quick coat of paint. A change of flag and name, plus an additional funnel added to a deception that was necessary for survival.

The ever-lurking danger of U-Boats was further highlighted when our Force F companion H.M.S. Dunedin, was torpedoed two days later by the U124 with the loss of 300 sailors. Many of those who got into the water were fiercely mauled in savage attacks by sharks and barracouta. The voracious fish caused prolonged and agonising deaths to the helpless swimmers, something we were to be alarmed about ourselves when it was our turn to be sunk.

Trawling the sea south of St. Helena, without finding the quarry, it seemed as if Captain Agar would be denied the chance to sink an enemy ship this time. He altered course eastwards and we began to prepare for another oiling stop at Freetown. The white skins of those who joined at Hebburn were now a golden brown, they were slowly coming to terms with the irritations of 'prickly heat', Chinese toe rot and 'gippy tummy'. They were also getting well acquainted with the familiar layers of weevils that settled on top of the pussers soup. The pests infested the peas and other pulses taken on at Freetown. Infestation was an accepted ingredient of West African foodstuffs. This included the hard-backed tiny black insects that got into the flour. The first timers abroad, like we first did, found the weevils repulsive to start with but with time it became an accepted way of life and the objectionable matter was just spooned off without comment.

On the afternoon of December 1st.1941, about 650 miles north-east of Tristan da Cunha I joined in with other seamen for a game of Tombola (Housey-housey).It was the one form of gambling officially allowed and only when a ship was south of Gibraltar. Although the prize money was modest, the game was well attended and generally enjoyed as a form of relaxation. This session was never completed because high up in the 'crows nest' the eagle eye of Ray 'Chippy' Carpenter picked up the tip of a mast on the horizon and quickly alerted the bridge. Nothing escaped 'Chippy's' attention, when he was on look-out he could be relied on to spot the smallest of objects long before anyone else. Speed was increased and action stations sounded, sending us scampering from the game to take up our battle positions. It was a necessary precaution against a surprise attack by a crafty German captain. The distance between the two ships closed as 'Dorsetshire' started to slowly overtake what was later identified as the armed U-boat supply ship 'Python'. Capt. Agar signalled the ship to 'heave-to' but she ignored him. Although caught off guard the German captain tried unsuccessfully to outrun the cruiser. Two other objects first seen from a distance on the surface and subsequently found to be submarines disappeared as we approached, prompting our captain to exercise extreme caution. Once we were within range 'A' turret fired two salvoes, one in front and another behind the 'Python' as a clear warning to stop her engines. When the German captain realised he was trapped he opted for an honourable alternative. Declining to hand over his ship he launched the lifeboats for his crew, and the survivors he was carrying from the Atlantis, to scramble into and row clear before priming explosive charges to set the ship on fire. Finally the seacocks were opened to complete the destruction of another important U-boat provider. We found out in time that when her captain Fregattenkaptain Lueders first saw 'Dorsetshire' approaching he desperately tried a manoeuvred to get the two submarines between himself and 'Dorsetshire' so that they could torpedo us. One of the U-Boats did fire off all its torpedoes in a vain attempt but luckily missed. The decision to scuttle saved a number of lives, it allowed Captain Agar to hold his fire that he would have been forced to use if the German kept running. We swept past the sinking 'Python' without stopping because all the telltale signs indicated the certain presence of U-Boats. This, with hindsight, was a wise precaution because the two objects seen on the surface earlier were the German submarines UA and U68. It was left to them to rescue their shipwrecked colleagues.

When 'Dorsetshire' was out of sight the two U-boats surfaced and carried out the rescue operation. The senior German captain was ordered to take the boats laden with Python and Atlantis survivors in tow and make for the Cape Verde Islands. There they would be met and assisted by two German and two long range Italian submarines. The German seamen had a precarious and uncomfortable journey before rendezvousing with their colleagues. After distributing the survivors between the six submarines the group set sail for Europe, finally arriving in port on Christmas Eve. Good fortune favoured them on the voyage. If they had passed Gibraltar a month earlier they would have had to run the gauntlet of Captain Walker and his famous flotilla. This legendary captain and his renowned destroyers were sending U-boats to their doom at a rate that alarmed the Germans. Fortunately for them he was off station when they made sailed northwards otherwise they might have never completed the journey. The loss of the armed cruisers 'Atlantis', 'Pinguin' and 'Kormoran', coupled with increasing U-Boat casualties, must have been a setback to the Kriegsmarine. The earlier capture of the 'Lothringer' by H.M.S. Dunedin and the sinking of 'Python' by H.M.S. Dorsetshire added to their troubles. The removal of these two invaluable supply and refuelling ships curtailed the scope of the raiders, without oil and provisions the enemy ships couldn't operate as far from their bases. The German High Command ordered the submarines back to waters nearer home for the time being, easing the threat to our ships using the South Atlantic routes.

There was an air of jubilation on board when 'Gussie' Agar told us we were on course for Simonstown. This was partly due to the sinking of the 'Python' but mainly at the prospects of a run ashore. Granted, the supply ship was not another 'Bismark' or 'Richelieu' but it added to the lesser successes like the 'Wakama' and the 'Mendoza'. We couldn't expect big fish every trawl. 'Dorsetshire' arrived at Simonstown on Sunday 7th.December the day the Japanese, with no declaration of war, attacked Pearl Harbour. Vice-Admiral Chuichi Nagumo commanding the Japanese carrier force under Admiral Isoroku Yamamoto, ravaged the United States Pacific Fleet. The unsuspecting attack will always be known to Americans as that 'Day of Infamy'. The unprovoked assault left President Franklin D. Roosevelt with no option but to declare war the next day, followed immediately by Great Britain. The news that the 'Yanks' had at long last come off the fence, pushed might be the better word, was heavenly music to our ears. Although their losses at Pearl Harbour were a devastating blow, eight battleships sunk or badly damaged, three cruisers and three destroyers sunk, as well as two auxiliary ships, a minelayer and 180 planes destroyed, they still possessed a vast number of ships to ease the overstretched commitments of the Royal Navy.

So far it had been a bloody sea war with hundreds of His Majesty's ships sunk, and this did not include the huge losses sustained by the merchant fleet. More important was the unaccountable number of seamen lost with thousands more still to die. Now with over two thousand killed and hundreds wounded in the one attack on Pearl Harbour the Americans were getting their first taste of warfare. I have to admit the tragic news did not spoil the enjoyment of my shore leave, "poor bloody doughboys" was about the extent of the messdeck sympathy for the Americans. Ships were being lost every day and it could be my turn tomorrow, if I could have only known how soon that was about to be. Everyone's complacency received a nasty shock a couple of days later when the whole ships' company was genuinely stunned by the news that the ultra modern battleship H.M.S. Prince of Wales and the Battle-cruiser H.M.S. Repulse had been sunk by the Japanese. A lot of our men had friends and relations on these ships that brought the reality of the loss much closer to home. The implications had a profound effect on all of us, if the Japs could sink such formidable vessels with aeroplanes what chance did we have. The general conversation focused on our vulnerability to the highly efficient planes of the Japanese navy. The consensus of opinion was that air protection had to be a necessity for all ships operating within range of enemy aircraft. It was a point well illustrated four months on when 'Dorsetshire' and 'Cornwall' met their doom without the loss of a single Japanese plane.

Originally the ill-fated Force 'Z' comprised of the battleship 'Prince of Wales', battle-cruiser 'Repulse', aircraft carrier 'Indomitable' and the destroyers Electra, Express, Tenedos and Vampire, when it was ordered to Singapore. It arrived on the 2nd.December without the all important aircraft carrier which had run aground on a reef off Jamacia on November 3rd. H.M.S.Indomitable was still having repair work carried out on the hull but was expected to catch up later. Winston Churchill considered the presence of a strong force a suitable deterrent to the aggressive overtones of the Japanese Government. He was wrong, five days later, on the 7th.Dec., Japan declared war on Great Britain, the Commonwealth and the United States of America. On the afternoon of Dec.8th, Admiral Phillips sailed from Singapore with the 'Prince of Wales' (Capt. Leach), 'Repulse' (Capt. Tennant) and a destroyer escort to carry out a surprise attack on a Japanese invasion fleet bound for Malaya. When the squadron reached the Anambas Islands it turned north for French Indo-China. Unfortunately as it passed the islands it was sighted by the I-65, a Japanese submarine on patrol. The submarine did not attack but reported the course of the ships, which was relayed to Rear-Admiral Matsunaga, commanding the Air Flotilla based in Saigon. Reconnaissance aircraft took off but failed to find the Allied ships, meanwhile Admiral Phillips sailed towards Kuantan to attack the reported Japanese landing. Unknown to him, his ships had been sighted again during the night by the enemy submarine I-58. This time the submarine captain, Lieutenant-Commander Kitamura, followed the ships for several hours and accurately reported their position and course. Admiral Matsunaga tried again, this time sending ten reconnaissance planes to pinpoint Admiral Phillips's force before despatching eighty-eight attack aircraft, guided by the spotter planes. Sighting the Japanese reconnaissance planes, Admiral Phillips realised that his surprise attack had been thwarted and he turned back towards Singapore. It was too late the Japanese aircraft attacked and destroyed the two prestigious capital ships within an hour. The 35,000ton battleship and the 33,000 ton Battle- cruiser were sunk for the cost of only four enemy aircraft. The escorting destroyers closed in on the doomed ships and worked frantically to rescue 1300 survivors. Eight hundred and forty men died including Admiral Phillips. It was a sad loss in men and material.

During our six day stay in Simonstown there was plenty to keep us busy with routine maintenance but it was obvious 'Dorsetshire' was waiting for something or someone because normally we would have been back at sea within two or three days. Our 'parcel' arrived in the shape of Convoy WS12X accompanied by a strong US naval guard. The American escort included two cruisers and six destroyers, an amazingly powerful bodyguard for the size of the convoy. With their unlimited resources the Americans did everything on a big scale and seemed to do it well. On the last day before we sailed or good behaviour record in the Cape was blotted when sailors from the two navies met ashore and fighting broke out. I don't know what started it nor did anyone else, but it was fierce in some places and only the intervention of the South African police prevented a riot. Considering the number of US ships in port our lads gave a good account of themselves, although the collection of bruised and battered faces on the messdeck the next day was a sure sign we didn't have it all our own way. The fighting was deemed serious enough for a delegation of officers from both sides to meet and smooth troubled waters. I suspect some of our lads were a bit jealous of the high standard of living on the American ships. A few ratings who had been on business to their boats brought back tales of seeing such things as washing machines, unheard of in the Royal Navy of the time. We were still dhobiing by hand in a bucket with a block of 'pussers hard'. On that day of the troubles I was late going ashore but had arranged to meet my oppos at a bar in Capetown. When I got there I went upstairs to the big lounge where we usually congregated but found it packed with Americans. One of them greeted me as I went in and asked if I would have a drink, which I accepted in the spirit of good-fellowship. At first everyone seemed friendly enough but their questions about America's part in the war got answers they didn't like and the mood of a few changed to one of aggression. Sir Richard Grenville's famous words "shall we fight or shall we fly" kept going over and over in my head. I wouldn't have stood a cat in hells chance of getting out of there with my teeth intact if I hadn't been rescued in the nick of time. Apparently one of our crew saw my predicament as he passed the door and quickly passed the word to a crowd of British matelots in another room who came in mob handed to ask if I was alright. The Americans let me pass and I made as dignified an exit as possible to join my buddies with a great feeling of relief. Unfortunately all such situations were not resolved as amicably hence the black eyes and bruises. By and large I think the Matelots enjoyed the punch-up it added spice to a run ashore.

'Dorsetshire' took charge of convoy WS12X single-handed and left Simonstown at 1400hrs on Dec.13th. I had a slight feeling of churlish satisfaction that we were doing what it had taken eight American warships to do. Some might have seen it as a moral victory for any defeats our ships' company suffered brawling the previous night. We were well away from land when the captain informed us that the convoy was en route for Singapore but we were only taking it as far as Bombay, from there it would be someone else's responsibility. The fourteen day voyage north went without incident including another uneventful Christmas Day at sea. On Saturday Dec.27th 'Dorsetshire' dropped anchor off the Bund in full view of the Gateway of India arch. The ship was staying for five days, long enough for the first timers to sample the colourful offerings of India. The Surgeon Commander, in keeping with his role as Senior Medical Officer, gave the younger members of the crew the benefit of his knowledge on sexually transmitted diseases. It was one of the regular lectures he relished to put fear into the hearts and minds of young seamen and midshipmen. "Remember. Don't go dashing ashore with your 'willie' in one hand and a half a crown in the other. 'Bag Shanties' will give you more than 'Crabs' and Chinese toe rot" he counselled. "Think of the planets, three minutes with Venus will get you two years with Mercury". The 'Snotties' were just as disillusioned with female company as we were when 'Bones' finished his talk. Those unfortunates who contracted venereal disease were in some ways treated like lepers, isolated and confined to the CD (contagious diseases) Mess. They were restricted to their own toilet and other facilities and forbidden to leave the ship. During their time of sickness they were not allowed to take part in the general running of the ship. 'Bones' had little sympathy with patients who ignored his advice and lectures, plus the fact that he provided unlimited condoms free of charge. They were placed on an unattended table by the ships' exits to be discreetly taken without facetious remarks from colleagues. It must be said that the Medical Officer's efforts were reflected in the very few residents of the CD Mess. In all the time I served on 'Dorsetshire' I can only remember three individuals being confined there. Two were older men who should have known better and the third was a young Petty Officer, who should also have known better.

I found Bombay a classic example of extremes in living conditions. The ostentatious wealth of the rich Indians rubbed shoulders with expatriate Whites to enjoy a luxurious lifestyle beyond the wildest dreams of the low caste natives. My first run ashore was in a party organised by the local English community and it was a day out to remember. I found everything hard to take in all at once when I stepped on to the Apollo Bunda. Every type of hawker, provider, beggar and tout, squatted along the extensive esplanade and by the commotion they made when they saw us, we were viewed as promising customers. Supervised by Leading Seamen, our group walked through the streets two abreast. Nobody was allowed to wander off on their own as we approached the sleazy quarter of the city known as Grant Road. Here people slept on the pavements or scavenged for food on equal terms with a host of mangy animals. Children were purposely deformed to increase their begging potential, with little wooden blocks under the palms of their hands as they moved around on all fours. In time the enforced posture became a permanency giving them a resemblance of a dog. Grant Road it was explained was notorious for it's seedy brothels which became apparent as we walked along it. It was a filthy place lined with open fronted shops displaying wretched collections of sad faced prostitutes waiting to be taken and used by the lowest types of the slum area. Why our hosts had included this part of the city in the itinerary left me puzzled, it was disgusting and made all the more poignant for those of us still celibate after the latest lecture from the surgeon.

From the dregs of humanity we were taken to the opulence of Breach Kandy with it's sparkling swimming pools and leisure complex. It was a world apart from the squalor of Grant Road. The tranquil difference to the noisy waterfront setting reminded me of that old Chinese saying:- "In the hustle and the bustle of the market place, there is much money to be made - but under the cherry tree there is peace". As I was driven through the avenues of palatial properties I saw my first Bengal Lancer in full regalia on guard outside one of the mansions. I could only assume it was of some important minister. I noticed that all the people in the swimming pool with us were white, apartheid was still practised by the remnants of the Imperial Raj. The use of Frogs, Wogs and Niggers was still socially acceptable to describe anyone born east of the English Channel, but times were changing. After an enjoyable meal our tour continued into the city to visit the museum. I was particularly impressed by a beautiful facsimile of the Taj Mahal which someone told me was the original of the famous masterpiece. Our day out finished with tea, English style, before making our way back to the jetty. I was sorry when our visit came to an end having witnessed the high and the low of Bombay society, things I would not have seen without the help of our kind hosts. Any further visits would be confined to the middle ground of the sprawling metropolis. Fred Ball and myself preferred to eat at one of the Chinese cafes in town where the food was good and cheap. I could never be persuaded to eat the local Indian cooking, having heard terrible tales of curried concoctions that dramatically increased the sale of toilet rolls. Most of the older members of our ship never ventured farther than Jimmy Green's bar and restaurant close to the waterfront. They had seen the sights many times and refused to waste good drinking time seeing them again.

It was customary that officers and men did not mix socially. In Bombay the officers laid claim to the grandiose Taj Mahal hotel and the other ranks gave 'Jimmy Greens' their seal of approval. Both sides observed the unwritten demarcation lines to avoid any form of fraternisation. One thing I did find repulsive was the dirty Indian habit of chewing Beetle Nut, and spitting the red juice with total disregard for the surroundings. It was especially distasteful to see so many women doing it. Although I had a lot of pleasure seeing the sights in the Indian city I was glad in my heart when we left. It was not a place I would hanker after or pay to visit, it made me realise why so many of the older sailors never bothered to go into the town centre, perhaps my trouble was that I expected it to be something like Durban or Capetown

Provisioning in Bombay proved to be something of a health hazard. The stores were hoisted inboard in large wicker baskets, which unknown to us were infested with big ravenous bugs. The pests quickly spread throughout the ship causing our Sick Bay to be inundated with complaints from badly bitten matelots. 'Dorsetshire' weighed anchor on January 2nd.1942 and as soon as we were at sea 'Bones' carried out a thorough fumigating and sanitising programme. The delousing also dispersed the shiny brown hoards of cockroaches, although we never looked on them as hazardous until they started dropping off the deckhead into our food at mealtimes.

21 MALAYA

News that we were returning to Durban for three days created an undercurrent of excitement that brought smiles to a lot of faces on the messdeck. There was a general buzz of elation and expectation with the usual preoccupations 'Walter Mittying' about food, beer, girls and leave, not necessarily in that order. Shore-going 'whites' were washed and pressed with fastidious care in preparation for at least one trip into town. There was also a possibility that mail would be waiting for us. The frequent calls by ships coming from England made Durban a good dropping off point for parcels and letters. Outgoing letters had to be in the mail office days before arriving in port. This was to allow them to be censored, and this caused a flurry of scribbling. Nobody underestimated the importance of preventing information getting into enemy hands even though men were sensitive about others prying into their private correspondence. Unwittingly something could be included in an otherwise harmless letter that might cost lives, and those lives might be our own. Snapshots received extra special scrutiny before having 'passed by censor' franked on the back. The censors were thorough, some more than others, using their blue pencils to obliterate anything minutely questionable in terms of security. Much of the thankless job of checking letters fell to the 'Sky pilot'. It was ideal work for a ships' padre, accustomed as he was to dealing with delicate personal matters. There were smiles and scowls when mail was issued and it was easy to pick out the ones not getting any. A letter from home was a precious commodity with every sentence to be savoured over and over again. Not all the news from home was good, I remember a friend getting a letter to say that his wife and children had been killed in an air-raid. He was sent home on compassionate leave and I never saw him again.

The return voyage from Bombay to South Africa went without incident, just a normal routine passage with a few extra exercises to keep the ships' company on their toes. We eventually arrived in port on the 10th.January, the day before my nineteenth birthday. I was beginning to feel like an old salt with some experience and I had to constantly remind myself how easily I could develop into a 'stroppy' sailor if I didn't watch my step. For many, a run ashore included visiting a tattooist to be adorned with something they could regret in time. One fatuous exhibitionist in my mess was tattooed with an item more impressive than the usual dragon, 'death before dishonour' or 'a sailor's grave'. He had a voluptuous female nude etched on his biceps that wiggled and danced when he flexed his muscles. His party piece provided a source of amusement, but the novelty soon wore off. The redundant nude wasn't a problem until be became friendly with a South African girl from a good family. Complications set in when he spent time at her parent's beach chalet. His reluctance to change into trunks for a swim brought facetious comments from her friends. The dilemma and embarrassment was a constant worry and a blight on the love affair. In a moment of weakness and desperation he did a very stupid thing, he asked his messmates for advice. Needless to say it was given freely with only his best interests in mind, at least I think it was.

My suggestion to change the nude into a palm tree with breasts converted into coconuts was considered the best possible solution. A tattoo of a palm tree with a couple of nuts would surely be acceptable to the family. The next time we docked he was off like a hare to find a tattooist to do the alterations.

Then all we could do was wait for the scab and bandage to come off to solve all the unfortunates problems. In the fullness of time the big day arrived and we gathered around to see the results, it was a disaster. The offending tattoo now resembled something that was part girl and part tree with two big coconut-like hairy breasts. Joining the legs together produced a disproportionate tree trunk that would have confused the most learned botanist. Even his closest friends laughed uncontrollably, adding further to the lad's misery. I kept out of his way fearing he might blame me. Suffice to say the love affair died, he was too ashamed to strip into swimming trunks and meld with his new found family. Fred Ball and I decided when we first met at sixteen years, never to be tattooed and we never did even with the constant cajoling of our friends to just have a little one done.

The day after we docked in Durban I completed part one of my evaluation exams for Leading Seaman. It included exercising a squad in forming and rifle drill on the Quarter Deck. The disciplines were exactly the same as those I had carried out dozens of times, as Leading Boy in charge of a class at the training ship. Later in the day the Divisional Officer sent for me to pass on Captain Agar's comments, unknown to me he had witnessed my endeavours and considered them worth an approving remark. This would undoubtedly be taken into account by the passing out officers and could only be to my advantage. I immediately started the second and final part of the exams, full of confidence that I would complete them successfully.

I noticed a couple of large packing cases being shipped ashore during our stay, when I enquired what was in them I was told it was the ships' silver and trophies being deposited for safe keeping. Perhaps Captain Agar had a premonition of the tragic events ahead or maybe it was just a precaution. On the afternoon of Tuesday the 13th.January 1942 HMS Dorsetshire cast off for the last farewell with the band playing that favourite South African tune Sarie Marais, the next time I visited Durban it would be under very different circumstances. Once again we were bound for Bombay with a convoy, but on the 21st. we were diverted to Aden to take on oil before rejoining the ships again the following day to complete the journey. It always seemed that whenever the ship was going to places like Bombay the whole crew went through a ritual of inoculations to combat every known tropical disease. The injections invariably caused unpleasant red swelling of the arms and high temperatures with flu symptoms. A visit to the Sick Bay was a waste of time because we all knew that the only treatment we would get was to be told to work the arm plenty and in time it would get better. Needless to say the aches and pains miraculously disappeared when land was sighted and the prospects of going ashore looked good.

At 0800hrs on the 26th.January the thunderous rumbling of the chain cables as they rattled along the steel 'scotchman', followed by a big splash as the close-stowing bow anchors hit the water, meant the two week voyage was over. During the afternoon the liberty boats were busy ferrying the off-duty watch ashore and I joined them. The unstimulating aroma and noisy chattering made me realise why old sweats referred to India as the land of bells, yells and bloody smells. I noted that the same reception committee of pimps, touts and slick salesmen lay in wait for any poor unsuspecting fool stupid enough to listen to their patter. Their persuasive charm differed little from country to country as they plied their wares offering girls, watches, cloth, carvings and postcards. I had a few runs ashore but none was as enlightening as the first.

One day while we were in Bombay, just after Divisions, I was detailed to take a crew of 'hostility only' recruits sailing in a Montague rigged whaler as part of my assessment for Leading Seaman part 2. My first reaction was irritation at being given an inexperienced bunch but this quickly evaporated when I realised it was a golden opportunity to show off skills I developed at H.M.S.Ganges. It could have been much worse, I might have been given a 34ft.Dipping Lug rigged cutter. Getting a few 'red inks' to boost my prospects of advancement outweighed any anxieties of a faux pas on the part of my crew. 'Knocker' White my divisional Petty Officer was highly amused at the thought of one of his nineteen year olds initiating much older men to the joys of canvas drill. There wasn't sufficient time to explain to them the most elementary rules for sailing, only just enough to make sure all the necessary equipment was in place and the bung firmly in. All too soon I heard the P.O. shouting "Turns for Lowering". "Start the Falls". "Lower Away". When the boat hit the water I took complete control of the situation and demanded silence. It was my responsibility and I would do all the talking otherwise there was the danger of an accident; nobody queried my directives, which was just as well. After securing to the boom I supervised the stepping of the masts and rigging the fore, main and mizzen sails. When the boat was 'made ready' the increasingly enthusiastic crew, carefully following my instructions to the letter, sprang the whaler away from the boom. With my heart in my mouth and my unskilled team squatting on the bottom boards, I pushed the tiller hard over and watched with incredible relief as the canvas billowed and we got under way.

Beating up wind I was too preoccupied with constant tacking to bother explaining the text book procedures for going about head and stern to wind. There would be time enough for them to know that sheets and shrouds were totally different to those in Civvy Street. When we reached the point for returning I gybed to get the wind abaft the beam, now we could relax and soak up the pleasures of boating by 'Running free' before the wind. It was an exhilarating sensation that increased the adrenaline and made it a moment to enjoy. My trainee yachtsmen seemed very pleased with themselves obviously feeling they had mastered the first steps for sailing a boat. As we swept past the ship and went 'about' coming back 'close hauled' I was unashamedly showing off, especially when I became aware of groups watching from the upper deck. With the whaler well over and the port gunwale nearly touching the water I knew I had done all that was expected of me. Keeping a weather eye on the ship, it seemed ages before I saw the boat recall signal run up. Now the tricky bit of getting back alongside without under or over shooting. I kept repeating to the men on the sheets that when I shout, "Let fly Sheets" they must release them instantly to spill the wind out of the sails. It would be up to me to judge that the amount of way on the boat was enough to take us to the boom to tie up. Too much speed and we could have a nasty bump, too little and we would be becalmed in an embarrassing mess. My worries were groundless I got the boat up to the lizard with just the right amount of movement for the bowman to make fast, it had been a successful and enjoyable sail for the whole party.

In Bombay, as had happened on more occasions than I care to remember, I was detailed off for town and pier patrol duty. In theory this meant maintaining naval good order ashore, in practise it meant using a lot of discretion when outnumbered by inebriated gangs of matelots. I couldn't help noticing that every time P.O.Schollett was responsible for shore patrols he always picked those of us who had been his charges on the boy's messdeck. Dressed with belt, gaiters, armband, and carrying an Admiralty pattern truncheon we were empowered to arrest and detain naval personnel caught misbehaving. It all sounded very grand when in fact we tried to keep out of the thick of any fighting until it had subsided to the exchange of a few verbals. Jim Schollett always tried the gentle approach to break up a fight or settle a dispute, but he could be tough when other methods failed. On this patrol we were called to a fight in bar, I think it was called the Lord Nelson. Jim assured the messenger that we were on the way 'chop chop' but like most punch-ups we were called out to, he held back waiting until the brawlers had knocked 'seven bells' out of each other before moving in. He always considered the welfare of his patrol before the needs of a bar owner who had allowed things to get out of hand by continuing to serve men who had already consumed too much drink. I first experienced the ploy in Freetown when a large number of sailors from different were battling it out. As we were only seven strong it was prudent not to rush in until they had tired themselves out. When a native came chasing to find us P.O.Schollett told him to run back as quickly as possible and inform the publican that we were hurrying to his assistance. Then he marched us in the opposite direction to kill a little time.

Another time on shore patrol I got my first insight into a brothel when we were called out to deal with a naval disturbance inside. I was eagerly curious to see what it was like only to be told to wait outside with a patrol from another ship. I pleaded with Jim Schollett to let me come inside with him, explaining that I had never seen inside a brothel before. "Alright Cannon, but stick close to me and don't give them time to put their *"!@#Š* trousers on. Do you hear".

"Yes P.O., I hear" We barged in ready for action of a milder nature, pushing open doors and ordered everyone, males and females, outside to the forecourt to be rounded up by the other patrol. The 'Madam' kept saying that everything was now under control but the P.O. told her to shut up and get out with the others. When we got to a veranda we found about four beds full of small children and this made P.O. Schollett very angry, especially when he saw the infants were in a filthy condition and exposed to the night air while the mothers were in the bedrooms plying their trade. He roared for the 'Madam' to be brought to him and he gave her a torrent of abuse like she had never heard before. He made her put the children into a comfortable room with clean sheets and warned her what to expect if she ever put the youngsters outside again. I was bitterly disappointed with my introduction to a brothel. I half expected a satin lined bordello with shapely 'ladies', it turned out to be a squalid repulsively depressing dosshouse with women who were long past their best. I followed Jim Schollett outside to inspect the two lines of sheepishly looking soldiers and sailors caught with their pants down. Jim was pleased to find that there was none of our men in the line-up and after a good dressing down he let them off with a caution and a warning not to get caught again. They scarpered like rabbits hardly believing their good luck.

On the 8th.February H.M.S. Dorsetshire arrived in Colombo, Ceylon, but left again two days later to find a convoy that was about to leave embattled Singapore. The Colony was under siege by the Japanese forces and was expected to fall to them soon. Steaming eastwards for four days 'Dorsetshire' sighted the ships, packed with women and children escaping capture from the advancing enemy. This convoy, with the destroyer H.M.S.ISIS towing the submarine H.M.S. Rover bringing up the rear, was said to be the last to leave Singapore before the island surrendered. 'Dorsetshire' found the ships 6 deg. South and 110 deg. East, just north of Surabaya, on the 14th. February; the next day Singapore capitulated. Fortress Singapore was the Gibraltar of the East, with a reputation of being impregnable and indestructible. It was a myth that was shattered when General Percival surrendered unconditionally to General Tomoyuki Yamashita. The Japanese could hardly believe their luck to get such a prize, with it's large new naval dock, airfields and vast quantities of war supplies. Much of the captured equipment was still in packing cases and unused, it was the ultimate reward for a victorious enemy. Thousands of Allied troops were either killed or captured and the Japanese lost no time demonstrating their supposed Nippon supremacy over the prisoners.

Large numbers of Allied servicemen were sent to build the infamous Burma railway. Amongst them was my elder brother Joe Cannon who had been serving with the Royal Corps of Signals in Indo-China. Years later when I met up with him I realised what the prisoners must have suffered, he looked gaunt and a thin shadow of his former self in appearance and personality. The notorious Burma construction claimed thousands of lives, many attributed to the brutal and inhumane treatment in the Japanese camps. Starved of nutrition, prisoners were expected to do heavy manual work all day in the sun. Without medical care the death toll was higher from a variety of tropical diseases brought on by malnutrition and dysentery.

The loss of the important base at Singapore was a blow for all the Services but especially the Navy who were now denied the use of the new docking installations and repair yards. Deployed to escort the convoy back to Colombo meant we narrowly missed the holocaust that was soon to follow in the waters of Indonesia. The Imperial Japanese Navy now dominant in the Pacific was committed to destroying the Allied navies to pave the way for the speedily advancing Nippon army. The island-hopping Japanese needed safe waters for their amphibious forces to land with the minimum of casualties. After the fall of Singapore the oil and rubber rich Indonesia was the next obvious target. The Allies were well informed of the Japanese preparations for invading Java. A small combined Fleet under the command of the Dutch Admiral Karel Doorman had the impossible task of stopping them. The Allies were outnumbered by at least two to one by the Japanese, and the enemy had superior fighting ships. The Dutch Admiral was a realist but undoubtedly very brave. He knew his inferior force was no match for the powerful enemy fleet. Undaunted, he was prepared to stake everything in an attempt to hold up the invasion fleet for as long as possible. On the 27th.February 1942 he engaged the Japanese Fleet in the Battle of the Java Sea. The outcome was total devastation, the Allied force including the cruisers 'Exeter' and 'Java', the destroyers 'Stronghold', 'Encounter', 'Jupiter', 'Kortenaer' and later the cruisers 'Houston' and 'Perth' were annihilated.

H.M.S.Exeter, of River Plate fame, was badly damaged at first. As it limped back to Surabaya it was spotted by a reconnaissance plane. The enemy fleet quickly caught up with the cruiser and her two escorting destroyers to finish the job of sinking all three ships. The captain of 'Exeter' asked for smoke and the destroyers swept around the crippled cruiser laying a thick screen. In a final desperate attack, her captain judged the position of the pursuing ships and came out of the smoke with guns firing to the last. The Japanese were waiting and I was told that the scene resembled the end of a stag hunt. H.M.S. Exeter went down fighting with the loss of all hands, although most of them must have been dead by the time the ship sank. Admiral Doorman, like so many of his men, also lost his life. If 'Dorsetshire' had been a few days late collecting the Singapore convoy there is little doubt what would have happened to us, along with the merchant ships carrying the women and children. It was a lucky escape that was too close for comfort.

The little convoy reached Colombo on the 19th.February where we left it, there was another to escort, this time in company with H.M.S. Glasgow before returning to Trincomalee. During our time at sea the ship carried out joint exercises with H.M.S. Emerald, including main armament shoots. It must have brought back a few memories to Captain Agar, earlier in the war when he was the captain of 'Emerald' it was used for shipping large quantities of gold to the United States for safe keeping. About this time 'Dorsetshire' was involved in a couple of off-beat covert operations landing small parties of commandos close inshore on the Burma coast. Once ashore their task was to harass the advancing Japanese in whatever way possible. We watched their boats being launched with mixed feelings knowing that these men were the real heroes of the war, they volunteered for missions that required the kind of courage few other men could claim to have. We could only hope they avoided capture and made it back home safely.

On Thursday 26th.February 1942 'Dorsetshire' sailed with her last convoy, taking reinforcements to the besieged city of Rangoon. It was a chilling feeling knowing that the city was already under threat, with Japanese soldiers fighting around the outskirts of the port. Arriving off Rangoon on the 3rd.March 1942 Capt.Agar didn't go right in but stood off and waited to see the merchant ships securely inside before returning to Trincomalee, his mission completed. Three days after the convoy arrived in Rangoon the city surrendered to the Japanese. H.M.S.Dorsetshire lays claim to having brought the last convoy safely away from Singapore before it fell, and taking the last into Rangoon before it surrendered. Sadly, the seagoing days of the County Class cruiser were numbered, soon hundreds of her crew would be killed and her services would no longer be available to the Allied cause.

22 The Japanese cometh

The Japanese, now convinced of their naval supremacy in the Pacific decided it was time to stamp their authority in the Indian Ocean. The British and Japanese High Commands both realised the importance of the arterial shipping lanes in these waters. The Allied war effort depended on the free passage of supplies and reinforcements to our beleaguered troops, fighting a desperate battle to contain the enemy advance towards the Indian sub-continent. Control of these seas was equally important to the Japanese. Their push through Burma depended on ships bringing the large amount of equipment needed to maintain their offensive. Admiral Nobotake Kondo was ordered to carry out a two-pronged offensive, with Vice-Admiral Chuichi Nagumo commanding the main carrier fleet attacking Ceylon and Vice-Admiral Jisaburo Ozawa a smaller squadron to harrass shipping in the Bay of Bengal. Vice-Admiral Nagumo was still enjoying the accolades of glory from his strike on Pearl Harbour. Commanding the carrier task force, under Admiral Isoroku Yamamoto, he had ravaged the United States Pacific Fleet. Fortunately for the Americans, Admiral Yamamoto and Admiral Nagumo failed to fully exploit their position of dominance at the time of the attack. Workshop installations and oil fuel supplies were left undamaged. More importantly, the American aircraft carriers at sea were not found and destroyed and this was a major blunder. Whatever his shortcomings, Nagumo was worshipped as a national hero in his homeland after Pearl Harbour.

On the 26th.March 1942 the main Japanese task force left Staring Bay in Celebus (Sulawesi), Indonesia. Once at sea Nagumo set a westerly course and the air crews drilled for battle. Pilots practised the Kyu-Ko-Ka technique of bombing, an important skill they had to perfect to achieve 100% accuracy. It meant carrying a full bomb load and diving almost vertical (75 degrees) at speed to as low as possible before making a sharp turn to climb upwards. The high speed of the diving plane and the momentum of the bomb were utilized to maximum effect on the target. Another integral part of their training was 'Self-explode' suicide to avoid capture. Planes were fitted with a special device for igniting a powerful explosive to destroy an aircraft completely and prevent it falling into enemy hands. The Japanese pilots were indoctrinated with the following instructions:-

(A) The Japanese warriors are to fight for the country of Japan by willingly sacrificing their lives with grace and glory any time in case of need. It is the most disgraceful and shameful for the Japanese warriors to be captured and become POW. Japan is not a signing country of the POW treaty.

(B) During the World War II, to rescue the Japanese pilots is not regarded as one of important measures to be undertaken with priority. Once a plane is disabled, the fate of the pilot is very clear - to die. For Japanese pilots, it would be even better to commit suicide than struggling in the sea in vain to be possibly captured as POW and later to be tortured by the enemy. No other means could be better than dying bravely with glory, and if possible, meaningfully, namely to steer the plane with bombs/torpedoes straight towards enemy target.

The outstanding successes at Pearl and in the Java Sea increased the morale and fighting spirit of the men who now felt total victory was theirs for the asking. The Southern Airforce escorted the fleet, giving it vital air cover at the start of the voyage and a Japanese Strike Force left Pandam Bay to capture Christmas Island, which they did on the 31st.March. This provided Nagumo's ships with additional security as they steamed one hundred nautical miles to the north on the same day. Nagumo, on the flagship 'Akagi' was confident of repeating his previous successes with his powerful fleet of :-

Five aircraft carriers: Akagi (Vice-Admiral Nagumo), Hiryu (Rear-Admiral Yamaguchi), Soryu (Rear-Admiral Hara), Zuikaku and Shokaku.

Four battleships: Kongo (Rear-Admiral Mikawa), Haruna, Hiyei and Kirishima.

Four cruisers: Tone (Rear-Admiral Abe), Chikuma, Abukuma (Rear-Admiral Omori), and Akigumo.

Eight destroyers: Urakaze, Tanikaze, Isokaze, Hamakaze, Kasumi, Arare, Kagero, and Shiranuhi.

Submarine squadron: I1, I2, I3, I4, I5, I6, and the flagship submarine I7.

The carriers had an additional 45 aircraft added to their normal compliment, making a total of 360 planes. This was made up of 105 fighters, 123 level bombers (Kates) and 132 dive-bombers (Vals).

With such a strong force the Japanese commander was justified to feel self-assured of another resounding victory. Taking a route past the west of Timor, the fleet rounded the southern tip of Java and headed towards Ceylon from the south. The course of the enemy ships sent alarm bells ringing throughout the Allied corridors of power. Not only was India threatened, the eastern side of Africa was now also vulnerable to attack. A fleet was hurriedly assembled under the command of Vice-Admiral James Somerville to combat the danger. Suspecting a possible attack on Colombo the Admiral moved his fleet 600 miles south-west of Ceylon to the Maldive Islands.

The ships were in two groups, 'A' Group was the fast section and 'B' the slow one.

'A' Group was made up of the battleship Warspite (flagship). The aircraft carriers Indomitable and Formidable, under the command of Rear-Admiral Boyd. The cruisers Dorsetshire, Cornwall, Emerald and Enterprise and the destroyers Panther, Paladin, Napier (Australian), Hotspur, Foxhound and Nestor (Australian).

'B' Group under the command of Vice-Admiral Willis contained the battleships Resolution, Ramilles, and Royal Sovereign. The aircraft carrier Hermes, the cruisers Caladin, Dragon and Jacob van Heemskerck (Netherlands). The destroyer escort was the Fortune, Griffin, Arrow, Decoy, Scout, Norman (Australian), Isaac Sweers (Netherlands) and Vampire (Australian). On paper the Fleet looked very commanding, in reality it was mainly an array of ageing warhorses. The battleships Warspite, Ramilles, Revenge, Royal Sovereign and Resolution were First World War vintage battle-waggons, affectionately referred to as the 'Wobbly R's'. If the Admiralty thought the display of thirty ships would impress and deter the Japanese Imperial Navy they were mistaken. Admiral Nagumo was well briefed on the ship to ship, and air to ship, capabilities of the British Eastern Fleet in comparison to his own. He had no misgivings about challenging Admiral Somerville to a sea battle and inflicting heavy losses.

On the 27th.March 1942 H.M.S.Dorsetshire entered the Graving Dock at Colombo for urgent repairs to the ships' steering and engines. It also provided a good opportunity for work to be carried out on the parts of the hull not accessible when the ship was afloat. During the stay, arrangements were made for part of the crew to have a few days shore leave. Invitations had been received from the tea planting community for the 'liberty' men to stay at their homes. It was a goodwill gesture, a way of saying "thank you" from the expatriate families to their countrymen.

There was plenty of light hearted banter on the messdecks. "Berry, don't drink the bloody water in the finger bowls like you did in Durban".

"Jan, cover that poxy tattoo, if a 'Sky-pilot' (Vicar) sees it he'll spew his guts".

"Don't suppose these girls will be willing to hawk their pearlies, least not to us lot. Wot you think Knocker"?

Finally the lucky ones passed inspection and were on their way to the estates around Kandy. Where I stood on duty by the Quarter Deck gangway I could hear a few 'snotties' and 'subbies' twittered like schoolboys going on their first date, nobody bothered to take the usual 'micky' out of them. The libertymen arrived at the cool mountainous region in Ceylon to find breathtaking scenery. Their welcome was a genuine one from the families providing accommodation that was luxurious and relaxing. Unfortunately the stay in the idyllic surroundings was short lived. Within twenty-four hours of arriving, everyone was ordered to return to the ship immediately. The Japanese threat to Colombo meant 'Dorsetshire' had to be made ready for sea as soon as possible. The work programme was cut short with 'hands' working at maximum speed to get jobs done, by Tuesday 31st.March we moved the ship out of the dry dock into the overcrowded harbour. As soon as the oiling, provisioning and ammunitioning was completed, the officers made their formal reports of readiness.

The returning libertymen were in a foul mood, knowing their chance to enjoy home comforts had gone. Nevertheless, they were all back on board and with something to grumble about they seemed to work that much better. Leading Seaman Bert Gollop, cast anxious glances around the harbour remembering a previous visit to Colombo. On that occasion, working along the ships' waterline with Able Seaman Watkinson, the unbearable tropical sun led him from the path of righteousness. He bartered with a passing boatman for bottles of beer for himself and his helper. After a furtively whispered conversation and the handing over of ten rupees with pleas to hurry the boatman set off ashore. The wayward matelots settled down to nervously wait, well aware of the punishment if caught with alcohol. The native never intended to fulfil his side of the bargain, when the ship sailed L/S Gollop was ten rupees lighter but wiser in the ways of dealing with native boatmen. Now as he looked around the harbour he was hopeful of renewing an acquaintance, which would prove painful for the Ceylonese. The off duty watch was granted afternoon leave ashore and most of them took advantage of a 'run'. Shortly after they had been landed a general recall was sent out for all hands to report back on board to prepare for sea. Shore patrols scoured the town rounding up our crew but a few, through intent or ignorance, failed to return and we eventually sailed without them. The consensus of opinion was that they were 'lucky sods', fortunately those who had gone adrift did not affect the ships' fighting capability.

The 'pipes' shrilled for special sea duty men to close up before calling 'all hands' to fall in for leaving harbour. Everyone moved in unison to share the overall task of putting to sea in a way we had done so many times before. The ever familiar chanting of 'Let go for'ard'. 'All gone for'ard', Sir. 'Let go aft'. 'All gone Aft, Sir' preceded the clanging of the engine telegraphs and the thumping of the engines as we got under way. Clearing the harbour at 1900hrs on March 31st.'Dorsetshire' streamed the paravanes as a precaution against mines. Meanwhile the duty watch closed up and checked their equipment and lines of communication. The smell of warm oil and grease again became familiar to the nostrils of the Gun House crews and the Stokers in the engine room. As the light faded, strict black-out procedures were enforced and this included the no striking of matches and cigarette lighters. Later the watch was ordered to "In PV's" and the ship settled down to a second degree of readiness for the night as Captain Agar set a course to meet up with the British Eastern Fleet south of Ceylon. I thought there was a peculiar atmosphere throughout the ship. Everyone off watch seemed to be spending their time furiously writing letters, as if for some reason they unconsciously felt time was running out to send a last message home. Joining the fleet H.M.S. Dorsetshire and H.M.S. Cornwall had the job of refuelling the destroyer escorts. We had some difficulty when the first refuelling pipe broke away as we steamed alongside a destroyer. Another pipe was rigged and fed across as the two ships kept their station with the fleet and eventually operation was successful. Afterwards the two cruisers left to return to Colombo and replenish their own fuel supplies.

Arriving back in port at 0600hrs on the 4th.April the crew were soon busy catching up on work not done previously. The general atmosphere was one of frantic activity as the men hustled and bustled with their labours. Stokers and Engine-room Artificers especially hurried to complete necessary maintenance work. Time was short, during the same evening 'Dorsetshire' and 'Cornwall' again made ready for sea and sailed. Captain Agar, the senior of the two Captains, set a course to the south of Ceylon to be reunited with the Fleet as soon as possible and get the air cover protection from the carriers; it was a rendezvous the Japanese stopped us keeping. Back at Colombo the Commander in Chief ordered the dispersal of all vessels capable of putting to sea. With hindsight this prudent measure saved a considerable number of ships. They would have been sitting targets when Admiral Nagumo attacked the island. Admiral Somerville's well kept secret to use the Maldive Islands as a base for his fleet foiled Nagumo's plans, believing his attack on Colombo was to be another Pearl Harbour. Meanwhile the second Japanese force had left it's base at Mergui, in Burma. This squadron of one aircraft carrier, six cruisers and four destroyers, under the command of Vice-Admiral Jisaburo Ozawa, was on it's way to the Bay of Bengal to attack merchant shipping. Ozawa's early successes was a bitter blow to the Allies and more so when he decided to split his force into three separate units. It wasn't necessary for his ships to remain as one force, the British fleet was no longer considered an imminent threat. Admiral Nagumo, off Ceylon, would engage the Royal Navy if Admiral Somerville elected to fight.

By dividing his fleet Admiral Ozawa could cover a much wider area before refuelling. The cruisers 'Kumano', 'Suzuya' and the destroyer 'Shirakumo' were assigned to Rear-Admiral Kurita to sweep north to the upper reaches of the Bay of Bengal. Ozawa with the carrier 'Ryujo' and the cruisers 'Chokai', 'Yura', 'Asagiri' and 'Yugiri' took a more central sweep and remained the main power base for the other two units to fall back on if necessary. The cruisers 'Mikuma' and 'Mogami' with the destroyer 'Amagiri' made up the third group under the command of Captain Sakiyama. His task was to search the lower part of the Bay of Bengal for Allied ships entering the wide span of sea across the Bay. During the hunt for merchant ships, aircraft from the 'Ryujo' were detached to bomb Kakinada and other coastal towns on mainland India. It clearly illustrated how desperate the situation was when the Japanese could operate unopposed so far west. As usual our grapevine was red hot with 'buzzes'. This suspect intelligence invariably had it's origins on the Lower Deck. No self-respecting officer would knowingly be a party to starting a rumour, so they say. Using the powers of clairvoyance the Lower Deck 'lawyers' combined a vivid imagination with a little eavesdropping to form a mixture based on facts from a 'reliable' source. It would imply that certain ratings were especially privileged, and like the Captain privy to confidential Admiralty reports. Travelling from mess to mess the repeated stories were added to on the whim of the teller. The extent they were believed depended on the gullibility of the listener. The current 'buzz' implied that we were to be joined overnight by a much larger Allied force to rout the ships of the Rising Sun. Home leave was in the 'offing' courtesy of the C-in-C.

The next twenty-four hours would prove how wrong the grapevine could be. It was true that the County Class cruiser was more than a match for larger enemy ships. The main armament of eight 8" guns was excellent in surface to surface engagements, even though their capability remained unchanged for ten years. Needless to say the big guns were of little use protecting the ship against air attacks. They lacked the rate of fire and the manoeuvrability to track and shoot down a fast moving aircraft. This was left to the secondary armament of eight 4" hand-loading, twin mounted guns. In addition there were two mountings of multiple Pom-poms, each carrying eight guns, and two single barrelled small calibre Oerlikon guns which had been taken on board in Ceylon and positioned one forward and the other on the Quarter Deck. The 4" fixed ammunition combining a shell and a long brass cartridge case was cumbersome and slow to load.

The Pom-poms, affectionately known as 'Chicago Pianos', were quick firing for putting up a barrage. Situated, one mounting on either side of the ship they were numerically inadequate for fast aircraft attacks. With hindsight, this shortcoming illustrated the vulnerability of British warships against the new age of planes. It must be said that the two small Oerlikons were little more than a gesture by the authorities to suggest they were updating the anti-aircraft weaponry.

Vice-Admiral Nagumo prepared to attack Ceylon hoping to destroy the Royal Navy in harbour before withdrawing from the Indian Ocean. His reconnaissance planes flew several missions to gather as much information as possible before the attack. At 1005hrs on April 1st, one plane reported seeing a small convoy being escorted by a single minesweeper.

Later the same plane noted the lack of protective air cover and anti-aircraft guns at Trincomalee, especially around the airport. About the same time the submarine I7, flagship of the 2nd.Submarine Squadron, was cruising at periscope depth outside Colombo on reconnaissance.

The submarine Commander sent a message to Admiral Nagumo, telling him that it was impossible to get close enough to the harbour to do a full survey because of the intensified anti-submarine activity. Instead he decided to lay off the port and check the movements of ships going in and out, unaware that the British Eastern Fleet had long since departed to the Maldive Islands. On the 3rd.April the Task Force completed the last refuelling from the fleet tankers Nippon Maru and Kenyo Maru before the assault on Colombo. The Japanese took the precaution of sending two ships ahead of the fleet to reconnoitre the area around Ceylon for possible danger.

By now Admiral Nagumo's finalised plan for the attack on Colombo was circulated to the Task Force carrier commanders.

A = Level Bombers   B = Dive-bombers Z = Zero-type fighters

Unit No.	Group No.	Commanding Officer	Name of Carrier	Planes No	Type	
1	A-1	Commander Mitsuo Fuchida	Akagi	18	A	To destroy ground military installations and enemy naval and merchant vessels
2	A-4	Lt.Commander Tadashi Kusumi	Hiryu	18	A	
	A-3	Lieutenant Heijiro Abe	Soryu	18	A	
5	A-15	Lieutenant Akira Sakamoto	Zuikaku	19	B	To destroy enemy ships at anchor -ground/airport military installations by bombing & shooting
	A-16	A. Takahashi	Shokaku	19	B	
9	C-1	Lt. Commander Shigeru Itaya	Akagi	9	Z	To cover the 1st. and 2nd. Groups, destroy enemy planes, and ground shooting
	C-3	Sub-Lieutenant I.Fujita	Soryu	9	Z	
	C-4	Lieutenant Sumio Kumano	Hiryu	9	Z	

10	C-6 Lieutenant Masatoshi Makino	Zuikaku	9	Z	To cover the first group & undertake ground shooting
	A-11 Lieutenant Zenji Abe	Akagi	17	B	To destroy enemy naval & merchant vessels
SP	A-13 Lt. Commander Takashige Egusa	Soryu	18	B	SP = SPECIAL VESSEL BOMBING TASK FORCE.
	A-14 Lieutenant Michio Kobayashi	Hiryu	18	B	Part of enemy vessels destroying task force specially assembled

According to Japanese naval records the first wave of strike aircraft would surprise and destroy any Allied planes on the ground, leaving the second wave free to bomb with less opposition. Nagumo felt so confident of dealing with any counteraction he ordered Captain Takatsugu Shiroshima of the carrier 'Shokaku' to prepare his 'Motayama' attack squadron of type 54 level bombers for a strike later on the Indian mainland city of Calcutta. On April 4th at 0840hrs (JT), the Japanese fighter pilots were put on standby. Although it was not considered necessary for them to sit in their cockpits all the time, the engines were kept warm for the planes to be airborne at short notice. This precaution for a quick scramble was rewarded when an alert look-out on the battleship 'Hiyei' spotted an RAF Catalina. The 'Hiyei' anti-aircraft guns started firing instantly but it was the Zero fighters that were quickly airborne to shoot it down. In the last dying seconds the Catalina W/T operator managed to get off a signal in plain language, it read "Three battleships - one aircraft carrier 305 ----. The Catalina ditched at 1920 hrs, two minutes later it burst into flames and sank leaving the crew to be picked up by the Japanese destroyer 'Isokaze'.

Intelligence gathering by the Japanese was going on all the time and being fed back to the flagship. At noon off Trincomalee, the submarine I7 sent a message to the 'Akagi' warning that the port was "fully vigilant". Scouting planes were over-flying large areas to make sure the skies were clear in preparation for the Easter Sunday assault on Ceylon. Early the next day, April 5th, the Japanese meteorological officer submitted his weather report to the Fleet Commander, it read :- Weather : Sunny. Sunrise (Japanese time): 0931hrs. Wind Speed : 7m/s. Visibility : Good. Wind Direction : Southwest.

As the aircraft engines roared and whined for the power to lift off, the eager Japanese fliers completed their checks, confident that today would be another 'Toro Toro'. South-west of Ceylon the enemy carriers turned into the wind sending steam jets along the centre of the flight decks to show they were correctly positioned for take-off. Signalmen on the flagship quickly pulled the halyards to send bunting fluttering from the yardarm. It was the message to commence the attack. Signalled to go just after 0900hrs JT (Japanese Time), the planes roared along the steel decks and into the air to form up and head for Colombo. Commander Mitsuo Fuchida, one of Japan's most experienced naval pilots, led the first wave of fifty-four dive-bombers, thirty-eight bombers and thirty-six escorting fighters. At 0945hrs JT, a patrolling fighter from the aircraft carrier 'Hiryu' intercepted an Allied seaplane about forty-five miles from the ships, using the clouds to hide in, the Jap planes had no difficulty shooting it down.

At 1045hrs.JT (Japanese Time) Commander Fuchida arrived over Colombo, disappointed and frustrated that Somerville's fleet was not at anchor. Alternative, but less prestigious, targets had to be found to justify the mission and he signalled to start the attack. About thirty Hurricane fighters were already in the air waiting for the enemy planes. The Japanese machines were superior but the Hurricane pilots were not deterred and soon both sides were twisting and turning in the air as they waged a war of attrition. British Fulmers and Swordfish joined the Hurricanes pushing their aircraft to the limits in a ferocious dog-fight. According to the Japanese account, twenty-one Hurricanes, nineteen Fulmers and ten Swordfish were shot down in the first thirty minutes with another nine listed as unconfirmed 'kills'. The British account was somewhat different, recording seven enemy aircraft shot down for the loss of nineteen Allied fighters and six Swordfish.

While the dog-fight was taking place the Japanese bombers commenced the destruction of the port installations and surrounding buildings. Ships that had remained in Colombo for unavoidable reasons were either sunk or severely damaged including the armed merchant cruiser 'Hector' and the destroyer 'Tenedos'. The bombers struck at the airport and runways, destroying three aircraft hangers. They also sank a large oil tanker in the harbour and set fire to five ships and the waterfront buildings. Ten Hurricanes attacked the bombers but, according to the Japanese, six of the fighters were shot down for the loss of five of their bombers. The dive-bombers had not been idle, between 1056hrs and 1113hrs JT, they reported the annihilation of several merchant ships, a bridge, and the railways. They also attacked the Naval Station and the barracks, causing a lot of damage. At 1118hrs JT, Commander Fuchida sent a message to the flagship to say there was now a thick layer of cloud at 1000m and requested the second wave of aircraft to attack the few remaining targets. These including the A/A guns still firing and the Allied planes left from the first assault. Admiral Nagumo duly ordered the final wave of attackers to take-off and complete the devastation of Colombo.

Earlier, as 'Dorsetshire' and 'Cornwall' made their way to rendezvous with Admiral Somerville, Chief Petty Officer Telegraphist Shaddick of 'Dorsetshire' reported to Captain Agar that he had intercepted Japanese aircraft signals. It confirmed the enemy were in the vicinity and probably coming our way. Capt.Agar, as the senior captain, signalled to Capt. Mainwaring of H.M.S.Cornwall to increase speed to 27 knots. Later he contravened standing orders and broke radio silence to warn Admiral Somerville of the close proximity of the enemy. The decision to use the wireless could have little bearing on the fate of the two cruisers. Already airbourne and preparing to sink us was an estimated fifty-five dive bombers and twenty-five fighters from Admiral Nagumo's 1st. Carrier Fleet. The British Admiral had no intention of risking the loss of his ships against such a superior force, hopefully the message provided him with enough information to avoid a confrontation with the Imperial Japanese Fleet.

23 Easter Eggs

Easter Sunday 1942 dawned delightfully warm and sunny. Beautiful blue skies with an abundance of fluffy white clouds painted a false picture of peace and tranquillity. We all knew the clouds could provide an excellent hiding place for marauding aircraft. Like everyone else that morning I had been at Action Stations before first light, now as the sun came up we reverted to Second Degree Readiness and set about our normal duties. There was a feeling of tension and expectation in the general conversation that something big was about to happen. South of Ceylon, at approximately 1100hrs, H.M.S. Dorsetshire sighted the first Japanese aircraft, a reconnaissance plane from the Japanese heavy cruiser 'Tone' (Capt. Tameji Okada). It quickly disappeared into the clouds but at noon another was sighted, this time from the heavy cruiser 'Chikuma' (Capt. Keizo Yoshimura). The pilot kept beyond the range of the anti-aircraft guns but there was no doubt he was reporting the position and course of the two British cruisers to the flagship 'Akagi'. The aircraft reconnaissance capability carried by the enemy cruisers allowed the Japanese to develop a technique for finding and shadowing opposing warships. They were the 'eyes' of the fleet before radar was fitted to ships. Paradoxically, it was the efficient finding of H.M.S. Dorsetshire and H.M.S. Cornwall that saved Admiral Somerville's fleet from destruction. The spotter planes concentrated on the two cruisers allowing the Allied ships to slip away while still within the range of the enemy aircraft. If they had searched just a little farther to the west they would have spotted Somerville's ships taking evasive action.

It was now generally accepted that an air strike was inevitable. In the minds of most of us was the hope that the Japanese would find a more attractive target little realising that we were seen as the best on offer. Everything on board was checked and re-checked in preparation for an attack. The Surgeons in the sick bay inspected and set out sterile instruments and dressings ready to administer to causalities. The Damage Control parties moved through the ship examining everything from the fire-fighting equipment to the watertight door fastenings. Stokers and Engine Room Artificers knew that when the attack started the Captain would be relying on their expertise to alter course and speed at a moments notice. Officers in charge of sections checked that all clothing and overalls was clean to minimise infection from wounds. 'Dorsetshire', like H.M.S.Cornwall steaming astern, was again at Action Stations. I had taken up my battle position high above the deck in the After Director Control with little to do except check instruments and lines of communication. I sat near the steel door trying to cool off in the heat of the day, watching with some disinterest the activities going on around the decks below. The Air Defence Controller initiated mock attacks, elevating and traversing the A/A guns to chase imaginary targets. This exercise eased the tension and provided the gun crews with a last chance to carry out checks. By noon the cloud formations became more numerous causing problems for the lookouts.

At approximately 1345hrs the bugler sounded "Repel Aircraft" and this was followed soon after by the sound of approaching planes, alerting everyone to the approaching danger. All eyes 'up top' looked apprehensively skywards as clusters of black dots could be seen passing between the gaps in the clouds. It was impossible for our gunners to sight and fire at such fleeting targets and we knew that any eggs we were going to get this Easter Day would not be of the chocolate-coated variety. At 1554hrs JT (Japanese time) the flight commander Lieu-Commander Takashige Egusa signalled the flagship "Enemy found" then at 1629hrs JT to his squadron "Attack, Tactic No.2 with 50 degrees, wind speed 6m/s in direction 230 degrees" The drone of aircraft engines got louder as the enemy pilots positioned to attack. Being dive-bombed was going to be a new experience for me but in my wildest dreams I could not have anticipated how savage and expertly executed the onslaught would be. Lead by the veteran Lieu-Commander Equsat the first group of Aichi D3 A dive-bombers (Vals) came out of the clouds into the clear sky plummeting down like hunger hawks screeching for their kill. Fascinated I first watched a plane diving on H.M.S.Cornwall, before releasing a bomb that went under the cruisers' bows. I didn't wait to see what happened after that, I slammed the Director door shut, adjusted my headset, and concentrated on the pointers of the control panel in front of me. Captain Agar, in textbook style, ordered a 25 degree turn to starboard and fire.

'Dorsetshire' responded, slewing sharply and at speed to avoid being hit but there was no escaping. The manoeuvre was anticipated by the attackers who screamed down and down, low enough for those on deck to see the 900 lb bombs unleashed from under the fixed undercarriage of the dive bombers. Our guns commenced firing immediately, but without effect. The ship's A/A armament was inadequate and numerically insufficient, a lesson learnt too late to prevent the loss of the ship and hundreds of lives. The initial assault on Dorsetshire struck along the centre line from stem to stern. It was this precise manoeuvre that prevented the A/A guns bearing on a target before it was too late. One of the first bombs exploded on the small arms magazine just in front of the After Director Control sending flames shooting skywards burning everything nearby, I certainly felt that one. Simultaneously a bomb hit the Supermarine Walrus still on the launching catapult, another in the same area struck the starboard Pom-Pom guns wrecking the guns and killing the gun crew.

Petty Officer C. Crosskey, the 'captain' of the port and starboard Pom-Pom gun decks, had good reason to remember that particular bomb. Concerned that the starboard gun had ceased firing he went to investigate and found a nauseating spectacle. Mangled guns hanging over the ship's side was bad enough but seeing the bodies of his men dangling from the nearby rigging made him feel sick. 'Cross' noticed flames coming from the Pom-Pom 'ready use' magazine and went inside to open the water spray valves. Unfortunately someone else also saw the flames and shut the magazine door not knowing he was inside. Coughing and spluttering he groped his way to the securing clips and managed to get out before being overcome by smoke. Wounded in the arm and left eye, as well as peppered with fragments of shrapnel, he made his way to the port side gun deck. Again he was faced with the hopeless situation of only one gunner still alive, trying to keep his guns firing with the help of a rating. It was a last defiant, but hopeless, gesture before the guns were silenced. P.O.Crosskey, still carrying some of the shrapnel in his body to the present day, cannot understand how he survived the carnage. Not normally given to emotion his eyes still moisten when he recalls the young men who died on his gun decks, it was a frightening experience for a young Petty Officer. A violent explosion outside the Director, superseded by several others, made the inside unbearably hot and the order was given to bale out. Being nearest to the door I opened it and got out double quick followed by the rest of the team. The Chief P.O. shouted at me to report to the Pom-poms and lend a hand.

Outside, everything seemed to be on fire and I wasted no time starting down the steel ladder. About halfway down, a mass of very hot thin wire dropped over my head and shoulders and brought me to a halt. Holding on with one hand I struggled to free myself with the other, getting very angry in the process but hardly noticing the small burns to my skin from the scorching coils.

When I did get free I quickly made it to the gun deck and pulled up short, the devastation made it obvious this area was beyond help of any kind, and most certainly not mine. The situation everywhere was the same as wave after wave of diving planes continued their assault with a ferocity that underlined the merciless tenacity of the Japanese pilots. I paused to look upwards and clearly saw bombs released from the underside of the dive-bombers. As they rained down on the decks the ship jerked wildly, I was convinced that my nineteen years was about to be the extent of my lifespan. The 'Chief' following close on my heels instantly assessed the situation and redirected me to the Quarter Deck Oerliken gun to help with the loading, it was firing intermittently instead of steady bursts. I didn't need to be told twice and I set off aft through billowing smoke and crackling fire, horrified at the shambles created by the bombing. On the way I heard my name called and approaching a huddled bloody mass I realised after close inspection it was a young seaman called Tom Murtagh, a friend since our days on the Boy's messdeck together. The lad was in a terrible state lying in a pool of his own blood, his arms and legs nearly severed from his body as his life ebbed away. He kept repeating "Don't leave me, don't leave me". It was tragically clear that he, like so many others, was about to make the ultimate sacrifice for his country, the torment of mourning his death would be left to his parents, Charles and Mary Murtagh of Manchester. I felt a great pity for Tom when I saw the condition he was in, unfortunately there was nothing that could be done except move him to another part of the deck. The Japanese were still bombing mercilessly and I had a gun to load, after a few words of sympathy I carried on to the Quarter Deck.

I found the Oerliken gunner trying to manage single-handed and asked where his loader was. He pointed to a body nearby, it told me all I wanted to know and I set about clipping on drums of ammunition. The gunner, a Liverpudlian named Grimes, was a born jester and a ready wit, he was also a good man to be with in a tight situation. As he pulled his gun round, firing all the time, he never once lost his good humour or level headedness. Possessed with a fanatical urge to kill, or be killed, the pilots were diving lower and lower before releasing their bombs. Their zealous determination overwhelmed H.M.S.Dorsetshire as the slaughter made the Upper Deck into a blood bath. The bodies of dead seamen rolled into piles along the guard rails as the ship started to heel. Seamen on the 4" portside gun deck slipped and slithered on the bloody surface as they made every effort to keep the remaining guns firing. It was all to no avail, beaten almost defenceless and burning fiercely 'Dorsetshire' began to list badly. By now, with the exception of the single Oerlikon gun on the Quarter Deck that I was loading and 'Scouse' Grimes firing, the rest of the guns had been silenced. I suddenly had a dreadful thought that 'Scouse', and I, might get singled out by the Japs. To boost my confidence I asked Grimes how many planes he thought he had shot down. Truthful to a fault he replied "Not a bloody one". The

Zero fighters made full use of this opportunity of the lack of firepower to complete the massacre. Sweeping unopposed, backwards and forwards along the ship, they strafed the decks with appalling effect. For me, the most terrifying sound was the cries and screams of the dying and badly wounded. Some only teenagers were horribly burnt. Pitiful appeals for help were far too numerous for them all to receive attention in the short time the ship remained afloat.

There was no answer to the remorseless and senseless killing. The ship was finished and settling in the water. The Bridge was a twisted mess and the Compass Platform shattered, the funnels had been blown away and the gun directors burnt out. Most of the upper deck and the superstructure was ripped apart allowing flames to seep through the deck from the hell below. Unable to halt the slaughter men viewed the total destruction with dismay, acknowledging reluctantly the supremacy of the Imperial Japanese Navy. The appearance of our beautiful 'Dorsetshire' had changed as if by magic, from a smartly painted cruiser to a blackened mass in a matter of minutes. Black smoke enveloped the ship like a shroud. It was a time of hopeless reality that revealed our helplessness. As I looked at the wilderness of jagged metal I felt dazed and sad.

Many had been trapped below decks when the hatches and steel doors were distorted and jammed by the bombing. Men could be heard hammering on the steelwork and shouting frantically to be got out. It must have been especially frightening for them to realise they would be entombed in a steel coffin because their chances of escape were nil. Other escapees, who found that ladders had been blown away, scrambled up pipes and other fixtures to get to the upper deck. Buckled, bloody, and a blazing inferno,

H.M.S.Dorsetshire was going down. A huge hole blown in the ships' side by an internal explosion allowed the sea to rush in as the vessel was torn apart. Flooding produced a destabilising effect and I knew the end was near.

The shouting of 'Abandon Ship' reverberated from stem to stern like the announcing of the Last Rites. Wounded were hastily dragged out on to the decks to give them a remote chance of survival. Burnt and mutilated bodies were spread around the decks in a horrifying scene, the kill was almost complete. Some of the badly injured were unable, or unwilling, to leave the sinking ship. They just settled themselves down calmly to accept their inevitable fate. I found it particularly strange and distressing to see this happen to a couple of youngsters who had only a short time before survived the sinking of H.M.S. Prince of Wales. Depending on our basic instincts when told to leave the ship, some jumped into the sea, others slid down the starboard side into the water. 'Scouse' Grimes and myself jumped over the port side at the same time. We both shared the general concern of being sucked under with the ship so we swam away from the immediate area as quickly as possible. It never dawned on me that we were about 200 miles from land and I hadn't got a lifebelt. As we dropped astern of the doomed vessel I were overjoyed that we both found something to hang on to. Neither of us had a piece big enough to climb on, but at least it was enough to keep our heads above the surface. The ship still had 'way' and we were left some distance behind before 'Dorsetshire' took the final plunge, away in the distance 'Cornwall' followed soon afterwards.

An eerie stillness settled over the whole tragic scene and remained for a seemingly long time. It was eventually broken by the calls of the swimmers to each other, mostly shouts of false bravado to boost our self-confidence. As Grimes and I started the long swim towards the main body of survivors we made a pact that the first time we met after getting out of this mess we would drop whatever we were doing and 'paint the town red' no matter the consequences. Two waterlogged boats had miraculously broken free from the ship but they could only hold about a dozen men at a stretch. There was an urgency to find some floating debris if men hoped to remain alive for any period of time. Part of the foremast surfaced to provide a lifesaver for many of the survivors. At first it rolled like a log sending them back into the oily water as too many tried to clamber astride it. The remarks of the seamen were unrepeatable Anglo-Saxon as the performance was repeated several times before they mastered the art of controlling it. As we swam around searching for flotsam, the roar of approaching aircraft interrupted us. I turned in the direction of the noise to see Japanese planes coming towards us in mass formation. Sweeping down on us, the pilots opened fire in a senseless gesture against defenceless swimmers. I dived under the surface as the first plop-plop-plop of the bullets hit the water and stayed submerged until I felt my lungs were about to burst.

By the time I came up again the enemy aircraft had passed to return to their carriers. The machine-gunning accounted for several lives and angered the men in the water. It seemed this scurrilous behaviour was mainly directed at 'Dorsetshire', H.M.S.Cornwall was spared. Ray Carpenter, a nineteen-year-old seaman at the time, saw in later years a funny side to the incident. Although an otherwise good swimmer, he always had difficulty swimming under water. When the planes swooped and he heard the rat-tat-tat of the machine guns he struggled to dive as deep as possible. In horror he realised that although the upper part of his body was under the surface, his backside was still up in the air. Fortunately he didn't get hit and came upright to see the enemy flying away. Despite their worries amid the death and destruction the morale of the men remained high. It is impossible to describe the unselfish behaviour of the oil covered seamen as they mingled with the dead and dying in a sticky, smelly mess, of oil fuel. Acting without supervision or instruction the more able helped the less fortunate, poor swimmers and badly injured with less chance of surviving were given a helping hand and provided with some piece of wreckage to hold on to. The case of Bill Howe, a Canadian midshipman, was typical. A powerful swimmer he took off his lifebelt and gave it to someone in distress. Later as he became tired he was given a lifejacket retrieved from a corpse. During the general hubbub going on all around, some orders were shouted from the boat but were inaudible to the widely scattered swimmers. Directives from someone in the relative safety of a boat were not practicable, or appreciated by men in the water clinging on for dear life.

Everyone capable of doing so, ignored well meaning suggestions and made up their own minds on the best way to stay alive. Word was shouted that the second in command, Commander Jack Byas, was alive. The news brought a spontaneous cheer of genuine feeling from all those in earshot. The generous response from dry and sore mouths was an indication of the respect and feeling the ships' company had for this officer. Commander Byas was invited to join the Captain in the boat but he refused, although suffering injury and burns he insisted on remaining in the water with the men. They tied him to a small float and put a piece of canvas over his face to protect him from the sun. The following day his condition deteriorated alarmingly and caused concern. The tired and blackened faced seamen decided to act and forcibly bundled him into the Captain's boat against his wishes to be cared for. Soon after the sinking Captain Agar, the ships' captain, had taken up position in one of the two overcrowded boats. He said prayers on the second day and called out to everyone to hang on until help arrived. Also in the boat was Surgeon Lieutenant Wood the only medical officer to survive, the other three were killed. He set up surgery in the boat to do sterling work including amputating a seaman's leg with a seaman's' knife. It was not the type of operation he could have anticipated performing but he coped well, unfortunately the patient died later.

Most of us had one article of underwear to put to good use covering our heads against the blistering sun. It didn't stop it burning our exposed shoulders and causing cracked lips and swollen eyes. During the night the daytime heat changed to bitter chill adding to the death toll of the injured, when many of the weaker succumbed to the cold. I tried to doze but it was too cold, my teeth chattered and I shivered as the nauseating oil lapped up my face and into my eyes. Weary and exhausted hanging on to my piece of wreckage I felt my arms getting heavier, for others around me it was too much and they let go. In a last token effort they thrashed about in the water before going to meet their Maker. Worn out from their efforts and numbed by the night cold, some lapsed into a semi-conscious stupor of delusion. A Boy Seaman called Jones could be heard shouting over and over again throughout the night "The Russians are coming, the Russians are coming". When daylight came his lifeless body was pushed away from the living. I could never understand why he shouted about Russians, they were our allies. There was some fears about a possible attack from sharks and barracuda, many of us remembering what happened to our colleagues on the H.M.S.Dunedin when they were savagely mauled by the big carnivorous fish. It prompted me, with my body in the water, to swim towards the main gathering of survivors for added protection.

If the predatory fish did strike then hopefully they would concentrate on the corpses. To encourage this the dead bodies were pushed towards the outer fringes of the survivors. Unfortunately they drifted back during the night and the whole process had to begin again in the morning. It was a necessary chore, if only to avoid the unpleasantness of looking into the bloated faces and lifeless eyes of dead comrades. Many acts of valour were recounted as the men exchanged information about good deeds they had witnessed, too numerous to be officially recorded or recognised. It would be left to the men to speak amongst themselves of the outstanding qualities of shipmates who made bigger sacrifices than was expected of anyone under such appalling circumstances. Acknowledgement would be for genuine and reliably authenticated acts, not tainted by political or social consideration, which so often demeaned the word valour.

On the second day an uneasy silence settled on the wretched scene as we took stock and addressed ourselves to the main task of staying alive and conserving our energies. I had doubts that a rescue would arrive in time to save the majority of us. Captain Agar, watching from his seat in the boat, must have had serious apprehensions that those of us labouring in the oily sludge would ever serve our country again. Seafarers have always found it easy to appeal to the Lord in times of danger and the crew of 'Dorsetshire' were no different, their spontaneous outbursts of hymn singing were really desperate cries for help. As fuel oil and salt water got into my mouth and stomach I coughed and retched to add to my misery. Rations were issued from the Captain's boat according to availability, the average was a quarter of a ships' biscuit and a sip of water for the whole two day period. I swam to the side of the whaler on the second day for my issue, it was a piece of biscuit the size of two postage stamps. Chief P.O.Yeoman leaned over the side with a mug of water and told me not to drink but to just dip my tongue in it to wet my lips, the mug of water had to serve about fifty others. He kept warning everyone not to hold on to the side of the boat as they waited their turn for fear of capsizing it. At about 1630 hours I heard someone shouting "Aircraft, aircraft" but thought it was another false alarm. There had been several during the night when shooting stars had fooled us into believing they were aircraft lights. This time it really was a plane, but was it friend or foe, everyone waited in agonising suspense and excitement. As it got closer I recognised the familiar lines of a Fairy Swordfish, it was one of ours. I had seen enough of the 'String-bags' when I served on 'Courageous' to be sure.

The plane signalled as it circled the survivors of 'Dorsetshire' and our equally unfortunate colleagues from the 'Cornwall'. They had suffered much the same fate and were also being kept alive by a stouthearted resolve to survive. It seemed as if the cheering would never stop as the plane waggled it's wings in acknowledgement before flying back to the fleet. It was stated later that the pilot broke radio silence to report the position of the survivors and was allegedly pinpointed by the Japanese and shot down by enemy aircraft. As we waited with a fresh sense of expectation that help would soon arrive we were unaware of this. In the distance, holding on to part of the mast with dozens of others, my pal Fred Ball had time to remember another sinking. Like me, at sixteen years of age he had survived the loss of the aircraft carrier H.M.S. Courageous. The deaths of over five hundred men on that occasion seemed far less traumatic than the present situation we were in. He was determined, despite the Japanese and sharks, he would survive once again to celebrate his nineteenth birthday in a months time. Thankfully he did and served his country in several other theatres of war before finally leaving the Navy as a Chief Petty Officer. H.M.S.Dorsetshire was the first sea-going ship of another pal of mine. His name was George Bell, later Warrant Officer Bell. He was sixteen when he came on board to be given the prestigious position of Captain's Messenger, a post usually reserved for a boy with above average ability. Due to a clerical misunderstanding he was also allocated the duties of masthead lookout without the Captains awareness. The error of his dual commitment was noticed when Captain Martin called for his messenger and was told that he was up in the 'crows nest'. A few crisp words from the captain instantly resolved the situation. At seventeen and a half the boy became a man and relinquished his messenger post to take up duties in the Gunhouse.

Floating in the Indian Ocean he reflected on the time he had spent on board H.M.S.Dorsetshire. Having never been to sea before he found the first few days extremely difficult, especially with two lots of duties. He recalled hanging on tight to the sides of the 'crows-nest' as the ship ploughed through a 'choppy' Bay of Biscay. High above the deck the movement of the vessel in the rough sea was far more pronounced. As it rolled and pitched he received his baptism to ' blue water' sailing. He was at his Action Station in 'A' Turret when 'Dorsetshire' was attacked and clearly remembered switching off his headphones and putting them back on their stand when told to abandon ship. With the rest of the turret crew he quickly left to slide down the tilting deck into the sea to begin the long ordeal. It didn't surprise me to be told that George remembered to have his lifebelt with him at action stations, he was more fastidious than the rest of his age group who tended to forget their lifesavers when they were most needed.

As the second day dragged on the waiting seemed endless, the Swordfish should have summoned help by now and although nobody complained our nerves were getting a little frayed. Lack of sleep and food, coupled with weariness and exhaustion, started to produce doubts that rescue ships would ever arrive and death seemed inevitable. Some chores continued, like stripping the lifebelts from the bodies of dead seamen to be utilised by the living. Unfortunately being young I was not considered a priority to be a recipient. Towards evening a startling cry rang out "Look, look, look", heads turned in the direction of the shouting and lo! and behold three objects could be seen coming our way at a good rate of knots. The question was whether they were Japanese warships on the prowl or British rescue ships. A voice called out near me "Please God make them ours", it was a time for praying. They were ours and they let everyone know it. The cruiser H.M.S.Enterprise, and destroyers Paladin and Panther hooted as if with joy at finding us. The cruiser and the Panther went to the assistance of the Cornwall survivors leaving the Paladin to concentrate on us. It slowed down and cautiously approached the swimmers, an officer shouted through a loudhailer for everyone to remain still and they would be picked up in time. Neither myself, nor the other impatient youngsters near me heard the announcement. We decided to swim to the destroyer not fully appreciating the amount it was still underway.

I could see boats being lowered and scrambling nets dropped over the side with sailors standing by on deck with heaving lines. I struck out with a few others of my age confident of swimming the distance to the destroyer but soon I realised I had made a grave mistake. The 33hrs in the water had sapped my strength, I tired very quickly and started to be left behind. It flashed through my mind that I was about to pay dearly for my impetuous stupidity and in desperation I struggled harder to make up some ground. Heaving lines were snaking out but none were coming within my reach and I started to despair that my bobbing head would not be seen. As the Paladin moved on I felt all was lost when someone shouted to me as he were being pulled through the water on the end of the rope. As he passed he reached across grabbing my hair and hanging on long enough for me to get a grip on his arm. Both of us were pulled to the side of the destroyer to scramble up the nets and on to the deck. I now discovered that my saviour was a South African RNVR Lieutenant called Geoffrey Berlyn. The fear of another attack from the Japanese meant the rescue had to carried out as quickly as possible and the ships to leave the area to return to the fleet. Once on board I joined the wretched looking collection of humanity to be treated with gentleness and kindness of immeasurable depth.

Willing hands removed as much oil as possible without causing too much suffering. Gallons of hot tea, rum, and lime juice was laid on to quench a two day thirst. Solid food was secondary, but it was readily available in generous quantities. The Wardroom had been converted into a Sick Bay to treat the rows of injured. Seamen with badly burnt bodies sat silently as attendants peeled off the blackened skin in strips. It was a painful process but a few showed no obvious signs of discomfort as they sat like zombies. When I mentioned this to an attendant he told me they were beyond feeling but they would recover with proper care and hospital treatment.

Emotionally drained and physically tired the rest of the 'Dorsets' found corners not being used, to curl up and lapse into deep sleep: the nightmare was over. The 'Paladin' Quarter-Master Bill Looker told me that another twelve men died while we slept. It was ironic, they had survived the trauma of 33 hours in the ocean and Japanese bombing to reach safety of the destroyer to die. According to Bill the bodies of the dead men were sewn into canvas bags and quietly returned to the sea without disturbing us. Hours later I woke feeling refreshed, but wondering at first where I was. It was a great relief to be told that 'Paladin' was making all speed for the Maldive Islands to put us ashore. Conversation 'buzzed' as groups gathered to relate the events of the past two days and enquire about missing friends and colleagues.

Ross Wilson the Canadian officer in charge of 'Dorsetshires' anti-aircraft control was furious when he recalled the Japanese shooting of men in the water. Swimmers near him were killed and others wounded, during the early morning it was especially upsetting when he turned to speak to men and found he was looking into the fixed stare of corpses. Ross was particularly shaken by the agonising screams of one seaman near him whose legs were partially severed, causing excruciating pain. Sailors in the sea nearest to him tried unsuccessfully to stem the flow of blood with strips of underwear, they were puzzled how the lad had managed to survive so long. It hurt them to watch him die without being able to ease his suffering during the final moments.

When the ship first started listing, the crew of 'B' Turret Shell Room escaped as far as the mess deck only to find a long queue impatiently waiting to get through the escape hatch. The electrical power had failed and lighting came from a dim emergency supply. Reg Turnbull decided not to join the waiting procession and made his way aft to find an alternative way out, but found his way blocked again. Then he saw a South African named Cessare climbing up a sloping mess table and disappearing outside through a porthole. Reg called to others nearby to follow suit and was just about to start climbing himself when he heard a junior seaman saying he was not going because he could not swim and that it would be hopeless to go into the ocean. Turnbull, an old salt who joined the boys training ship at Shotley in 1923, dropped back to the deck. In undiluted naval language he told the seaman, (when translated it meant) that if he did not make the effort and climb up the mess table as quickly as possible, he would receive a kick in his arse strong enough to send him all the way to Bombay. The fellow didn't dare hesitate, he went up the escape route at an alarming pace followed by his more seasoned colleague. Swimming away from the ship Reg saw another head bobbing about in the water and he called out to it. It was a Stoker Petty Officer who replied "Wotcher Jan, never a bloody dull moment is there" and in the midst of all that was happening around, it made Reg laugh out loud.

Bert Gollop felt exceptionally lucky to be alive. His battle station was assistant to the Air Defence Officer on the exposed part of the Bridge behind the Compass Platform. He remembered the speed of the attack and huge explosion seconds later before being knocked off his feet. In a state of semi-consciousness he heard the deafening roar of the planes and the detonating bombs. He got up in time to see flames streaking upwards from the 4" Gun Deck and went to the rear of the Bridge to look over. Bodies were strewn around the guns and then it registered how desperate the situation really was. When he was given the order to go by the Lieu. Carver, the Torpedo Officer, he left with mixed feelings. Seeing the twisted steel and burning superstructure, he knew the ship he had been proud to call 'home' for the last five years was doomed. Picking his way over the corpses he unintentionally stood on the stomach of a dead sailor and it made a noise like exhaling air. Bert felt sick and mumbled an apology, hoping the dead man's soul in heaven would forgive him. Jumping into the water he swam away, turning later to see 'Dorsetshire' slipping to the deep.

At the time Able Seaman Wright D/JX 146883 was a very angry man. As he helped Petty Officer Monks to rig an escape ladder for the men to get out of 'A' Turret Shell Room and Magazine he fumed and cursed. He had only recently got his new kit together to replace the one he lost when he survived the sinking of H.M.S. Prince of Wales, now he would have to start all over again. The navigating officer, Lieutenant Bryan Durant, was wounded when the Bridge was hit but he got back on his feet and continued directing operations until told to abandon ship. He survived to reach Flag Officer rank in the Royal Navy.

'Taff' Charles's apprehension when he was told to leave the ship was not due to the fact he was a non-swimmer, or that the ocean looked menacing. It was the unrecognisable figure near his feet. 'Taff' recalled that the man, burnt black, was still conscious and he was uncertain what to do under the circumstances. As he knelt down to talk to the poor unfortunate he was taken aback to hear it speak "There is nothing you can do for me, so sod off". Moments later 'Taff' jumped into the sea and started to 'dog paddle' as frantically as his arms would allow. It kept him afloat until he found something to hang on to. When he left the navy 'Taff' Charles became an ordained minister of the church, but nobody from the crew of 'Dorsetshire' would dream of referring to him as Reverend, only Shipmate 'Taff'.

Engineroom Artificer Norman Wilkes was waiting on the main footplate of the Engine Room when he received a call about 1345 hrs., to attend to an overheating solenoid coil on the steering motor. Hurrying aft he found the fault and repaired it without any difficulty. Just as he finished an explosion badly shook the ship to such an extent he thought it was being lifted out of the water. As other explosions followed he decided to check the levels above for damage as lights started to go out and the ship started to list. Checking through the different areas finally brought him to the Upper Deck where he was faced with a sight that left him momentarily stunned and perplexed. That so much damage could have been done in such a short time was difficult for him to comprehend. He recalled how everyone hurried about their business but stayed relatively calm, there was no panic or loss of discipline.

Fred Plenty, coxswain of the 'Paladin' rescue cutter, was the very much-toasted man of the day. He worked his men hard rounding up and filling his boat time and time again with survivors. At reunions his name is probably mentioned more than any other, and with good reason. This does not take anything away from the rest of the destroyer's crew. Everyone one of them was magnificent in their concern for our well being.

The endless telling of events by witnesses to the facts, often about a third party, finally came to an abrupt halt when the masthead look-out with the voice of a Town Crier was heard bellowing 'Land in sight bearing ------'. It brought smiles to our faces as we waited to set foot on dry land and enjoy the safety, out of reach of Admiral Nagumo's warships. The Paladin crew prepared to drop anchor in the coral basin of Addu Atoll and complete their part in saving the remnants of our ships' company.

It was said later that Captain Annesley of H.M.S. Enterprise, knowing that seamen were in the water waiting to be rescued, ignored an earlier directive to abort the seemingly fruitless search. If he had rejoined the Fleet, when he was first told to, it would have meant a death sentence for us all. Having exceeded his brief without sighting the survivors the captain set himself a time limit of one more hour. After that he would have to comply with instructions and turn back. It was within that period that his lookouts roared " Objects in sight, bearing....". Captain Annesley was a very happy man at that moment in time and so were we.

Perhaps the most fitting tribute to those who lost their lives from the two cruisers H.M.S.Dorsetshire and H.M.S.Cornwall on that Easter Sunday 1942 are the words inscribed, under the Dorset crest, on the memorial at Kohima.

        When you go home
        Tell them of us and say
        For your tomorrow, We gave our today.

On the 9th.April 1942, one hundred and thirty planes from the Japanese carriers launched an attack on Trincomalee. This was Ceylon's second major port and a prime target but again the Admiral was disappointed, the harbour was deserted. Before the Japanese arrived the aircraft carrier H.M.S. Hermes, the Australian destroyer 'Vampire' and the corvette 'Hollyhock' had put to sea. As they steamed south to find Somerville's fleet they were joined by two tankers glad of the warships protection. Several Blenheim bombers made an unsuccessful attack on the Japanese ships, losing five of the bombers in the process with nothing to show for it. The few Hurricanes and Fulmers protecting Trincomalee were outnumbered and badly mauled by the high performance Zeros but worse was to come. Enemy reconnaissance planes found 'Hermes', escorts and tankers, hugging the coastline trying to avoid contact with the Japanese. Nagumo was alerted and eighty dive-bombers with fighter escorts took off to sink them. The strike was swift and deadly as the jubilant enemy pilots swooped down to annihilate the British ships. There was little the Allied Command could do against this superior Japanese force except continue to count the heavy loss in human lives and shipping. Nagumo was free to trawl the Indian Ocean like a latter day pirate, sending shivers down the spines of our seafaring fraternity. Roaming the seas like a hungry predator he was becoming impatient and frustrated in his search for the British Fleet.

After sinking 'Hermes' and the accompanying ships, Admiral Nagumo decided there was little to keep him any longer in hostile waters, it was time to bid 'Sayonara' and return home. Admiral Somerville had despatched the slow 'B' Force of his fleet as far out of harms way as possible to Kilindini

Creek in Mombasa. His fast 'A' Force went to the safety of Bombay to wait developments before risking a confrontation with the enemy. H.M.S. Enterprise returned to the 'A' Force with Captain Augustus Agar, captain of the ill-fated 'Dorsetshire'.

The Japanese Navy sank about 150,000 tons of shipping during their short foray into the Indian Ocean and with a huge cost in human lives. Vice-Admiral Ozawa's smaller force had destroyed twenty-three merchant ships, mostly carrying vital supplies to our army in Burma. On the 10th.April Ozawa, reinforced with the cruiser Sendai and the destroyers Fubuki, Hatsuyuki and Murakumo, passed through the Strait of Malacca homeward bound. Two days later Admiral Nagumo followed, leaving a submarine squadron as the sole Nippon representative in the Indian Ocean. Another triumphant homecoming was waiting for the Imperial Navy following the devastating defeat they had inflicted on the Royal Navy. It would be unfair to suggest that Nelson, Drake, Hawkins and Grenville turned in their graves but Nagumo's victories over two of the most powerful navies in the world, at very little cost to himself, was humbling. In a matter of months he had left a trail of destruction from the coast of Australia, Java, Pearl Harbour to Ceylon. He arrived home to a tumultuous reception, to the people of Japan he was worthy of the title 'Samurai'. It might have eased the hurt we all felt if we could have forseen the future. A year later on June 5th. 1943, in the Battle of Midway, Nagumo lost four of his carriers, Kaga, Soryu, Hiryu, and Akagi. It was the beginning of his downfall, and on the 7th.July 1944 he committed the honourable suicide act of Seppuku (Hara-kiri).

24 An unwelcome return

Situated approximately 400 miles south-west of Ceylon the Maldive group of islands was difficult to see from a distance, being only six feet above sea level. The inhabitants were mainly of Indian descent and spoke in a local Dhivehi language, not that I was about to have much contact with them. H.M.S. Paladin eased her way into Addu Atoll and joined other warships already at anchor. From a distance the gleaming white sand and clear water made a favourable impression of picturesque restfulness, unfortunately it didn't last long. As we were put ashore the buzzing of millions of flies greeted us. It was an unpleasant welcome, especially for those with open cuts. A plague of hungry insects soon covered cuts and blood stained dressings in a revolting black mass. Swotting them was a waste of effort because dead flies had ever-eager replacements to settle on lacerations. A meal of stew was prepared on a field kitchen for us. Although it was hot it didn't stop the persistent pestilence from swooping on that as well. In all my travels I had never experienced insect attacks anything remotely like these kamikaze flies. The only course of action was to run as fast as possible into tents and dive under the mosquito nets. Any flies that had managed to get under the netting could then be killed before the food was eaten. Fortunately in later years when the islands became a tourist resort the flies were controlled. The tents and mosquito nets were provided by the Indian Army resident on the island. I think most of us landed in just a pair of oil stained underpants which we were glad to discard if possible, although with hindsight we should have kept them.

The army unit issued me, and many others, with a shirt, a pair of shorts and a pair of rope soled shoes, the only three items of kit I was to get for some time. There was no issue of other basic needs like soap and towel, headcovering, razor or change of clothing, it would be weeks before any of us would enjoy such luxuries. Nevertheless, after the happenings of the last few days I was grateful for what little I had. Under the circumstances it was trivial to remember the loss of all the presents and souvenirs I had carefully collected on Dorsetshire. My locker was full of things to bring smiles to the faces of the family at my next homecoming. Looking like tramps at a Salvation Army hostel for waifs, the bedraggled assembly was classified according to injury. Eventually when the sorting was completed the motley looking crowd embarked in groups for ports in mainland Africa. I was in a party of twenty sailors and one Royal Marine that left the white sun-bleached coral atoll, and the hordes of serenading flies, bound for Mombasa. From this point in time the disgusting treatment we received from the authorities left much to be desired and fell far short of common decency to men who days earlier had been through a fairly rough time. Cable forms were given to us to fill in to let our families know we had survived, but there was a snag. The cables could not be sent from Addu Atoll for security reasons, they had to be shipped back to Mombasa to be dealt with. This delay was unfortunate because the cables arrived home some time after the Admiralty's announcement of regret at the loss of both H.M.S. Dorsetshire and H.M.S. Cornwall. After the BBC radio broadcast the families waited for confirmation with the anxiety always experienced by loved ones in similar circumstances.

Our little group of twenty-one arrived at H.M.S. Tania, the naval base in Mombasa. There was a distinct feeling that nobody wanted to be bothered with us. Overnight we slept on the floor of an empty and dilapidated harem, requisitioned from some obscure Sultan who had no further use for it. Mombasa, the second largest city in Kenya, had a hustling, bustling, waterfront with dhows still trading between Zanzibar and Madagascar and ocean going merchantmen unloading goods from around the world. Occupied by the Portuguese after Vasco de Gama laid claim in 1498 it was later settled by the Omani Arabs and their influence was still very evident. The following day our party was transferred to the army transit camp at Nyali. This was a crude establishment, situated in a bush clearing about six miles from the naval base. The hotel complex on the present day site bears no resemblance to it's humble origins. We were housed in huts, adapted from the packing cases of lease-lend trucks shipped from abroad. Holes were cut out for doors and windows and the roofs thatched with palm branches. Snakes that were everywhere had a frightening habit of slithering through the huts at night. We still had the problem of personal hygiene, lacking towel, soap, comb and razor. Having only the one shirt, shorts and canvas shoes given to us in Addu Atoll, clothing had to have dual roles. When we washed it meant using our shirt as a towel and when our shorts needed washing the shirt had to double as a skirt. Now that the naval authority was aware of our existence, we felt an issue of fundamental necessities was the least we could expect.

Time passed but nothing in the way of kit arrived from the base in Mombasa and we were puzzled by the lack of consideration. The Colonel in charge of the transit camp commiserated with us. He was just as bewildered by the negative attitude of those deemed responsible for our welfare. The Colonel repeatedly approached the Navy for something to be done for the hapless group. He received one concession, an issue of fresh meat twice a week specifically for our use. In fairness to the Colonel, he could hardly be expected to deplete his stocks to clothe naval personnel. He did arrange for his Quarter-Master to supply us with fruit, vegetables and cooking facilities. There was also a limited supply of Victory V cigarettes and the use of transport to Mombasa when it was available. Eventually we reached a stage when enough was enough, it was decided to send a deputation to H.M.S.Tania to make those responsible fully aware of our plight. The Petty Officer and two others hitched a lift in an army truck to ask the authorities for essential needs and pay. They set off with great expectations, knowing we had a good case for quick action. Nobody in their right mind could refuse instant help with clothing and toilet requisites when confronted by the hairy matelots. When they arrived back their silence and the look on their faces said it all, they had received little sympathy from the supply office. The air was alive with suggestions what should be done to the desk bound, pen-pushing, administrators.

"The bastards said that there was nobody of sufficient rank to sign for a bulk issue of kit. The sods said we must wait until we get to the Cape". "We treated the Germans a damn sight better then our own treat us" said one lad remembering the Bismark sinking.

Our Robinson Crusoe appearance was a source of amusement to the other servicemen passing through the camp, especially the Royal Air Force who seemed well provided for. Some of the airmen took pity on their less fortunate compatriots and were fairly generous with any soap they could spare. They must have thanked their lucky stars they were unlikely to be naval survivors, even the Swahili 'boys' around the camp found it hard to come to terms with our dishevelled appearance. It was rare for them to see anyone less affluent than themselves, especially a European. One day our Petty Officer, who shall remain nameless, called us all together for a council of war. Something drastic had to be done to improve our situation and it was unanimously agreed that a shoplifting expedition into Mombasa was the only solution. We were split up into two groups to operate independently, each with a list of requirements needed to maintain some form of human dignity. Next day twenty of the party hitched a ride from the ever obliging army drivers into town. One man had to remain behind in case the Colonel had news from the Naval base about a possible departure to South Africa. It was a simple business to keep shopkeepers busy while nimble fingered 'dodgers' appropriated the needs of His Britannic Majesty's Navy. When the groups returned, razors, combs, soap and head coverings appeared as if by magic. Later towels and other items also 'just happened'. The Colonel must have had serious thoughts about the origin of these things, but he was discreet enough not to ask questions. We had a good relationship with him and the other army officers, discipline amongst ourselves was well maintained never giving the Army cause for concern. Captain Agar fared better than his men. On his own recorded telling he was taken from the Maldives to Bombay to receive exceptional treatment. Wined, dined, and given the best suite of rooms in a prestigious hotel his social calendar was full. It can only be hoped he thought his rescued crew was being accorded the same excellent care. Being a good man I am sure he would not have enjoyed such high living if he knew people like us at Nyali were shoplifting for combs and razors.

I had a nasty gash on the front of my left leg that showed no signs of healing and the leg had become badly swollen. The Petty Officer arranged for me to be taken by truck to the No.6 Army General Hospital in Mombasa for treatment. When the doctor examined me he ordered me to bed until the leg could be X-rayed to see if a fragment of shrapnel was causing the trouble. The doctor said I was lucky. The X-ray equipment had only recently been captured from the Italians. Being in hospital was like heaven on earth, sleeping in a bed with clean sheets and under a mosquito net was paradise even if it was a short stay. The use of a net might have come too late, I had a strong suspicion of having been already well bitten by the malaria carrying pests. One of the highlights of my stay in No.6 was witnessing the constant battle between the ward Sisters and the Swahili attendants regarding footwear. It was natural for the natives to walk around barefooted but the English Sisters wanted to change the habit of a lifetime by insisting the 'boys' wore their regulation issue boots for hygienic reasons. When the natives heard or saw a Sister coming they quickly slipped into their boots but as soon as she was past they took them off again. It was funny to see an attendant rendering to the needs of the sick with a pair of army boots around his neck. On the rare occasion when they were caught barefooted, the blast from an Army Sister's reprimand could be heard from end to end of the single-storied building.

After a couple of days I returned to Nyali, still limping but with a clean dressing on the wound and an appointment to have it changed. To make the lads green with envy I told them about the food, the clean sheets, and the beautiful English Sisters. Admittedly I lied a little about their beauty. My reminiscences of the hospital comforts sparked off an idea that was to prove fruitful for the rest of the party. Usually when any of our lot found it difficult to get back from a trip to town it was the standard practise to ask at the police station for a bed for the night. The local constabulary was obliging if a cell was available, and a cup of tea was always on hand before we left in the morning. When I happened to say that there were beds without patients in some wards, the quick-witted decided that a spare hospital bed was preferable to the solid board at the local nick. It was easy to slip into the unused wards and tuck up for the night to enjoy a comfortable sleep. The free lodgings came to an abrupt halt when the Army staff discovered that more beds were being used than they had patients. We had to beat a hasty retreat through the windows one night when orderlies decided to do a thorough inspection after lights-out. It was too risky to continue with the present accommodation arrangements but we soon found an ideal substitute in the hospital ground. Rows of ambulances were parked there that never seemed to be used. For the rest of our stay in Kenya they were to provide the answer to our sleeping problems in town. We always left the vehicles in as tidy a condition as we found them, which might have accounted for us not being detected.

Another group shipped from the Maldives to Mombasa was fortunate enough to be taken straight to the converted transport ship SS Mendoza. This was the French merchantman captured by 'Dorsetshire' in January 1941 and put to good use by the Allies. I didn't know it at the time but my long time friend Fred Ball was one of the lucky ones to be on board, albeit their lack of clothing was much the same as ours, for a quick passage to the Cape. After a period of time that seemed 'for ever' the Colonel mustered the survivors to say that a ship called the 'Westernland' had arrived in Mombasa and would take us to Durban. We wasted very little time getting aboard an army vehicle to be driven to the docks, but not before paying a final farewell to the Colonel who had done his best for us. At least we had no kit and belongings to pack and transport. Our band of 'jolly' jacks walked up the gangway of the 'Westernland' with our worldy possessions in the pockets of our shorts. We were grateful that at long last something was happening that might improve our lot. For a couple of days I had been sweating with fever and I guessed it was malaria. When I heard about going to South Africa on the 'Westernland' I decided to stick it out for fear of being left in East Africa. As soon as I got on board I reported to the Sick Bay and was given enough quinine tablets to last me until the ship reached Durban.

There was plenty of time to reflect as the Westernland steamed south. The deaths of hundreds of my shipmates, the burning inferno that had been my home and the thirty-three hours in the water holding on to a piece of flotsam I could accept as the price of war. What I found repugnant and unacceptable was the insensitive treatment my fellow travellers received and myself when we reached the naval base at Mombasa. Nobody from the base came to see us off to make sure we were safely on board the 'Westernland'. That we were an inconvenience was made all too apparent. The fact that H.M.S. Dorsetshire and H.M.S. Cornwall had been left to the mercy of Admiral Nagumo when the Allied Fleet scattered seemed to have been forgotten. My badly swollen leg and a wound refusing to heal coupled with the onset of malaria was no more hurtful than my feelings for the staff at H.M.S. 'Tania'. With time to think and take stock of my intentions for the future I came to a conscious decision to leave the navy when the war was over. There was no doubt in my mind about my ability to scale the ladder of promotion but I had lost the appetite to realise my full potential. Psychologically I had reached the ultimate point of disillusionment with the service I had been proud to join.

On arriving in Durban we were taken to Clarewood Camp on the outskirts of the city. It consisted of lines of army tents previously used for housing Italian prisoners of war. The survivors already there gathering around us in surprise, they had been told that any of the crew not already accounted for must be 'missing presumed dead'. There was a lot of chattering as I was brought up to date with what had been going on before my arrival. Apparently, being late, our little party had missed all the 'fun'. The Canadian gunnery officer Ross Wilson, with a party of fellow officers, came direct from the Maldives to South Africa through the Mozambique Channel. Like everyone else he received two blankets, but no groundsheet, to be billeted under canvas at Clarewood. Ross and the other officers found the general conditions totally unacceptable, especially the sleeping arrangements. The blankets got damp through direct contact with the ground and the sand flies were making life a misery. The officers got together and agreed to walk out, after making their complaints known to the Camp Commander. The South African Lieutenant, Geoffrey Berlyn, had family connections in Durban and he took the disgruntled officers to the Jewish Y.M.C.A. where they were welcomed with open arms. After a slap-up meal the kind hearted Springboks installed them in luxury beach apartments.

Like others still waiting for uniforms, they were wearing the same items of kit issued to them on Addu Atoll. Most had no money but their benefactors made it clear that this was not a debatable issue, everything was free and this included civilian clothing. Another group of sailors who arrived just before our party found it difficult to prove their identity to the reception clerks at the depot because they had been officially listed as missing, presumed killed. The endless quizzing and questioning to prove they were not infiltrators, coupled with a lack of consideration, unleashed a fury of pent up anger and frustration. Their spokesman, Petty Officer 'Polly' Hopkins, refused to be, as he said, 'piddled' about by an unfeeling authority. Threats, counter threats, warnings and clenched fists amounted to a serious confrontation. In isolation the grievances would have been accepted as the usual bloody mindedness on the part of clerks but collectively they were tantamount to harassment at a sensitive time in the aftermath of the sinking. A major disturbance was only averted when the incensed sailors were promised an interview with a very senior officer. The C in C of the Cape, Commodore Martin, was informed about the fracas and the plight of men he once captained. He came personally to speak to them and vouched immediate action. In double quick time his pledge was honoured and the survivors were given some clothing and told they could have two weeks leave. In some ways I was glad it had happened before I got to Durban, more problems with the authorities was something I could do without.

The South African Women's Voluntary Service also heard about the sailors' predicament. They quickly took over the responsibility for providing free holiday accommodation, a supply of spending money, and travelling arrangements to include sleeper trains. Homes as far away as Zululand, and right across Natal, eagerly offered to care for us. In the heart of the African veldt the names of towns, like Dundee and Glencoe, was a reminder of home to those who went there. This did not mean that the welcome at Amatakulu or Vryheid was any the less enjoyable. The hospitality of the South African people was overwhelming, it restored my faith in the human race; excluding Naval administrators that is. After the leave and a belated issue of full uniforms, the refreshed matelots returned to sea. A large number of draftees went to the battleship H.M.S.Valiant, others joined lesser known vessels. Except for the NAFFI canteen manager, none to my knowledge were fortunate to get a draft chit back to England. The old 'Dorsetshire' crew was spread out in all directions across the world. Nevertheless, they retained a bond of comradeship that distance and time did not diminish. Sailors in general talk about the many ships they have served aboard, affording a degree of allegiance to each. 'Dorsetshire' men mention other ships but keep their total loyalty for that special County Class cruiser H.M.S.Dorsetshire.

Arthur Davies, a young Ordnance Petty Officer, was the sole survivor from his mess. His story of the Easter events was similar to other accounts, nevertheless, his grief and sadness merits the telling. His Action Station was the Shell Rooms of the for'ard gun turrets, with special emphasis on the grabs that lifted the shells. They had to work smoothly, lifting the 250lb. missiles from the steel bins to take them across the Shell Room to the conveyors. Arthur was not especially pleased with his station, preferring the Gun House to the 'dungeons' below the waterline encased in three inches of armoured steel. However, he accepted his lot philosophically and gave the job the benefit of his engineering skills. On Easter Sunday, during a twenty-minute break, he took his dinner up on the deck to enjoy it in the open air. Dinner was a mug of soup, a corned beef sandwich and his tot of rum. As he munched away his close friend joined him, a young 'Tiffy' from the 4 inch gun deck. For some unexplainable reason he offered Arthur his rum. Afterwards the pals separated and returned to their posts, it was the last time they would sit and chat together. A sudden increase in speed and the ship turning hard over to port, followed soon afterwards by several colossal explosions, told Arthur that an attack had started. One Shell Room optimist was heard to remark "I think that was a near miss" and got the quick reply. "If that's a bloody near miss then thank the Lord we haven't been hit". 'Tiffy' Davies realised that the hydraulics had packed up just as the lights went out and the ship started to keel over, sending everything crashing to one side of the Shell Handling Space.

P.O.(P.T.I.) Monks in charge of the Shell Room ordered the magazine door opened to let the crew out, then he told the anxious faced assembly to evacuate in an orderly manner. By the time they got to the upper deck the ship was well over. Like others coming from down below, he was appalled at the scene of the holocaust. As 'Tiffy' Davies made his way amidships he was sickened by the sight of the dead, the whole mounting of a 4" gun was completely wrecked. His pal who had earlier given him the tot of rum was lying near his station with his head nearly severed from his body. Arthur clearly remembers taking off his overalls and shoes and placing them in a neat pile before jumping into the water. He had still not come to terms with the fact that he was leaving everything behind and would not be coming back. Swimming clear he looked back to see the ship rearing up to expose a huge hole in the starboard side, as he said "Big enough to drive a bus through". He watched in disbelief as 'Dorsetshire' went down, and contrary to popular theory there was little or no drag as she sank. As he swam towards a group of swimmers the Japanese planes came back machine-gunning. He recalled seeing the sea boiling in long streaks as the bullets hit the water, killing several near him by an unnecessary act of barbarism. The 'lap of honour' by the Japanese pilots against the helpless men achieved nothing but contempt for the flyers.

He received a quarter of a biscuit during his time in the water, and like everyone else he was overjoyed to be picked up by H.M.S.Paladin. As he walked around the destroyer in his underpants, a sailor on board gave him a pair of shoes. They were size 9 and he needed a size 11 so the seaman cut the toe caps off to make them usable, at least it stopped his feet getting blistered on the hot deck. After experiencing Addu Atoll, but missing out on an issue of clothing, he was shipped in his underpants to Mombasa and put on the 'Mendoza'. South African troops on board, returning from the fighting in North Africa, took pity on him and gave him a shirt, a towel and a pair of shorts. There were no prospects of 'slops' in Mombasa, Durban seemed the most likely place to get kit. He wasn't pleased to receive the same treatment as the others when he arrived at Clarewood Camp. Walking through Durban in his 'tatty' clothes, he was stopped by an elderly lady who asked him why he was dressed in such a manner. When he explained, she marched him into the nearest outfitters and bought him two shirts, a pair of shoes, grey flannel trousers and some socks. She also bought him a towel and a few other incidentals and insisted that she must not be thanked because it was her pleasure to do this good deed for a serviceman.

Stoker 'Bungy' Williams also suffered the trauma of the sinking. As he left the ship, a little later than most, he became entangled in the ships' ensign. The thought flashed through his mind that he was about to be buried with full naval honours draped in the White Ensign. Self-preservation perished the thought, he freed himself and struck out to get clear and join the other swimmers.

When the Japanese planes flew over, firing their guns, he was holding on to a piece of wreckage with two others. The man next to him was killed by the bullets, it could easily have been all three of them but for that strange quirk of fate. The one thing that kept flashing through his mind, as he hung on to his piece of wreckage, was if he let go he would not pick up his Leading Stokers' Hook that was due to him. He arrived in Durban dressed in an old boiler suit overall that had been given to him by a stoker on the 'Mendoza'. Like Petty Officer Davies, he was approached about his unbecoming appearance. In his softly spoken Welsh voice he explained the circumstances and was taken to the shops to be kitted out. A few days later having a drink in a local bar, looking resplendent in his 'man about town' civilian clothes, he was given a white feather by a South African serviceman. Taken by surprise by the accusation of cowardice he demanded an explanation. "Because you should be in uniform and fighting for your country" he was told. Looking into the eyes of Stoker Williams he realised that a better reason was necessary if he did not want two black eyes so he quickly added. "My brother gave his life a couple of days ago, he was killed on H.M.S. Dorsetshire". "What was his name" asked 'Bungy'. "Harry Sewell, a stoker" "Yes I know he was a stoker, he was a pal of mine and he was in my mess". The Springbok was dumbfounded, speechless and ashamed when his insult backfired. Suffice to say Bungy William was 'adopted' for the remainder of his time in the city he didn't have to find a 'tikki' to buy a thing. His stay in Durban as a celebrity was all too short-lived, the Navy found him a more conventional mode of dress and a little piece of paper called a 'draft chit' for a return to sea.

I received the bare essentials of kit and told to muster at the local railway station that evening, to join a party going on leave to Empangeni for two weeks. Still sweating with a fever I had high hopes that it would go away but at the station I collapsed and was taken to Addington Hospital in Durban. It was diagnosed as possible Blackwater Fever caused by the lack of treatment for earlier Malaria. I lost consciousness for three days, although I had a faint recollection of coming around a couple of times in a fog to find nurses sponging me down and then covering me with several blankets to start me sweating again. The nurses were very pleased when I finally woke up, feeling very weak but glad to be back in the land of the living. The doctor came immediately and asked me a lot of questions about where I had been. He was an Austrian who had lived for many years in South Africa and had no wish to be associated with the part his country was playing in the war. It didn't matter to me where he came from as long as he got me better. As a 'battle-blooded' nineteen-year-old I got a lot of fussing from the nurses and a fair amount of motherly affection from the Matron and Sisters. I loved every minute of it, it was the place to stay for ever or at least until the end of hostilities. Every night I had Ovaltine before being tucked up in bed, often by one especially delightful young nurse with skin like the inside of a cream jug, it was a sailor's idea of paradise. The food was fantastic and geared especially to get me back to full health and strength. I had a full audience the day I was allowed to stand out of bed and I build up my part to get maximum sympathy. It was an opportunity that might not come my way again and I had to make the most of it. My progress was rapid, including the healing of the leg wound, but the doctor was in no hurry to discharge me and I was in no hurry to leave.

When I was fully mobile I visited the other wards where Dorsetshire crew were in bed. There was plenty to talk about not the least being the time we would be going back to sea. One survivor, Able Seaman 'Pony' Moore, badly wounded in the Japanese attack was fighting a losing battle to save a leg. Before 'call up' he was a schoolteacher with a promising career. He was very unhappy when the doctors told him that gangrene had set in and it was necessary to amputate to save his life. The night before the operation I visited him but he was too distressed and depressed to be consoled. The pungent smell of gangrene filled the single bed ward, it was overpowering and sickly. I was very relieved when a nurse came and asked me to go because she had to give him injections. 'Pony' came through the operation and returned to teaching after his discharge from the navy. He eventually became a Headmaster of a school in the Manchester area and no doubt had plenty to tell his pupils about his experiences on 'Dorsetshire'. I did visit him after the war and came away pleased that the loss of a leg was not making any appreciable difference to his normal life.

25 Dundee

When I was deemed fit, the hospital contacted the South African Women's Voluntary Service to arrange a holiday to replace the one I missed out on when I went sick. A courtesy car took me to the station to meet a lady from the SAWVS for a briefing on what was to be an exciting vacation.

I was put on a train for the overnight journey to a place called Dundee, a small town about thirty miles from Zululand. First I received my ticket, spending money and reservations for a sleeping cabin and meals on the journey. Before the train set off the WVS lady introduced me to two fellow travellers sharing the compartment. They were Afrikaners (Boer) farmers returning north to their homes, and far from being hostile to a British serviceman they assured the lady that I would be in good hands during the journey. They were true to their word and although I found their heavy guttural accent difficult to understand at first I got used to it and the conversation throughout was enlightening. I knew the name of the family I was to stay with, but when the train pulled into Dundee my two companions stepped down to the platform to make sure someone was there to meet me. A homely mature woman accompanied by two young ladies approached and greeted me as if they had known me all my life. After a lot of handshaking and light-hearted chatter the two farmers re-boarded the train to continue their journey and I was driven 'home'. My host Mrs.Wang, a widow, was Norwegian by birth but her two daughters, Hjordis and Ann were born in South Africa. Her sons were at present in North Africa fighting with the Allied Forces but were expected home soon on leave. Mrs.Wang was everything a mother could be and the girls willingly accepted the role of chaperon taking me out and about to meet people and see the sights. Just as important, the larger than life black housekeeper, Josephine, took a liking to me and treated me as one of the Wang family. She brought me a cup of tea in bed every morning and put a packet of cigarettes on the bedside table. She cleaned my shoes, washed my clothes and thought it was her God-given right to fatten me up. A British sailor was a novelty so far from the sea, and I enjoyed the celebrity status of strangers stopping me in the street just to shake my hand and wish me well.

One day a Mr. Smith called at the house to ask Mrs. Wang if I would like to go shooting with his son Joe. She saw the expression on my face and agreed, providing I was taken special care of on the veldt. The next day Joe arrived and drove me to his father's farm to meet the rest of the family and a few of his pals going on the shoot. Before the party set off I was given a .22 rifle and a bandolier of bullets for shooting Buck, a shotgun and bandolier of cartridges for Guinea-fowl, and a very obedient gun dog. On the way to the starting point Joe Smith gave me a few pointers. "Don't wander too far in front of the other guns. Hesitate before firing at a Buck to make sure it wasn't a dog bounding through the bush retrieving a bird. I could get lost but the dog would always find it's way back if commanded. Never shoot a sitting bird or a Guinea-fowl running along the ground. If in real trouble fire several volleys into the air and wait for help". As the guns spread out and moved through the bush the South Africans made loud clucking noises, mimicking the call of the Guinea-fowl. The birds clucked back in reply revealing their position and the dogs were sent to flush them out. Once the fowl were airborne the guns blasted away and the dogs, on command, sped off to fetch the fallen birds. I couldn't hit a thing and felt annoyed and disgusted with myself, even the dog looked fed up. Worse still, when I rejoined the party later for refreshments they had all bagged several brace and they didn't hide their smiles at my lack of success. When the Springboks spread out again to resume the shoot, Joe Smith called me aside and gave me a couple of brace from his bag which I reluctantly accepted to safe face with the others. Guns kept popping away but by the end of the day I could only show a couple more brace for a mountain of spent cartridges. Nobody managed to shoot any Buck, which was something of a consolation. It meant the sharpshooters hadn't achieved everything they set out to do. That evening roasted Guinea-fowl graced the dinner table, expertly prepared by Josephine. I basked in the glory of complimentary remarks from the girls without revealing Joe Smith's contribution to my triumph.

Another evening Joe and his pals took me to a campfire party out on the veldt where a lot of people had gathered to eat, drink and be merry. A large vociferous group near the fire started giving vent to their feelings with songs in Afrikaans. I asked Joe what they were so enthusiastically singing about and felt somewhat concerned when he casually said. "Oh! just some anti-British songs". Noting the size of most of the Afrikaners bellowing like bull elephants I was anxious about my safety and mentioned this to Joe. Unperturbed he told me not to bother, the singers were mainly Ossewa Brandwag supporters, an anti-British militant wing of the Opposition Nationlist Party still 'fighting' the Anglo-Boer war of yesteryear. He assured me I was amongst friends, and he was right. Several of the group came to speak to me in English instead of their usual Dutch and they could not have been more friendly. It did cause a few smiles when I sang my few lines of

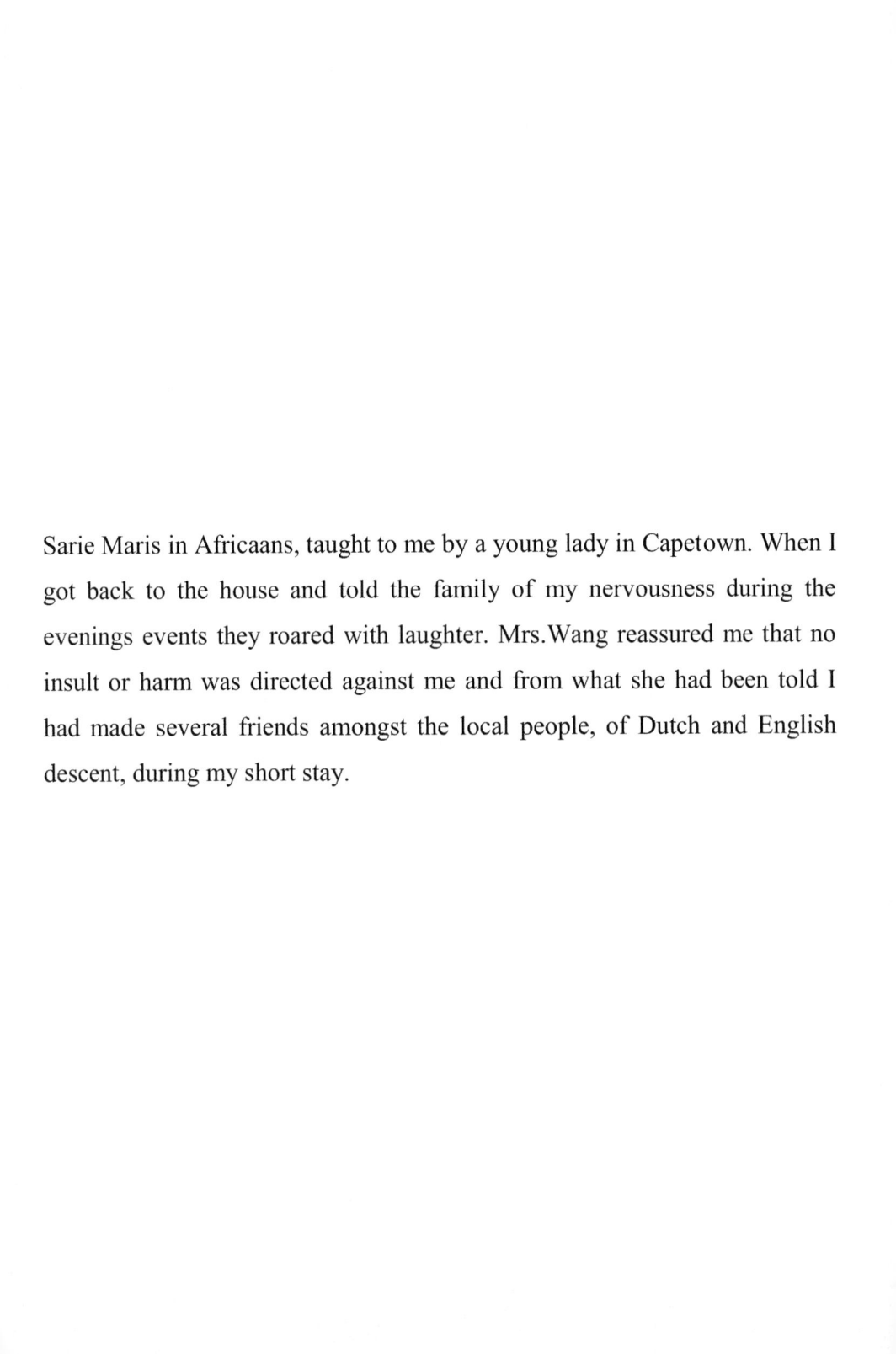

Sarie Maris in Africaans, taught to me by a young lady in Capetown. When I got back to the house and told the family of my nervousness during the evenings events they roared with laughter. Mrs.Wang reassured me that no insult or harm was directed against me and from what she had been told I had made several friends amongst the local people, of Dutch and English descent, during my short stay.

26 A funny shaped coal burner

While I was still at Dundee, Joe Smith and two of his pals received their papers to enlist in the South African Airforce as trainee pilots. They opted to wear the orange/red flash on their uniforms, denoting their wish to fight outside the Union for the Allied cause. Inevitably my leave came to an end and time for me to report to Snell Parade the South African barracks in Durban. In my absence all the survivors had been moved from Clarewood Camp to the better housing at the barracks. When I first arrived in Dundee I had a kit bag with very little in it, now as I packed for leaving it didn't seem big enough to carry all the presents I had been given, mainly from the Wang family. The last item to pack was a very large wrapped fruit cake that Mrs.Wang had baked especially for me, it was a bit of a squeeze getting it into the kit bag. The next day, waiting for the train, I got so many big hugs I hated having to leave. When the train pulled into the station I turned to say my last goodbyes to Mrs.Wang and found her unashamedly sobbing, then Josephine and the girls started crying and finally I started. It was a very emotional and tearful send off, a weepy spectacle curiously watched by the people already on the train. The company that seemed attentive to increasing my knowledge about the towns and districts we passed through made the return journey all the more comfortable. The time went quickly and I arrived in Durban to find a SAWVS car waiting to see me safely into the hands of the authorities. The SAWVS wanted to know all about my holiday and I was able to tell them that it was the most wonderful leave I had ever had.

Snell Parade barracks housed a varied collection of servicemen in an atmosphere of anticipation as they waited for postings. Most of the 'Dorsetshire' survivors had already been drafted, the largest number going to the battleship HMS.Valiant including my pal Fred Ball. Enough were still around to make me feel amongst friends, but the numbers were reducing every day. I went to the mail office on the off chance and was pleasantly surprised to be given several letters and a parcel. A couple from my Mother with the usual gossip about everyone in the neighbourhood, she also mentioned that there was still no news of my brother captured by the Japanese just before Singapore capitulated. The parcel containing a mixture of non-perishable 'goodies' was from Kay and very much appreciated. I made a mental note to give her a special treat the next time I took her out. Letters from Helen in Hebburn were warm-hearted and caring with a longing to see me as soon as possible. There was also a letter from her Mother saying how unfair I was not to have written recently and would I state my long term intentions towards her daughter. I don't think the censor would allow me to say where I had been and what I had been doing or that I didn't expect to return to Hebburn for a very long time. A young lady in Torquay wrote to say she was sorry but she had now taken up with an airman and she hoped I understood. She forgot to say if he was Yank, British or Pole but in my mind I wished her well particularly as I had always fancied her sister more than her. Maureen with the lovely eyes, also from Torquay, assured me of her undying love but my sister had written to say she had seen her out with an American. I pondered over how fickle women could be and wrote a long letter to my girl friend in Capetown telling her how much I missed her, it made me feel better. Obviously nobody knew where I was because of the restrictions on information but it seemed as if everyone expected me home in the near future. Unknown to them I was to travel thousands of sea miles before I saw the shores of England again.

A couple of days after arriving at the barracks I was sent for by the Divisional Officer for a talk, more of an assessment I would say. He said he was fully conversant with my record on 'Dorsetshire' but unfortunately the final part of my Leading Seaman's exams had not been ratified prior to the sinking and I would have to sit the exams again. It was made clear that it would be a mere formality, more so with the need for fully trained ratings to accept advancement to a higher grade to fill the gaps left by the mounting death toll when ships were sunk. He was taken aback when I told him that I was not interested in promotion. I said I wished to apply for the submarine service but he told me not to bother wasting my time, Durban was a non-submarine port and there was already about 400 hundred on the waiting list in the Cape. The talk got nowhere and in the end he told me to go away and reconsider my irresponsible attitude towards upgrading. Later the Chief Bosun's Mate sent for me and called me every stupid, stubborn bloody-minded fool, he could think of. Then he tried the gentle approach telling me how well I had worked under him on 'Dorsetshire' and how he could always rely on me to do a good job. He told me I had to report back to the Divisional Officer the next day and I was to show up in a different frame of mind or else. I told the DO the same as before and he took it on board that I meant what I said, there was little point trying to convince me that the treatment I received after the sinking of 'Dorsetshire' could be reconciled with promotion. It must have appeared I was acting like a spoiled brat, but at the time I was determined the might of His Majesty's Royal Navy could make up the shortfall in skilled lower deck supervisory personal without involving me.

The same evening a messenger found me and gave me a draft chit, to take effect immediately. I was to pack my kit and report to Transport to be taken to HMS.Barrymore, a coal-burning Boom Defence vessel of about 700tons. Before that evening I had never heard of HMS. Barrymore. A little miffed I went to see the Chief 'Buffer' and told him a few home truths. He said it was an emergency, 'Barrymore' was short of crew and I was only going as far as Mombasa. I would leave the ship there and await passage back to Durban for drafting to something more prestigious. When the truck dropped me off at the wharf I could have deserted there and then when I saw what passed as a Royal Navy ship. The dirty looking heap of metal was tied up alongside her sister ship HMS. Barfount. Having never served on anything less than a 10,000 ton cruiser I stood viewing my next berth with some trepidation. It crossed my mind to go back to Snell Parade and 'land one' on the drafting officer, but the inevitable consequences would have only made matters much worse. My day-dreaming was interrupted by the emergence of a huge fender-bellied individual through a hatch on deck. We eyed each other for a few seconds, long enough for me to take stock of his oil stained boiler suit trousers and singlet. The rag around his neck looked as if it had been used to great effect to soak up sweat. Then his face spread into a big genial smile. "You must be one of the new lads, I'm Chief Stoker, welcome on board son". "Why how many more is there to come". "Oh! just you and another, he hasn't arrived yet but if he doesn't come soon we'll bloody well sail without him".

The Chief pulled back a tatty old curtain screening a door and spoke to someone. A Wavy-Navy Warrant Officer came out and I introduced myself. He took my papers and jotted down all the particulars before directing me to the mess deck in the fo'c'sle to report to the Coxswain. Over the next twenty-four hours I was introduced to the rest of the thirty-man crew that made up the ships' company. They fell into two distinct categories, those who were Riggers and those who were not. With the exception of the other rating who arrived later, the Chief Stoker and the Captain, everyone else had been recruited for wartime service only. The Captain was a Lieutenant and the other two officers were R.N.V.R. Warrant rank. One had worked for Burtons the tailors before call up and the other a commercial traveller. They were fairly nice chaps, weekend sailors with no real seafaring qualifications who got in through the back door to get commissions. The Petty Officer Coxswain was previously a trawler skipper out of Grimsby and a good seaman, his right hand man had been a freelance photographer in Fleet Street. The riggers were something different, real professionals, the finest I had ever seen with wire. A rigger splicing on his own did what normally took three of us to do on a General Service ship. They were either Scots or Irish who had served their time in the shipbuilding yards as riggers. The way they manipulated the huge wire hawsers used in boom defence work deserved an Admiral's commendation.

H.M.S.Barrymore was a workhorse with no pretentious aspirations to resemble a warship. Except for the obligatory White Ensign and the two horn like gantries protruding forward over the bows, it could have been any old coastal tramp. In general the crew were an unruly lot but loyal to a man and ever supportive to each other. Discipline was not their strongest attribute but the ability to work long hours in the tropical heat without complaining made up for any shortcomings. I knew from the moment that I took my place in the Mess that living with this zany lot was going to be a different lifestyle to one in the 'proper' navy. Fortunately for me, 'Barrymore' had already taken on as much coal as she could carry, including the rigging of a large wooden box-like structure on the fo'c'sle to hold additional fuel for the journey to Mombasa. All traces of coal dust had been washed away and the ship was ready to sail at short notice.

When it was time to go the crew cast off without the formalities of 'piping' special sea dutymen. The Skipper asked those men on deck to wear a white shirt and cap instead of the usual singlet and khaki shorts, to show some conformity with the Royal Navy. The two unusually shaped vessels finally slipped their moorings and chugged towards the open sea. There was no Royal Marine Band to play us out with 'Anchors Away', neither was the Lady in White standing on Maydon Wharf to sing a sentimental farewell ballad. We hadn't been at sea a day when the captain heard about one of the lads having a pet rat called 'Nelson' that he took everywhere. He ordered the rodent to be thrown overboard but nobody had the heart to do it. As a compromise the men built a sturdy little raft with a flagpole through the centre and lashed a container of water and a large portion of cheese to it. Then they tied 'Nelson' to the post with enough slack to move around without getting washed away and gently lowered the lot into the water to disappear astern. The Skipper had a pet himself that he liked to show off to visitors, it was a West African Grey parrot with a knack for picking up words. To get their own back the crew started teaching it vile swearwords when the captain was busy and out of earshot. When he heard his bird giving forth in vulgar Anglo-Saxon he was furious. He let it be known that anyone caught educating his parrot in the unspeakable would have his 'Bloody guts made into garters'. By the time we reached Mombasa the captain's pet was fully conversant with every profanity in the nautical wordbook and had to be locked away when callers came on board.

The captain was much older than the normal run of Lieutenants, and probably came up through the ranks from the Lower Deck. He was good at his job and the crew respected his competence. The only weakness in an otherwise flawless character was his unquenchable thirst for whisky. It was known that he drank a lot of the golden spirit, and without it he was inclined to be unbearably crotchety. It was a standing joke that he never shared a bottle with the other officers, preferring his own company in the tiny cabin under the Bridge. I was told that he sat in from of a mirror and treated his reflection as a real person. I didn't believe the story when I first heard it so one night a member of the crew took me to see. We crept quietly up the ladder and peeped through a chink in the curtain. The Skipper sat, as I had been told, in front of the looking glass with two glasses on the table in front of him. As I watched he emptied his glass before looking into the mirror and asking his image "Do you fancy another". Then refilling both glasses, he drank his measure and swapped the glasses about and downed the other. I crept softly away without any preconceived or opinionated notions about his abilities, the fact that the crew thought he was a "Bloody good Skipper" was sufficient recommendation for me. When I was accepted as part of the ships' company, they confided in me about their exploits before leaving England. One rendering was the close shave they had with the law just before setting out, when a full keg of navy rum 'happened' on board in mysterious circumstances.

Nobody accepted responsibility for it's presence and it was considered too dangerous to return it to where it rightfully belonged. Instead, help was enlisted from the stokers to secret the spirit away before the inevitable police search began. The 'bubbly' was skilfully locked into a section of the fresh water system between two valves with a secondary piping installed to bypass the section. As expected, the local C.I.D. searched all the vessels in the vicinity including 'Barrymore'. The lads confessed they sweated 'drops of ink' as the ship was combed from end to end, including turning on taps hoping to flush out rum. The diligent police officers found nothing and 'Barrymore' was given a clean bill and allowed to sail. When the ship was well clear of land the precious liquid was retrieved and enjoyed in small doses for most of the passage to Durban. Having already been to Mombasa I was constantly quizzed about what was there to see and do. My previous experiences in the place would hardly allow me to give it the 'gold star' award but I offered to act as guide on a run ashore.

My messmates were naturally curious about the East African port and it's people, especially the girls, food and beer. I told them to forget about the first two but the ever warm beer was acceptable. 'Barrymore' chugged into Mombasa and made her way up the Creek to the coaling wharf, followed by 'Barfount'. Both ships attracted so little attention they might as well not have existed. The stop over was expected to be just long enough to refill the bunkers and take on fresh water. I asked the 'Skipper' about the arrangements for me to return to Durban but he said my replacement hadn't arrived and I was staying with 'Barrymore' until one turned up. He did divulge that our next port of call would be Mahe, off the East African coast north of Madagascar. The mention of the Seychelles island allayed any misgivings I had about staying with the 'old tub'. Even though the quarters were cramped, the 'heads' inadequate when more than three had the screaming abdabs and wanted to use the toilet, and the washing facilities poor. It was a price worth paying to visit the islands again. Coaling ship started early the next day, it was an unpleasant job shared by everyone, officers and men alike. I was given sound advice to liberally apply Vaseline around my eyes, nose and ears. This was essential to minimise the effects of the gritty dust that got into every crevice and orifice of the body. It was an essential safeguard to ease the cleaning process later. When the last of the coal had been taken on board the ship was hosed down to remove all traces of the black dust before an inspection by the 'Skipper'. Only then could we start scrubbing ourselves clean and allowed a 'make and mend' for the rest of the day. About twenty went ashore to use their precious afternoon leave in what ever way they fancied. On all ships there is the 'bagging off' brigade who seek the flesh-pots in every port of call. One could only hope they were wise enough to take the precautions and advice given to them about the effects of loose living. On 'Barrymore' the 'brothel creepers' could be counted on one hand and by natural selection palled together when going ashore. They were constantly under the eagle eye of the Coxswain after a stay in port for any signs of sickness.

I often wondered how much of their shore-side activities was fact and how much was plain old fashioned bragging and bravado. A pair of knickers draped from the hammock bars the next morning was no proof they had been acquired in the manner told. I suspected in most cases they were bought to add spice to the tales of conquest and a warped humour for anyone who saw the funny side of their stories. After cleaning myself I changing into 'whites' and joined up with three close mates of the same mind who wanted to find a restaurant and bar to have something to eat and drink in peace and quiet. Most of the eating places were third rate by English standards, the locals were accustomed to the food but newcomers to the area ran the likely risk of a touch of Delhi-Belly or Montezumas Revenge with every mouthful. There was one place I remembered from my previous visit. Although I couldn't afford to eat there on that occasion I did recollect it had a reputation for providing an acceptable cuisine with a lesser chance of bellyache. Frequented by the better off it tried to maintain a degree of up-market pretentiousness to encourage a 'nicer' clientele. We arrived to find the entrance blocked by a well-built individual who made it perfectly clear we were unwelcome in the establishment. "No, no, not here Jacks, you no come in here O.K. You kick up too much peace and quietness O.K." That it was not O.K. was made quite plain. The two riggers with us, with arms like wire hawsers, lifted the protesting doorman and deposited him in the road. I felt a pleasing comfort that he wasn't the recipient of their infamous 'Liverpool Touch', perfected by so many of the 'Barrymore' crew. This amounted to a swift head butt followed by a knee in the 'balls' that was guaranteed to floor the strongest of men if delivered correctly.

Once inside we sat quietly in one corner of the bar section and waited patiently before being served with beer and eats. It was supposed to be a leisurely afternoon away from the confines of the ship, instead it turned out to be ruined by the arrival of a crowd of 'Aussie' matelots. From the noise they were making and the high spirits it was obvious they had been drinking, and when Australians drink too much they cause a commotion disproportionate to their numbers. This time was no different, all the signs indicated trouble with a capital T. I kept a weather eye peeled for the first signs of a disturbance and warned the others to do the same, particularly as we were grossly outnumbered by about five to one. A discreet exit was high on the agenda if 'things' started to get out of hand, best to leave it to the memorable exploits of Sir Francis Drake and Sir Richard Grenville to uphold the good name of our navy. The peaceful atmosphere was shattered when the Aussies 'cast loose' and the first empty bottles crashed against the restaurant wall. It was the call sign for me to take shelter under the table. Peeping over the top I saw our Antipodean friends, now out of control, breaking the legs off the chairs and tables to hurl them indiscriminately around the room. We weren't being picked on but we were in danger of getting hurt. After a quick discussion under the table the four of us decided to retaliate and then make a hasty departure. We stood up and pelted the Colonials with everything that came to hand before disappearing on all fours under the tables to the door as a hail of missiles came our way. Outside we reckoned we were lucky to have got off lightly and in a happy frame of mind we made our way back to the ship, run ashore over.

HMS.Barrymore cast off and left the Creek with 'Barfount'. What was expected to be a sedately jaunt from Mombasa to Mahe turned out to be the roughest sea journey I ever made. It was supposed to take less than a couple of days but in fact it took six and a half. The voyage had hardly got under way properly when we ran into what Capt. Rawlings told us was the tail end of a typhoon. Low in the water and bow heavy 'Barrymore' was not built to behave gracefully in very rough weather. Every inch of the vessel groaned in protest as the storm whipped the sea into a boiling frenzy that sent giant waves crashing down on the little ship. Decks were awash day and night making it impossible to move from one part of the ship to another without being fastened to a safety line. The pounding waves, testing endurance and stamina to the limits constantly buffeted the ship and everyone on board. 'Barrymore' balanced herself precariously on the top of each huge wave before nose-diving into the pit of every advancing deep-sided trough of water that threatened to engulf us. Men going on deck were soon knee deep in foaming water that swirled along the port and starboard waists, it was a miracle that nobody was lost overboard. When it was my trick on the helm, a rope was lowered down from the bridge to the hatch by the fo'c'sle messdeck. At the appropriate moment the officer on the bridge shouted down the voice pipe 'to go'. The hatch was opened long enough for me to tie the rope around myself before being hauled up ahead of the next incoming wave. As she pitched and tossed violently, mostly refusing to answer to helm, I spun the wheel hard over from side to side to keep the bows into the wind and waves to prevent her yawling broadside on to the big rollers and capsizing. Lieutenant Rawlings shouted down the tube to try and keep the ship on a resemblance of a steady course, agreeing that it was virtually impossible under the extreme sea conditions. I had great difficulty keeping my balance as 'Barrymore' lurched, bounced and wallowed her way through the waves. Most of the time I had to fight the wheel to stop it spinning out of control from the sudden pressures on the rudder.

As visibility deteriorated we lost contact with 'Barfount' although she was in close proximity. During the night the skipper did a most unusual thing in wartime, he shone a masthead light to let the other vessel know where we were as a precaution against collision. I suppose he judged that no enemy submarine would dare venture on the surface under such atrocious circumstances, and most certainly they could not carry out an attack. The stokers were in greatest distress, battened down and shovelling coal in intense heat from the boiler room fires, their strength was sapped after a couple of days. Volunteers were called for to help with the stoking and, as was expected, everyone said they would do a spell. When I went below to do my trick with the shovel I found it backbreaking work that I would not have wanted to do for too long. I must have lost pounds in weight as the sweat poured from me sending rivulets of perspiration trickling down my body from head to foot. The dust from the coal and the arid smoky atmosphere convinced me that any job on board was better than this. To add to our problems the ships' pumps couldn't cope with the volume of water that must have found it's way through the vents into the bilges. It meant working in shifts to bale out by hand. From the smell I don't think the bilges had been properly cleaned out since leaving England. The nauseating stench caused a few of us to 'spew up' as we worked on our knees in the bowels of the ship, adding a little more to the vile stink. The two cooks worked wonders with the limited resources from tins, mostly herrings in tomato sauce. Using the stoves to prepare hot meals was far to dangerous under the circumstances although they did make valiant attempts on a couple of occasions.

The gale continued for most of six days and when it finally abated we took stock of the storm damage. Above deck every inch was encrusted in layers of salt, but damage was superficial, the Barboats were well constructed albeit not ideal for sailing in tempestuous weather. Birds that had taken refuge on the after deck during the storm instinctively flew off before the islands came into sight. One very large Heron had stayed with the ship for most of the journey and we had become quite attached to it, feeding it scraps at regular intervals.

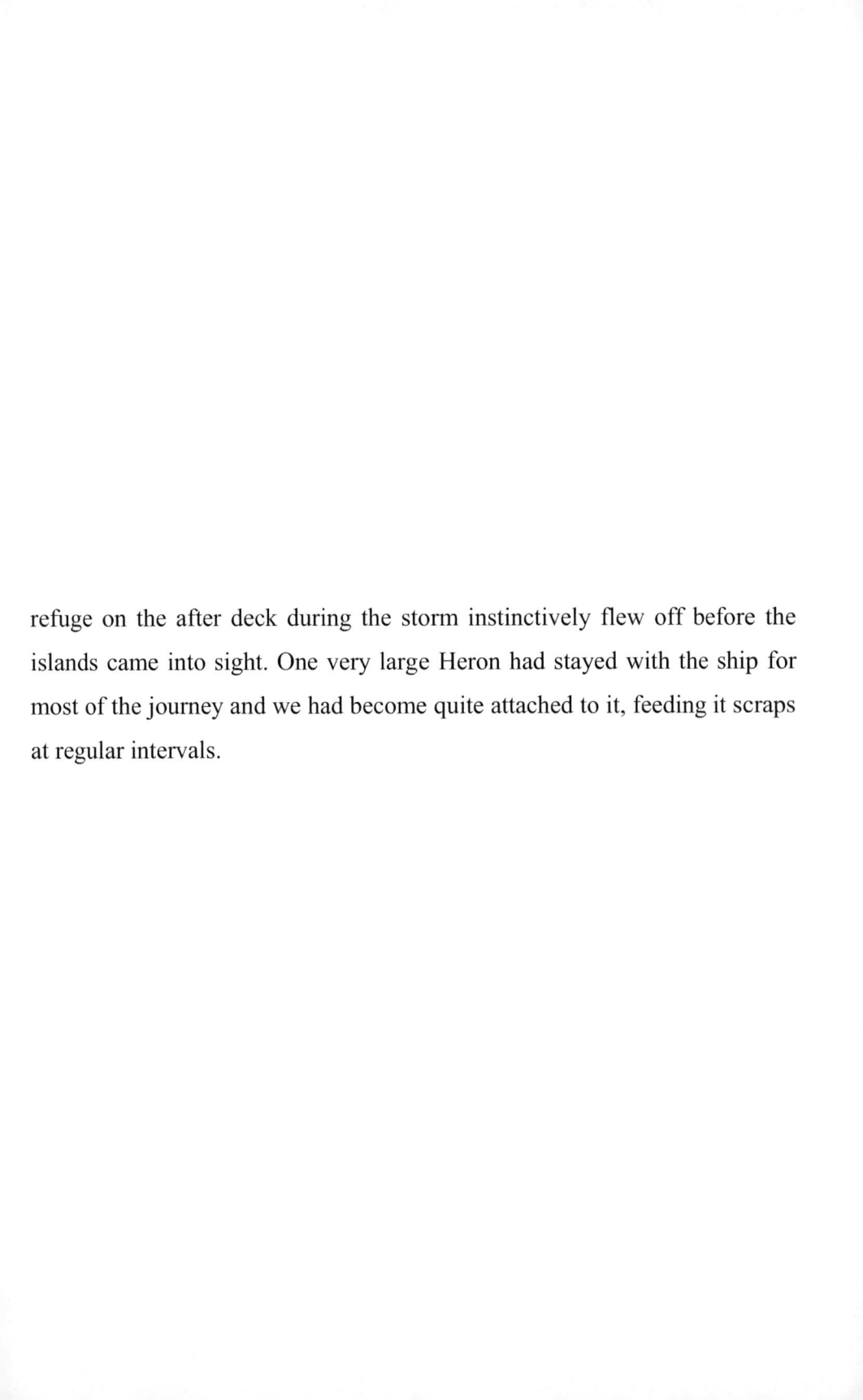

27 The Seychelle Islands.

When the anchors rattled and splashed into the water off Victoria at Mahe it was the end of an unpleasant journey that I didn't want to repeat in a small ship. Looking around, the harsh conditions of the previous few days were soon forgotten. 'Barrymore' and 'Barfount' had come to the islands to prepare a safe haven for Allied ships by constructing a boom defence system between the smaller islands around Mahe. Both Bar-boats now had to wait for the arrival of the boom supply ship 'Ethiopia' with the necessary equipment to start the work. Large concrete blocks about the size of an average room had to be placed on the sea bed to hold the network of wire hawsers to protect ships against possible submarine attack. The operation required accurate positioning to avoid the loss of half a days work retrieving a block dropped out of line. The first job after anchoring was to scrape away the thick covering of salt that encased the ship. Then it was clean down and repaint overall to remove the last signs of continuous battering before relaxing to weigh-up our new surroundings.

The Seychelles comprised two distinct group formations. One concentrated around Mahe and the other scattered across 150,000 square miles of the Indian Ocean. The Mahe region was the archetypal concept of a tropical paradise. Grouped into sun-kissed coral clusters the islands portrayed the perfect hideaway. The luscious greenery, isolated beaches, secluded coves, fabulous bird and plant life in breathtaking scenery suggested this could be the original Garden of Eden. Discovered in 1609 and colonised by the French in 1770 the group was named after the French nobleman Viscount Seychelles. Surrendered to the British in 1810 they retained a delightfully strong French influence. The language and local customs was a mixture of English, French and Creole with the majority of the people embracing the Church of Rome, the religion brought in by the early settlers. The first time I went ashore with another Catholic for Sunday Mass I realised how many customs were retained, the service was in the Latin version of the time but the sermon was in French. Island names reflected their earlier subjugation, La Digue, St.Pierre, Felicite and Curieuse intermixing with Bird, St. Anne's, Round and The Sisters.

Swimming below the surface in the crystal clear water was an inexpressible experience. Shoals of brightly coloured fish shared the coral reefs with an abundant assortment of marine life. Seychelles was world renowned for the variety of magnificent seashells that washed up in large quantities on the deserted beaches. Giant tortoises put there it was reputed by the famous Captain Cook freely roamed the out islands. Another unique feature was the indigenous Coco-de-Mer, the double coconut that grew nowhere else in the world. The Seychellois, or as we called them Seychellees, lived a laid back existence that differed dramatically to the turbulent happenings in the world outside. White and Creole mixed freely in their everyday life whilst retaining social demarcation lines that only time would change. Everything about the islands was exciting and appealing, it was easy to imagine the stories of pirates burying their treasures here in years gone by. The remoteness of the place held a special fascination for me, away from the regimented and regulated life on a large warship. Creole children, who only knew about things like trains and buses from the pictures in books because of their isolation, were eager with their questions about the outside world. Some of the older French children had visited Europe before the war and were knowledgeable about life in big cities. The infrequent arrival of a merchant ship, with the prospects of mail, was looked on as a pleasurable event for us as well as the Seychellois.

While he waited for the 'Ethiopia', Capt. Rawlings surveyed the area to decide the exact positioning of the new defence system. In the meantime the crew worked a normal day carrying out the necessary maintenance to keep the ship in good condition. Being a small vessel in the islands, regular shore leave was allowed when it fitted in with the work programme, and everyone took advantage of time away from the confined space on the Bar-boat. The capital Victoria had the shops, bars and bustling market that could be noisy, but within a few minutes walk along the dirt road in the direction of Cascade village lay real placidity. Walking barefoot on the soft clean sand of the foreshore, shaded by palm trees that grew right down to the waters edge swaying gently in the warm breezes, was magical. With only the sound of the lapping tide to disturb the stillness, the seclusion was sheer seductive bliss.

Soon after coming to this enchanting place, a magnificent Barque under full sail was sighted bearing down on Mahe captained by a local man called Morris. Our captain told the Coxswain to muster half a dozen men in white shirts and caps, at the double. Having been a training ship boy, it was automatically assumed that I knew how to pipe on a Bosun's Call. It was fortunate I did because the Skipper lent me a 'Call' to do the honours, mine having been lost when 'Dorsetshire' was sunk. I was told to stand by to pipe the 'Still' as the ensigns were dipped to observe maritime courtesies to the homeward bound vessel. My 'piping' must have proved satisfactory because

I got the job on a permanent basis. Watching the elegant Barque taking in canvas before coming to anchor close by was a bonus for that day. It didn't spoil it when I overheard Rawlings muttering as he watched " Now they are proper bloody sailors".

I got lumbered with one job that I hated doing more than any other, it was doing shore patrol single-handed. Why I was picked on to do it so often, especially on my own, was puzzling. I asked myself time and time again "why me", but when I approached the Coxswain for an answer he just shrugged and said "Yours is not to reason why lad". Enforcing law and order was a farce, I had about as much chance of controlling a bunch of unruly riggers on my own as I had of flying to the moon. The worst part was keeping an eye on the boisterous behaviour of the habitually wanton 'bagging off' brigade hell bent on enjoying the favours of the Mahe Jezebeles. Dealing with sailors who had supped a tipple too much was easier, all I had to do was sober them up to an acceptable degree and point them in the general direction of the jetty. After the first day of patrolling the streets I conceded that winkling wayward shipmates out of houses of ill-repute was virtually impossible. I had reported to the police station to receive instructions, a truncheon, armband and whistle. The sergeant told me the name of the area most affected by sailors who drank too much, cavorted with loose women and caused a disturbance. I was assured that police backup, one constable, was available should he be needed. As I made my way up a dusty road a native woman drew my attention to singing and shouting coming from a nearby house. She assured me it was English sailors with naughty ladies, which meant it came within my powers of jurisdiction to sort out. Brave as a lion, and with all the authority invested in me, I went up on the veranda and banged hard on the door. A giggling coloured girl opened it and looking past her I recognised four or five of Barrymore's crew sexually frolicking with Creole girls. I called them "stupid prats" and ordered them all outside at the double, in return I received several two worded replies, all ending in "off". To maintain some form of dignified authority I settled for telling them to keep the noise down or I would report them. My conciliatory warning only caused loud howls of laughter and promises of what they would do to me if I didn't "#!*"@Š off". I gave it up as a bad job and went for a walk in the town contemplating how much of the island's electricity problems could be solved if that mobs insatiable 'humping' power could be harnessed to a generator.

Seychelles fishing was reputedly so good that I decided, three days after arriving, to try catching a shark. I bought the line with tracer and hook from a local fisherman for a couple of rupees and he gave me a few fishing tips and some bait for good measure. Returning on board and eager to get started I baited the hook and cast, paying out the number of fathoms recommended by the fisherman. I tied the line with a bowknot to the guard rail wire and sat down to watch for it to release. Quicker than I expected, the loop disappeared and the line snaked away too fast for me to get hold of, evidence that something big was on the hook. I let it carry on until it slowed down before I took over and pulled in the slack. My shouts of delight brought several of the crew on deck to see what was happening. I enjoyed holding centre stage, determined to show them how to land a big fish. The fisherman had warned me to let it run at first if I thought I had hooked a shark, otherwise it could snap the line along the roughness of it's back. Eventually it would turn and that was the time to exert plenty of pressure to haul it in.

For over an hour I fought the struggling fish before it started to weaken. That was until I pulled it to the surface and it found renewed strength that set it off again like a race horse. Later when I got the shark close to the ship, with the accompanying pilot fish, everyone shouted instructions of one kind or another what to do next. I had never caught a shark before and neither had anyone else so the excitement was understandable. I played my catch to and fro for an hour and three quarters before it gave up and I got it alongside.

Getting it inboard was the big problem because it was far too heavy to be lifted out of the water with the fishing line. Words of wisdom were plentiful with so many wanting to be involved. One suggestion was to tie running loops of rope around the shark line and drop them into the water to sink down over the it's body, then the fish could be pulled up by the many willing hands on deck. It worked and I claimed the distinction of being the first to land a shark on board H.M.S. Barrymore. As it came over the side it had another spell of life, it's tail lashing out and clearing everything lying loose on deck. Someone hit it several times on the head with a hammer but that only seemed to aggravate it all the more. Only after I had my picture taken with my catch did I realise that my hands were blistered by the struggle, until then I was oblivious to everything except landing a shark that weighed approximately 500lbs and measured 9ft.4 inches in length. A native, standing up in his dugout boat near the ships' side watching the whole episode, said he could help and was allowed on board. He pounced on the shark's back and swiftly severed the tail with a big knife. He wanted the fish and offered me three rupees, which suited me, providing he gave me the teeth. He expertly decapitated the fish and the lads lowered the headless and tailless monster gently into the dugout that looked too frail to take the weight. The fisherman paddled away pleased and the cook boiled the head to extract the teeth for me to keep as souvenirs.

I had enough for one day and willingly lent the tackle to someone else. Within half an hour he produced a catch that created confusion out of all proportion to it's size. It was a Hammerhead shark and although it was fairly easy to land, being half the size of mine, it was uncontrollable once it hit the deck. Someone with a warped sense of humour suggested flooding the small washroom and putting it in there 'for fun'. After plugging the drain and pumping in salt water the peculiar looking thing was dragged in snapping and lashing out, and let loose. Once it was back in water it went mad with renewed vigour. Nobody wanted to get near it, that was until the Skipper heard the noise and frivolity and came to see for himself what was going on. Anticipating the damage it could cause, he called everyone stronger things than "bloody fools" before ordering it to be got rid of immediately. There was a lack of volunteers to go in and get a hold on it and I must admit I was well down the queue. Eventually with the aid of iron bars keeping it to one side, two brave souls managed to unplug the drain and let the water out. Then followed a hilarious performance as they tried to lasso the beast by the tail. As they leapt backwards and forwards trying to avoid the threshing hammerhead it closely resembled a rainmaking ritual dance. In the end one of them got lucky and the struggling fish was pulled out and pushed over the side to live and fight another day.

The supply ship arrived soon afterwards with her holds full of wire hawsers and some of the very large concrete blocks for anchoring the anti-submarine netting to the seabed. Preparation was carried out with meticulous care to avoid the serious accident that was always waiting to happen when working with big wire. As long as 'Ethiopia' provided the equipment long hours were worked. Stripped to the waist with the sweat glistening on bronzed backs, every man Jack heaved and hauled the heavy cables to keep on schedule for completing the work. I had rarely seen team work on such a scale, as if getting the job done was a personal thing for every member of the crew. A typical day started early with Capt.Rawlings impatient to pull alongside the supply ship to take on a chunk of concrete mass that had to be 'wired up' before we set off for the dropping zone. One of the first blocks to be laid was close up to the beach at St.Annes Island, which I was informed was the women's leper colony. As we worked a large group of them, chaperoned by St.Vincent de Paul nuns, stood at the head of the beach to watch. Shouting greetings and waving they stayed for a considerable time looking on, it must have provided a welcome diversion to their normal routine on the small island.

In the evenings when work was finished the men relaxed and indulged in a variety of activities, model making being the most popular. Gnarled hands produced intricate detailed replicas of every type of ship from the times of sail to modern day warships. One chap used his expertise to put fully rigged windjammers into clear electric light bulbs after the filament had been taken out. He intended boxing them up and sending them to a deserving charity to raffle. The easy discipline allowed gambling to thrive unchecked. 'Schools' were most active on, and just after, pay days that came once a month. Being paid in the local currency of rupees gave the illusion of getting a handful of money because of the low value of the notes. It was not uncommon at weekends for a game to start in the early evening and continue through the night until breakfast the following morning. Players came and went as some ran out of money and others took their place. Meals were eaten without leaving the game, players frightened to miss a hand that might be the 'big one'. A whole months pay could disappear in one game, leaving the loser 'subbing' until the next pay day and the winners relishing the prospects of having extra to spend for the next couple of runs ashore. The tension charged atmosphere made players aware that an ill-timed comment during a game could lead to a nasty rebuke in the shape of a fist from a bad loser. Like most, I enjoyed the thrill of a gamble and in the main was pleased with my winnings. Never winning a tremendous amount neither was I ever out of pocket.

Whatever the outcome of the gambling 'schools', the team spirit never faltered with the defence system project. Each time 'Ethopia' emptied her holds, she weighed anchor and returned to the mainland to replenish the stocks needed to carry on with the work. I was always glad to see her go because it meant a welcome change in routine. The riggers still toiled with their marlinspikes and fids splicing wire and rope, but the rest of us went about the less arduous everyday maintenance. During one period of waiting for the supply ship to return, the captain decided to carry out a 'shoot' with the ships' 3" gun. This sole piece of ordnance was the main armament and looked pathetically small to be used in anger. It was a far cry from the chest high shells that came up on H.M.S. Dorsetshire's hydraulic lifts to produce ear-splitting broadsides. Captain Rawlings took 'Barrymore' away from Mahe before starting. The crew, with the bizarre spectacle of some bringing stools to sit around in a half circle to watch treated the exercise as a novelty. There was a buzz of excited anticipation when the Leading Seaman came along with a shell under his arm and put it into the breech with the charge. With no electrical firing mechanism, a percussion method was used operated by firing lanyard. When loading was completed, the lanyard was struck and a muffled bang sent the small missile flying away accompanied by a rousing cheer from the spectators. If they were impressed by today's performance what would they think if they ever saw a capital ship firing off tons and tons of steel in one salvo. Mac, the other general service lad who joined 'Barrymore' with me, sidled up and quietly whispered "Did you ever see any 'bloody' thing like that before". We both had a laugh, keeping our thoughts to ourselves. The 'shoot', over it was never repeated while I was on board, which was a shame because I enjoyed it. I made a mental note to relate the days happening the next time I sat in the gunhouse of a big ship, not that anyone would believe me.

'For everything there is a season' and at the end of November Mac and I were told to get our kit together and be on standby for drafting, it was time to return to the navy proper. An Australian sloop, H.M.A.S. Cessnock, was making a stop at Mahe to pick us up and ship us back to Mombasa. In some ways I was glad to be returning to the navy I was best suited, on the other hand I deeply regretted leaving the idyllic islands and the friends I had made amongst the crew of the 'Barrymore'. Also the people ashore who had been so kind to me during my stay, the young ladies of the French speaking Seychellois community who spoke English in the most captivating way without seeming flirtatious. I was grateful for what I had learnt and experienced during the months on the little ship. Oddities, like eating flying fish, shark and turtle steaks, approaching the ships' captain without conventional formalities, the lack of regimentation, and the lackadaisical form of dress on board. Barrymore's crew was more of a family than a ships' company. I had come to respect their seamanship and skills with wire and rope. I valued the support and unquestionable trust of loyal shipmates, even if I didn't condone the bad habits of a small minority. They were rough diamonds but with hearts of gold. When the H.M.A.S. Cessnock arrived the transfer was swift because her captain was anxious to get under way again. There was just enough time to go around everyone and say our last farewells. In this case it really was goodbye, I never came across any of them again.

The journey was uneventful although we must have deviated from a direct course to the mainland because it took much longer than I would have expected from such a fast ship. Mac and I were well treated on board and I found it easy to mix with the crew, although I preferred the company of the Tasmanians to the Australians. They were less 'loud' and foul-mouthed when holding a serious conversation. As soon as the sloop reached Mombasa, Mac and I were taken by ships' boat to the submarine depot ship, H.M.S. Adamant. Built under the 1938 Estimates she was a comparatively new ship with luxurious facilities. She was designed to provide for the needs of the submarine crews returning to port after punishing patrols. 'Adamant' was a stopgap while I waited to join the Colony Class cruiser H.M.S. Gambia as soon as she entered harbour, she was my next draft.

Whatever the outcome of the gambling 'schools', the team spirit never faltered with the defence system project. Each time 'Ethopia' emptied her holds, she weighed anchor and returned to the mainland to replenish the stocks needed to carry on with the work. I was always glad to see her go because it meant a welcome change in routine. The riggers still toiled with their marlinspikes and fids splicing wire and rope, but the rest of us went about the less arduous everyday maintenance. During one period of waiting for the supply ship to return, the captain decided to carry out a 'shoot' with the ships' 3" gun. This sole piece of ordnance was the main armament and looked pathetically small to be used in anger. It was a far cry from the chest high shells that came up on HMS. Dorsetshire's hydraulic lifts to produce ear splitting broadsides. Captain Rawlings took 'Barrymore' away from Mahe before starting. The crew, with the bizarre spectacle of some bringing stools to sit around in a half circle to watch treated the exercise as a novelty. There was a buzz of excited anticipation when the Leading Seaman came along with a shell under his arm and put it into the breech with the charge. With no electrical firing mechanism, a percussion method was used operated by firing lanyard. When loading was completed, the lanyard was struck and a muffled bang sent the small missile flying away accompanied by a rousing cheer from the spectators. If they were impressed by today's performance what would they think if they ever saw a capital ship firing off tons and tons of steel in one salvo. Mac, the other general service lad who joined 'Barrymore' with me, sidled up and quietly whispered. "Did you ever see any 'bloody' thing like that before". We both had a laugh, keeping our thoughts to ourselves. The 'shoot', over it was never repeated while I was on board, which was a shame because I enjoyed it. I made a mental note to relate the days happening the next time I sat in the gunhouse of a big ship, not that anyone would believe me.

'For everything there is a season' and at the end of November Mac and I were told to get our kit together and be on standby for drafting, it was time to return to the navy proper. An Australian sloop, H.M.A.S. Cessnock, was making a stop at Mahe to pick us up and ship us back to Mombasa. In some ways I was glad to be returning to the navy I was best suited, on the other hand I deeply regretted leaving the idyllic islands and the friends I had made amongst the crew of the 'Barrymore'. Also the people ashore who had been so kind to me during my stay, the young ladies of the French speaking Seychellois community who spoke English in the most captivating way without seeming flirtatious. I was grateful for what I had learnt and experienced during the months on the little ship. Oddities like eating flying fish, shark and turtle steaks, approaching the ships' captain without conventional formalities, the lack of regimentation, and the lackadaisical form of dress on board. Barrymore's crew was more of a family than a ships' company. I had come to respect their seamanship and skills with wire and rope. I valued the support and unquestionable trust of loyal shipmates, even if I didn't condone the bad habits of a small minority. They were rough diamonds but with hearts of gold. When the H.M.A.S. Cessnock arrived the transfer was swift because her captain was anxious to get under way again. There was just enough time to go around everyone and say our last farewells. In this case it really was goodbye, I never came across any of them again. The journey was uneventful although we must have deviated from a direct course to the mainland because it took much longer than I would have expected from such a fast ship. Mac and I were well treated on board and I found it easy to mix with the crew, although I preferred the company of the Tasmanians to the Australians. They were less 'loud' and foul-mouthed when holding a serious conversation.

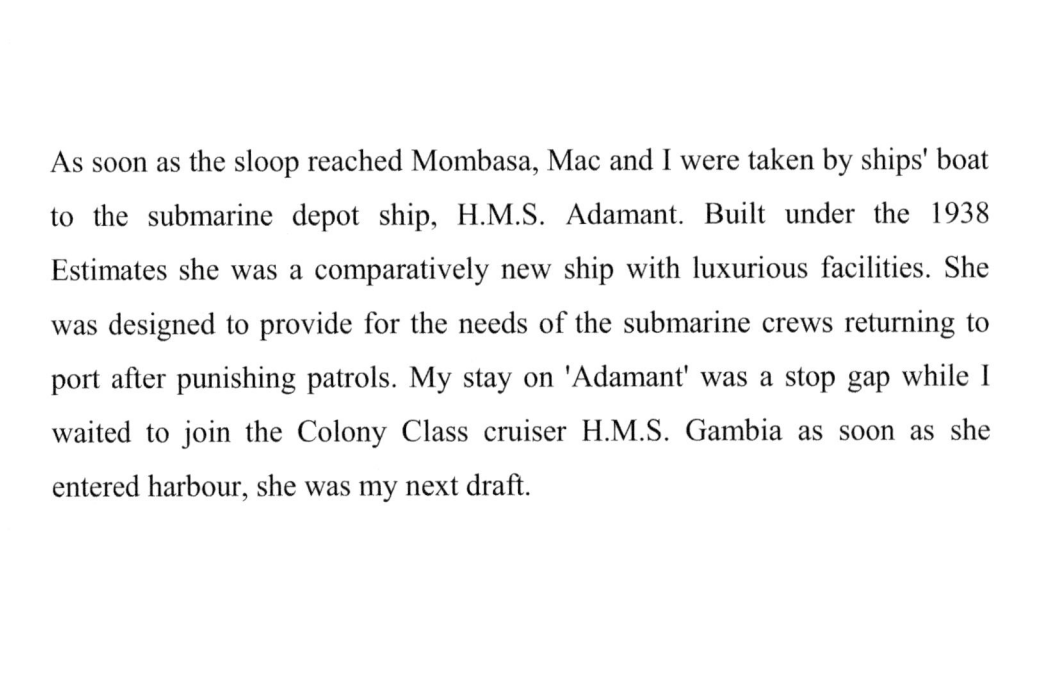

As soon as the sloop reached Mombasa, Mac and I were taken by ships' boat to the submarine depot ship, H.M.S. Adamant. Built under the 1938 Estimates she was a comparatively new ship with luxurious facilities. She was designed to provide for the needs of the submarine crews returning to port after punishing patrols. My stay on 'Adamant' was a stop gap while I waited to join the Colony Class cruiser H.M.S. Gambia as soon as she entered harbour, she was my next draft.

28 H.M.S.Gambia

When H.M.S. Gambia came up Kilindini Creek I liked what I saw, a sleek fighting ship with distinctive lines, similar to the H.M.S. Edinburgh and H.M.S. Belfast City Class cruisers. One noticeable difference was the two funnels standing upright instead of raked backwards. Four turrets, A, B, X, and Y, housed triple 6" guns, smaller than H.M.S. Dorsetshire's but later to prove very efficient. It was a comparatively new ship having completed the builder's trials in February of that year. Officially my draft to 'Gambia' took effect from December 6th. but in reality, because she was still at sea, I didn't join her until she arrived back in port on the 14th.December. On that day, with no preconceptions, I humped my hammock and kit bag on board and reported for duty. I had left Mac on the 'Adamant' and never saw him again although I have some recollection of being told he later deserted. I wondered what life would be like on a cruiser again, after my 'Harry Tate Navy' time on 'Barrymore'. Any misgivings were groundless. I slipped back into the familiar spit-and-polish routine without any effort. The smell of warm new paint and the constant sound of noisy fan motors and generators made it feel as if I had never been away. Daily orders and procedures varied little from warship and warship, and one bluejacket is much the same as another, at least to look at. 'Gambia' had it's quota of hard cases, 'rum rats', hostility onlys, lower deck lawyers, and three badge ABs of the old school who knew it all. A new face in the Mess was always a welcome diversion. It stimulated a mutual exchange of gossip and information that put fresh life into messdeck conversation. As expected, I was quizzed about the ships I had been on, to assess if I was green enough for a little micky-taking.

Being a 'stroppy', early matured, nineteen year old, I could stand my corner with most who wanted to 'swing the lamp' and talk of blue water sailing. First impressions mattered, I casually mentioned that I was an X-Ganges boy, survived the sinking of two ships, seen action against the Germans, Vichy French, Japanese, and Italians, done my share of 'sea-time', and served on a coal-burner. It was a character reference that automatically precluded me from the usual leg pulling that awaited the arrival of a 'sprog'. In return for my contribution to the messdeck chinwagging I was brought up to date with recent events on board. It was surprising to hear about the unrest during the previous months before I arrived. On Sunday, September 20th., Commander Riley pinned a notice on the board reprimanding those who had written home criticising the ships' food. The Commander reminded the crew that people back in England were not enjoying the best of food themselves. The following Saturday he 'Cleared Lower Deck' and warned the men again about putting complaints in their letters. It had to stop, in future anyone doing it would be punished. It didn't: On the 23rd.October Shipwright Rowley was charged for writing about the ship in his letters. He was sentenced to 60 days imprisonment ashore with the loss of one good conduct badge. I found the conditions palatial after the austere simplicity of the tiny 'Barrymore'. Although H.M.S. Gambia was an excellent ship in every way I didn't feel at home on her, not in the way I had felt on H.M.S. Dorsetshire. Perhaps it was because I was still unsettled, determined to get out of the navy as soon as the war was over.

During an assessment by the Divisional Officer I was asked about promotion, but refused to be considered. The Lieutenant apparently asked my Divisional Petty Officer to have a 'quiet' word with me to explain the error of my stubbornness. He fared no better and gave up in despair. His summing up said it all and the matter was closed, "I don't know what keeps your *"#Š!<+? ears apart Cannon but it can't be brains, you stupid %$!"@#Š". Not so long before, promotion had been of paramount importance to me, now it was a meaningless exercise, a reminder of other values. I did my work to the best of my ability and kept out of trouble. I steered clear of the 'awkward' squads and made a point of never agitating or teaming up with scabs and lower deck lawyers. I picked my oppos, not them pick me, which is why I ended up with Dave as a shore going pal. He and I got on like two peas in a pod and being in the same part of the watch we were able to go ashore together. We realised we had a lot in common from the start. He didn't associate with the local coloured girls, the forbidden fruit commonly referred to in the Navy at the time as 'black ham' and dangerous to get involved with. We liked saving money for the same fondness ashore; eating a big plate of eggs, peas and chips followed by a 'few' pints and a sing song. We also shared a sense of humour and enjoyed doing similar things, which always makes for a good friendship. Sometimes I thought he was as daft as a two-headed parrot but he must have seen funny sides to me as well.

On Sunday the 20th.December 1942 Admiral Tennant came on board to unfurl his flag and the next day we weighed anchor. The tropical sun beat down on the well-scrubbed decks as the crew lined up for leaving harbour, accompanied by the Indian Navy Fleet minesweeper HMIS. Bengal. A fascinating array of vessels, from the East and the West, rocked backwards and forwards from our wash as we swept past towards the sea. 'Bengal' was a proud little ship that had shown her fighting spirit a month earlier when escorting the Dutch tanker 'Ondina'. The 672 ton minesweeper sighted two 10,000 ton heavily armed Japanese commerce raiders, the Hokoku Maru and Aikoku Maru, and although greatly outgunned altered course to engage the enemy and protect the tanker. The early success of the minesweepers single gun set fire to one of the raiders, but not before the 'Ondina' was hit and set on fire. When she started to list and settle in the water the crew was forced to abandon ship and take to the lifeboats. 'Bengal' quickly returned to lay a smoke screen around the tanker before continuing the fight and forcing the damaged Japanese to disengage and withdraw. With Bengal's assistance the 'Ondini' was reboarded and stabilised, eventually making it safely into Fremantle. When the little ship returned to Kilindini the news of the gallant encounter had preceded her and the other warships cheered her in, an accolade reserved for special occasions.

Now as we put to sea we knew we were in good company. Both ships joined forces with the battleship HMS. Valiant, the carrier HMS. Illustrious, and four destroyers to carry out a series of exercises that included night encounters. Night 'shoots' always reminded me of tropical thunderstorms. The loud booming and banging of the firing resembled thunder, the gun flashes that lit up the darkness took on the facsimile of lightening. Although I found the drill fascinating to take part in I was always glad when it was over and the ship reverted to normal. On this occasion the exercises lasted two days before 'Gambia' left for Diego Suarez to refuel, arriving at the Madagascar port at 0715hrs on Thursday the 24th.December (Christmas Eve). The Vichy French naval port had been the scene of a combined Allied landing earlier in the year as the first stage of occupying Madagascar. 'Gambia' had taken part in two subsequent operations transporting troops to consolidate the invasion to thwart Japanese plans of using the base to attack the vital trade routes through the Mozambique Channel. While Madagascar remained under the control of the Vichy French government there was a constant danger that the Japanese, with the help of Vichy sympathisers, would use the facilities on Madagascar. Subsequently, the invasion codename operation 'Ironside' was put into effect to secure the island and safeguard the supply lines to the Middle and Far East. As 'Gambia' picked her way carefully around the obstacles on her way to the refuelling tanker the funnels and masts sticking up out of the water was evidence of the assault on the port. Two Vichy warships were sunk along with merchant ships during the previous operations. I was told by a reliable source that some scuttled to avoid capture by the Allies. As soon as the fuel oil was taken on board 'Gambia' cast off and returned to sea to relieve H.M.S. Frobisher of two troopships while she came into port to refuel.

Friday December 25th.1942 was yet another Christmas Day at sea for me, not that it mattered, it wasn't the time or the place for funny hats and crackers. At 06.30 hrs. the hands stood to for dawn action stations with a lack of enthusiasm for it being a special day. After breakfast, the normal routine of cleaning the messdeck by the off duty watch was finished before a chapel was rigged up in the aircraft hanger. Divine Service with Holy Communion was held for the ships' company at 1000hrs, excluding 'Holy Romans' and Jews. The Roman Catholics had an informal prayer meeting of their own in the recreation space, I couldn't say where the Jews disappeared to. After the service, as a special concession, the watch below were allowed to 'Pipe Down'. To mark the occasion Captain Mansleigh provided an issue of nuts, previously shipped in at Colombo. Before we had a chance to enjoy the little treat a warning was broadcast saying they were infested with grubs and not eat them. At 1300hrs. 'Frobisher' caught up with us and three days later two destroyers also joined us. Their presence signified the political importance of protecting the troopships against attack. They were laden with South African servicemen, the first to return home on leave from the Middle East. The precaution was fully justified soon after the destroyers took up their stations when a positive ASDIC sounding sent us scurrying to 'Action Stations'. Twisting and turning at speed the escorts churned up foaming wakes as they circled, probing and dropping patterns of highly explosive depth charges. After an hour the concentrated attack was called off when the captains were satisfied the enemy submarine was destroyed. The next day the alarm bells had us again scrambling to First Degree Readiness when a Flying Boat on patrol sighted an unidentified submarine on the surface ahead of the convoy. 'Gambia' turned on the speed and dealt with the now submerged enemy in a most efficient and thorough way, leaving the course of the other ships unaltered as they made their way to Durban. When we arrived there at 1800hrs. on Thursday the 31st.December we received a rousing welcome. News had spread like wildfire that the ships were carrying South Africans, their returning heroes. The local people showed their joy with an emotional homecoming that was overwhelming.

On January 9th. 'Gambia' accompanied by H.M.S. Frobisher, nine transporters and a destroyer escort, sailed majestically out of Durban on a northerly course. The stay in port had given me the opportunity to renew a few past acquaintances and enjoy the unstinting hospitality of the Victoria

League Club. Two days later on the 11th, I reached the ripe old age of 20. I didn't bother to mention it to the others, on reflection it might have been difficult to find someone interested in my birthday. Other things taking place were more important than hearing someone wish me a happy birthday. When the convoy decided to split up, 'Frobisher' and two destroyers took four of the troop ships leaving 'Gambia' on her own with the other five. The rest of the escort wheeled around and after blowing a cheeky farewell returned to Durban; the lucky devils. Unperturbed, our reduced in size convoy sedately continued it's passage with nothing to report out of the ordinary, until the 14th. The day started like all the others at sea when the crew mustered for dawn actions stations at 0505hrs. At 0700hrs. the ships' Commander was found unconscious by his orderly. Despite the efforts of the surgeons, his sudden death at 1000hrs from a stroke was received with some disbelief. As preparations were underway for his immediate burial a call came in for medical assistance for a native soldier on the 'Cap de Tourane', one of the ships in the convoy. The captain quickly responded and ordered the 2nd. whaler to be lowered to bring the soldier and an interpreter to the cruiser. As soon as the transfer was completed 'Gambia' increased speed and rejoined the convoy. At 17.07 hrs. the engines were again stopped and Commander Riley was committed to the deep with full naval honours. His cemetery was the Indian Ocean and his plot approximately 15 degrees South. 43 degrees East. I never got used to the eerie atmosphere surrounding a burial at sea. Watching the canvas covered body slide down the plank into the water with a splash of farewell always left me with a knot in the stomach, I think I took it too personal.

Reality soon returned as another day drew to a close. At 1837hrs., with the light fading, 'Action Stations' sounded, followed ten minutes later by the call to 'Darken Ship'. Then the ships' company settled to normal watchkeeping hoping for an uneventful evening. The next morning the convoy was turned over to H.M.S. Ramatura and we returned at speed to Kilindini. Admiral Tennant came on board with his staff and 'Gambia' left, this time with a small armada of warships for gunnery exercises. These lasted for two days then it was back to the Creek to offload the 'top brass'. We didn't see him again until the 28th. when he came back on board and we put to sea for another 'shoot' and night exercises with 'Frobisher' and 'Devonshire'. The ship seemed to be in and out of Mombasa like a runaway yo-yo, with the Admiral coming and going as if he couldn't make up his mind to stay or leave. His presence added another dimension to the tension below decks. It was a constant worry that he might find something amiss, particularly when he did his rounds of inspection to see if 'Gambia' lived up to it's flagship status. On the Saturday after the Admiral's arrival, Stoker Cottingham, for sensitive reasons that need not be mentioned here received six days detention in the ships' cells.

The cells must be one of the most sterile and inhospitable places on a seagoing ship. They were mainly for short stay confinement, anything longer than a couple of weeks usually meant the defaulter going to a Provost Establishment ashore. I was not too familiar with the 'brigs' on H.M.S.Gambia but I was well acquainted with the same type of cage-like lock-up on H.M.S.Dorsetshire. Not from the viewpoint of an inmate but from my many visits accompanying the Commander on his inspections when I was his messenger.

The bare interior of the well-scrubbed cells consisted of a board for sleeping and sitting, and a latrine bucket. The only reading material allowed at the time was the bible, which prisoners made full use of to relieve the boredom. It was often said you could detect habitual offenders from their extensive knowledge of the holy book when religious matters were discussed. Besides studying the scriptures and reflecting on the errors of their ways, prisoners had a daily task to perform, picking Oakum. This was a piece of stiff tarred hemp or manila rope that had to be unpicked and teased for caulking the seams between the deck planking. Hot pitch was poured into the seams before the fibres were rammed down between the planks with a caulking iron and a heavy hammer. Picking Oakum was slow, tedious, and extremely hard on the fingers, the only tools provided. The naval authorities had no intention of letting a custodial sentence be seen as a respite from shipboard duties. Watched over every hour night and day by a Marine sentry, a prisoner was permitted out on deck in his white canvas suit for a limited period of exercise. After the ritual of emptying his latrine bucket he was allowed to pace backwards and forwards in silence on the fo'scle under the watchful eyes of his guard. No doubt Stoker Cottingham would deliberate on his misdemeanour, the cause of his punishment, and the black mark on his record sheet. He might console himself with the fact that he was not the first or likely to be the last to be incarcerated on board H.M.S. Gambia.

Except for the drills and exercises, nothing much happened to ease the monotony of patrolling the trade routes until we arrived at Adu Atoll on Sunday 7th.February to join up with an impressive collection of liners that arrived from the war zones of North Africa. They included the 'Queen Mary',

'Acquitania', 'Ile de France', 'Nieuw Amsterdam', and the AMC Queen of Bermuda. Code named 'Pamphlet' the convoy was carrying the 9th.Australian Division home for some well-earned leave. Twenty-four hours later we sailed with the convoy and an escort of two destroyers and three corvettes. H.M.S.Devonshire also joined the convoy with an additional three ships. Soon the islands disappeared astern and we were out in the sea lanes heading south. It gave rise to a lot of speculative rumour, fuelled by the lower deck sages. We didn't have long to wait, away from land the captain informed the ships' company that we were staying with the convoy all the way to Fremantle in Western Australia. After another days steaming, the destroyers broke station and returned to port, leaving the two cruisers and the AMC to guard the convoy. I realised how well the waters in the area were patrolled when we passed the battleship H.M.S.Warspite and the cruiser H.M.S.Mauritius, albeit it didn't stop the enemy sinking ships.

The convoy barely had time to settle down to cruising stations before the weather worsened, blowing rough, and continued to do so all the way to Fremantle. Two days from landfall a Dutch cruiser and two Dutch destroyers came to join the convoy for extra protection. Early in the morning of Friday 18th. the ship was already closed up for dawn stations when the drone of an aircraft increased the alertness of the A/A gunners but it turned out to be friendly. Things really got under way after breakfast when the messdecks were thoroughly scrubbed clean and the upper deck hosed down. When the PVs' (Paravanes) were streamed, a necessary precaution against enemy mines being laid in the harbour approaches, I realised that Australian terra firma was not very far away. From the shellrooms to the crows-nest a general sense of goodwill and excitement prevailed throughout the ship fuelled by the prospect of shore leave in Fremantle. The hundreds of men on board set about their specific duties for entering harbour and securing the ship with a well practised order and disciplined routine that needed very little officer supervision.

When the paravanes were later recovered, the big ships steamed down the swept channel in line ahead formation. I could well imagine the flurry of activity on the troopships as the Australian soldiers waited impatiently to be with their loved ones. At 1335hrs. 'Gambia' passed through the boom and everything became uncannily still. After ten storm-tossed days it was a pleasant relief to have crockery staying on the tables without having to be held to stop it crashing to the deck.

Ten minutes later 'Devonshire' followed ahead of the armed merchant cruiser Queen of Bermuda. The troop carriers, now in the safe care of the port authorities, were no longer our responsibility. Sailors, smartly turned out, lined the decks fore and aft as H.M.S.Gambia nosed her way up the Swan River. The Marine band struck up 'Hearts of Oak' as people crowded on to the quayside to wave. It was painfully obvious that most of the ships along the waterfront were flying the Stars and Stripes, it emphasizing the growing American influence in Australia. The White Ensign fluttered proudly from Gambia's stern to remind the people of the Mother country and their roots. As she edged towards her berth, 'H' shed close by the railway bridge that spanned the river just outside Fremantle, a passenger train crossing the bridge came to a halt and blew several whistles in greeting. Passengers opened the carriage windows to cheer and wave, as if we were a relief column arriving at a besieged city. I think everyone on deck was taken aback by the unexpectedly warm reception, especially after being warned to expect a hostile reaction. When the train resumed it's journey it left us totally bewildered by the demonstration of affection. Like my shipmates I was unaware at the time that our popularity was partly due to an undercurrent of resentment against the American servicemen dominating so much of the local life and economy with their spending power.

Trades people enjoyed the mini-boom but everyday folk begrudged the preferential treatment the affluent Yanks could buy with their 'goodwill' allowances. One instance of this was the block booking of taxis to ship huge numbers of US servicemen into town at the beginning of their liberty. Locals were unable to find a cab when they needed one because the drivers concentrated on the lucrative dockside trade. In isolation this might seem a trivial thing to get annoyed about, but collectively with the many other small irritations it produced a backlash against the Doughboys. Another vexation was the hoards of young ladies who jettisoned their Australian boyfriends for Americans, to enjoy the rich pickings that were plentiful and easily available. The Aussie males could not compete with the over generous sailors.

According to what I was told later, it applied to a large proportion of the local female population who were determined not to miss out on the cornucopia of rings, watches and expensive jewellery. The Yanks had so much to give materially for the return of the usual 'favours'. The animosity it created worked to our benefit, with our pay we were never likely to be a threat to anyone. The girls who went out with our lads didn't do it for money or presents, as least I don't think they did. Unfairly the more envious local 'joeys' put down the American's insatiable need for female company to sexual promiscuity.

As soon as Gambia 'made fast' a delegation of town dignitaries came on board to exchange greetings and partake of the usual Wardroom hospitality. It must have gone down well because the next day invitations arrived for members of the crew to spend a few days leave with families. Dave and myself went to a Mr. and Mrs. Coles in Fremantle. He was a Customs Officer and they had two teenage sons a little younger than us. We were treated like two of the family and felt at home the moment we moved in. The sons were eager to show us the best things in the district and especially the water sports that took place most days on the beach. Being reasonably good swimmers we could join in without showing ourselves up. H.M.S. Devonshire returned to sea after forty-eight hours, leaving 'Gambia' to enjoy the benefits of being the flagship of the 4th.Cruiser Squadron with an Admiral and staff on board.

The three days flashed past and it was back to the ship to let someone else have a break. With so much to see and do Dave and I took ever opportunity to go ashore and get to know more of Fremantle and Perth. Forewarned that we might be called 'Pomms' or 'Pommie Bastards' depending on the standard of a persons vocabulary, the crew were not unduly perturbed by name calling. It was important to make allowances for those were direct descendents of felonious 'blacksheep' and convicts.

Fortunately the nastiest remarks were confined mainly to the bars where alcohol stimulated the 'dutch' courage necessary to make the jibes. The natural wit and repartee of the British sailors quickly responded, giving as much as they got. In reply to contemptuous remarks, the Aussies were reminded that they were 'sons of convicts' and we nicknamed them 'kippers', meaning two-faced and no guts. I have to admit it didn't always go down too well, even when it was said in jest. Happily, any clashes didn't arise when we mixed with the more respectable families.

The language of the colonials was easy to understand, being a form of English, but the colloquialisms were hard to grasp at first. 'Cobber', 'Dinkum', 'Schooners' and every girl called Sheila or 'Cow' were easy enough but the Australian tendency to abbreviate everything over four letters was perplexingly difficult to comprehend.

Although most of our crew were reasonably well acclimatized, with skins hardened by the tropical sun and salt air, a large number were badly bitten by mosquitoes that caused dreadful swelling around the eyes. Luckily they were not the malaria carrying type that I had experienced in East Africa. Apart from the 'mossies' everyone remarked how enjoyable the visit was going, a few spoke about emigrating there after the war but it might have been just talk.

In later years I was asked about contrasting types of people I had met on my travels. Without hesitation I could justifiably say that the kindest and most gentle were the Maya Indians of the Yucatan, the coarsest and crudest were without doubt the Australians of the time I was there. At a social evening in the Catholic church hall, Dave and I introduced ourselves to a couple of attractive young ladies. They came from neighbouring families and after getting the seal of approval from the Mums and Dads, we were invited home. It was suggested that the next time we called, the girls should take us to the tennis club in Fremantle. I was a bit apprehensive and openly confessed I had never played real tennis. Dave said he had played 'quite a bit' and I was assured it didn't matter, there were other things to do at the club. If I did want to try my hand the girls would look after me, and besides it was only for fun.

On the way back to the ship Dave convinced me he could handle a racquet and not to worry, I could leave it to him to sort things out. Afterwards I cogitated on my gullibility not to have realised he couldn't have played serious tennis. It never dawned on me at the time that he was showing off to impress the girls, going through the motions with no intention of playing. Eventually he admitted his lack of tennis skills but assured me he would come up with a plausible excuse for us to wriggle out of playing. A few days later we met the girls again and went to the club carrying our gym shoes, shorts and a towel as a token of our good intentions. The 'Sheilas' brought a couple of spare tennis racquets and a good supply of balls. After a lot of Aussie back-slapping and amiable greetings we signed the visitors book and got changed. I was anxiously waiting for Dave's opt out plan to rescue us from a catastrophic situation, but nothing was happening. He seemed to be leaving it very late to do his limping routine, especially when we ended up having a knock-about with the girls on an outer court. Then the Secretary came to tell us that we were down to play two young lads on an inner court. My knees didn't exactly play a tune but I was alarmed at the prospect of getting involved in a proper game. When I saw the two youngsters I felt much better, their tender age and diminutive size made the odds more attractive in our favour and boosted my morale. Dave decided we should play, now that he had seen the opposition. According to him it was a no-go contest, just a matter of making mincemeat of them.

Dave kicked off but the ball came back like a bullet, too fast for me to get to it. He served again and in a vain attempt to hit the return I collided with him and we both ended up on the deck. The spectators, increasing by the minute to see the slaughter of two 'Pommie Goliaths' by the pipsqueak 'Aussie Davids', thought it very funny. The young lads had us running around aimlessly, like a pair of headless chickens. The final humiliation came at the end when Dave decided to do the 'proper' thing and jump the net to shake hands with the winners. He took off alright but caught his foot in the mesh and crashed down on the other side. The place erupted with shrieks of laughter at the the undignified spectacle, I wanted the ground to open up and swallow me. Beating a hasty retreat to the shower room I intended leaving the club as quickly and as quietly as possible, preferably without Dave and the girls. He was in another cubicle making all kinds of conciliatory utterances that fell on stony ground. On the way out I was stopped by the Secretary who invited me to the bar for a drink. At the risk of being seen as a bad loser I had no option but to accept. When we entered the lounge, followed by Dave and the girls, we got a rousing cheer. Then we were told that the two youngsters we had played against were in fact schoolboy champions destined for big things in the tennis world. We had been set up and the girls had been in on it from the start. I saw the funny side to the whole episode but, disregarding the pleas of those who had been onlookers and now wanting to see more of the same, I declined the offer of a rematch. Dave and I were invited to visit the club any time we were ashore, and not necessarily to play tennis. Apparently we were seen as good sports and accepted as 'cobbers' by the members.

Normally by stealth and long practise I kept my nose clean and out of trouble on board ship, but not so on one occasion in Fremantle. It was close to midday when I lowered my bosun's chair to 'B' gundeck and finished painting. Looking up admiringly at the shining paintwork, all the way down from the wheelhouse, I was joined by a seaman Petty Officer. It was someone I hadn't worked with before, from another part of the ship. He studied my handiwork before asking what I intended doing next. "Just finished P.O., I'm watch ashore so I'll get cleaned up". "I don't think so. You've missed an up and down stroke half way down. Go back up and do the lot again". I was thunderstruck, it meant going down over wet paint and getting covered in it. Scrutinising the whole section carefully I couldn't see anything wrong with the finished job and I protested in the strongest possible way at his fault finding bloody-mindedness, implying he was a 'prat'. His answer was to march me aft to the Quarter Deck and report me to the Officer of the Day for insubordination. When asked to reply to the charge I explained the situation, denying I refused to carry out the order but merely questioned the incredulous instruction to work down over fresh paint, making a terrible mess of the most viewed part of the ship. Before putting me into the Commander's Report the young Sub-Lieutenant decided to see for himself what it was all about and went for'ard to look. In silence he meticulously inspected the area before passing judgement. As a face-saving compromise for the Petty Officer's muddle-headedness he pointed to a place at the very bottom and said "Just touch it up there". I tried hard to suppress a smile, the spot he picked out was easy to reach standing on the deck and was nowhere near where the PO claimed it needed repainting.

The 'Subbie' realised the charge was an unwarranted figment of the doolally imagination of a vindictive bonehead, but he was duty bound to be seen to support the PO. I went through the motions of touching-up the paintwork and the officer nodded his approval and told me to dismiss and get cleaned up. As I walked away I overheard him say to the Petty Officer "I want a few words with you later". Careful not to be a bellwether for others I never, in the normal course of events, challenged authority or discipline. Nevertheless, when unjustified malicious conduct by those in charge affected me personally I was not afraid to sort it out, officially or unofficially.

As far as the authorities were concerned the incident was over and the matter closed, but not by me. I would come across the insufferable bastard ashore at some future time and the issue would be put to rest when he got his comeuppance.

29 Beating the Retreat

The crew had created a lot of goodwill during the stay in Western Australia. We got off to a good start with the local community who saw 'Gambia' as the guardian angel that protected the ships bringing their men safely home from the war. Inevitably preparations got under way for us to leave and return to the more dangerous areas of the sea. On the day of leaving, the Royal Marine band accompanied by a Guard of Honour, marched into the town centre playing stirring tunes. It was the ships' way of saying thank you and farewell as crowds gathered to listen to the music. Marching back to the ship the Marines gave a heart-rendering display of 'Beating the Retreat' to loud appreciation from a large number of people that followed the band, right down to the dockside. H.M.S. Gambia slowly drew away from the quayside to the cheers and waves of hundreds of well-wishers who had turned out to see us off. Sirens wailed, hooters reverberated, and steam whistles screeched as the ship conned her way down the Swan River to the open sea, it was an emotional send off. All too soon it was back to the routine of watchkeeping and drills to get us back on our toes. Once over the horizon the pledges of everlasting love and affection with the possibility of a gold band on the finger, the promises of avidly penned correspondence, the vows of celibacy until meeting again, were forgotten. For most, the names of the girls they loved so truly would be hard to recall by the following week. The general chatter was more about the number of possible unborn children left behind, the amount of booze consumed at the shanty-roaring evenings in the beer joints, and the number of Aussies floored in fights. Some were gracious enough to comment on the nice surroundings and the generosity of the people we stayed with, but that was well astern.

Captain Mansleigh was determined to remove any apathy or slackness from our association with shore life, he ordered prolonged exercises in all departments including a full shoot of the main and secondary armament. When it was completed to his satisfaction, and volumes of rich language from the gunhouse 'captains', the ship took up station to shadow the Queen of Bermuda escorting a northbound convoy. The lads were elated when it was announced we were to dock in Durban on the 17th.March. I put the good news down to the luck of the Irish because it fell on St. Patrick's Day. The joy turned to disappointment when the captain announced a change of destination. We were going to Kilindini instead with a stop over enroute to refuel in Mauritius. The passage went without incident except for the usual 'flaps' and interceptions. 'Gambia' chased one unidentified ship with every hope of it being a German or Japanese supply vessel. Unfortunately it turned out to be the Abraham Lincoln, an American merchantman sailing from Fremantle to Abadan, another of many disappointments. All in all as commissions go I felt happy with the way this one was progressing. The patrolling was monotonous, broken only by the alarm bells that always rang at the most inopportune times, too often when I was just coming off watch and ready to get my head down. Every call out created a certain amount of tension with the possibility of attack from a submarine or disguised surface raider.

Now and again my thoughts turned to home but it was an extravagance unbecoming a twenty year old 'sheelback'. It was an indulgence that could produce homesickness and was best put out of ones mind. We put into Mauritius and went alongside an oiler to take on fuel. The stay was just long enough to allow one watch to have a run ashore and this time Port Watch got lucky with liberty granted from 1300hrs until 1800hrs. They made the most of it, judging by the inebriated state of the returning Jacks the local brew was very strong or they drained the island dry of alcohol. Normally, anyone coming back on board jibbering or staggering could expect to end up on a charge. On this occasion the numbers involved and the possible terminal embarrassment with a Flag Officer on board, called for a measure of discretionary clemency. Wisely, the Commander suggested turning a 'blind eye' unless things got out of hand. Gangway sentries duly showed an enforced indifference to anyone hauling themselves inboard with difficulty. No action was taken against remarks for them to 'get knotted' from exuberant tanked-up sailors enjoyed a rare relaxing of discipline. There would be another day and another place when retribution would be exacted for the caustic remarks. Those of us on duty had the thankless job of persuading the pie-eyed merry-makers to be ushered for'ard and out of sight as quickly, and as quietly, as possible. H.M.S.Gambia cast off early the next morning with a noticeable lack of chatter. Many of the Port Watch were feeling decidedly tender after their high jinks ashore. Those like me who had to deal with the near drunks the night before were hoping for deep swells and choppy waters to help the recovering revellers spew their breakfasts over the guardrails.

When I sighted the island of Aldabra on the 16th. I knew we were getting near our destination and sure enough we arrived the next day in Mombasa. Now it was my turn to go ashore and self consciously walk down Salim Street remembering the time the 'Dorsetshire' survivors were forced to go shoplifting to preserve their dignity. One particular day, draft notices started to appear on the boards causing more than a little consternation, there were bound to be winners and losers. Although nothing had been said officially it was openly discussed that 'Gambia' would soon be returning to the U.K. The lucky ones staying with the ship would be going home, draftees going to ships remaining on station were put on standby to await the arrival of their replacements. Messdeck conversation changed from the everyday seafaring trivia to one of serious discussion. The likelihood of being on any subsequent lists was a matter of concern to some. To me it flew in the face of logic to split up a crew already melded into a well-oiled, efficiently integrated fighting machine. The ship was just 14 months into her first commission and changes were being made. It didn't make sense, but mine was not to reason why.

The next couple of weeks were an endless round of Fleet exercises involving every aspect of the ships' weaponery, including torpedos and aircraft. I thought we had finished when the battleship H.M.S.Resolution left for England but on the 4th.May 1943 H.M.S.Gambia put to sea to continue firing practise before starting the first stage of a long voyage home. Steaming southwards there was another three day shoot that left my ears ringing from the din. Then the ship unexpectedly returned to Mombasa, much to the crew's surprise. It turned out the C in C had been taken sick and Admiral Tennant was going ashore to take charge. In some ways it was a bonus for the lower deck, there was too much forelock touching and genuflecting by the upward mobile young officers when the top brass was on board. It made for a much too 'pusser' a ship that could be a pain in the 'butt'. We sailed again after breakfast the next day as more draft notices on the board caused another buzz of gossip and speculation. Cutting through the Mozambique Channel 'Gambia' went into Durban and tied up at Maydon Wharf, leaving again for Capetown just as our sister ship H.M.S. Kenya arrived.

Outside the harbour the captain issued a warning that U-boats were reported in the vicinity. Lookouts were told to be 'on their toes' at all times, especially at dawn when the ship was silhouetted in the early morning light. Thankfully nothing happened to cause any undue alarm and the journey went without mishap. When the ship tied up in Simonstown, five vans pulled up on the harbourside closely watched over by a strong Royal Marine guard and a squad of local detectives. Under their careful scrutiny wooden crates were unloaded and hoisted inboard. Word got out that the boxes contained gold bar in excess of £3.000.000, an astronomical amount at present day value. Once the bullion was safely stowed the mooring lines were cast off and 'Gambia' rounded the Cape into the Atlantic Ocean heading north. Buzzes continued to fly around the ship thick and fast speculating on the likelihood of returning to the UK, why else would we be carrying gold in a northerly direction. As I watched Table Mountain disappearing in the distance I wondered if I would ever see it again. When it was announced that the next port of call would be Bathurst, 400 miles above Freetown, I was certain we were making our way home. In preparation for the visit Captain Mansleigh appealed to the ships' company to adopt a courteous and friendly attitude towards the Gambian people, both ashore and on board the ship. They had already collected £700 for our immediate comforts and, at a later date, for a permanent reminder of their relationship with the ship. £200 had been spent, mainly on sports gear for us. In view of this the captain asked everyone to make every effort to show their appreciation and foster a pride in the ship named after Britain's oldest colony by behaving in an exemplary manner at all times.

Life on board soon fell into a steady routine with seemingly few people changing their duties once the ship was under way. Steaming through the clammy Doldrums and on towards the Equator the lookouts strained their eyes, particularly during the early morning and evening gloom for the slightest thing unusual. This was U-boat hunting ground where Allied shipping was sent to the bottom of the ocean at an alarming rate. H.M.S. Gambia arrived on schedule at Bathurst (now Banjul) the capital of Gambia to make the goodwill stop. It was obvious the mooring facilities were totally inadequate for a vessel the size and weight of the cruiser. Additional hawsers had to be manhandled up the street leading from the beach and tied to palm trees. Initial efforts proved a failure, when the ship moved with the tide it uprooted the trees. Extra lines and firmer palms resolved the problem and the ship was opened to the general public, which was an unusual event in wartime. First on board, in a blaze of brightly coloured costumes, came the local Head Chiefs and self-important 'big-wigs' accompanied by their retinues. Then came the hordes of lesser mortals from the Mandinka, Jolof, Fula and Jolo tribes to swarm all over the ship like a plague of locust. Talking to the locals I was amused to learn that they genuinely thought they owned the ship because they had subscribed money to it.

For security reasons all sensitive areas were closed off and most of the not so sensitive places as well. Sentries strategically positioned watched carefully to make sure the natives didn't 'collect' souvenirs as they wandered aimlessly about satisfying their curiosity. A large party of native drummers took up position along the foreshore in front of the ship beating out ear-splitting rhythms of welcome. The monotonous throb was bearable for the first few hours but it became intolerable as it continued late into the night, so too was the language the sailors used to express their feelings about the din. Dawn brought little respite as the drumming started up again. Fortunately it came to a stop when the Bishop of Gambia and a choir arrived for a service that included the blessing the ship. Then the Governor of Gambia came on board to add his two pennyworth by making a typical speech suited to the occasion. In addition to the goodwill call, H.M.S. Gambia took on board Sir Hugh Stevens the Governor of Sierra Leone for passage to England, although we didn't know this when he embarked. A party of seamen had the dubious pleasure of a trip up the river Gambia on a local steam boat to see the original white settlement. I didn't want to go, preferring to take in the scenery from the comfort of the fo'castle capstan. Judging from the number of Sunderland Flying Boats I could see moored in the estuary, Gambia was an important base for the RAF. Strategically, the flying boats were ideally placed to give the convoys cover, vital against the ever present threat from Italian and German submarines off the African coast.

After two days in port we said our farewells and thankfully put to sea. Only then did the captain confirm over the speaker system, that we were on course for Liverpool to dock in Cammell Lairds. Sceptics said they would believe it when they saw the windows of the Liver Buildings. The vast majority of us were not so disbelieving and couldn't wait to get home. The next week dragged on slowly, although it wasn't without incident. There was the everyday alerts for one reason or another I had come to expect at sea. On the

Monday, June 7th., the gunners got a chance for some target practise when a suspicious object was sighted some distance away and we closed for action. It didn't instantly dive and was soon ruled out as a possible submarine, in fact it turned out to be an abandoned raft. I often wondered what happened to the many rafts and boats that littered the seas after ships were torpedoed. This raft was quickly destroyed with a burst of gunfire and everyone carried on with their work. Later in the day at 1915hrs. two submarines were sighted on the surface ahead of the ship. When they spotted us they knew what to expect and crash-dived to escape. Travelling at speed 'Gambia' cut between the last sightings on the surface and fired off depth charges. The ocean thundered, sending up giant fountains of water as the sea erupted from the explosions. With £3,000,000 in gold and the Governor of Sierra Leone on board the captain decided it prudent not to take risks by hanging about, he kept going as fast as he could away from the area, a decision that pleased us all. Picking up survivors was far from our minds with the thoughts of leave and family reunions. One could only imagine the terror we were inflicting on the enemy submariners down below, but sentimental considerations are rare in wartime. The day after the attack the captain spoke to the crew again to say the schedule had been changed. Instead of making directly for Liverpool, we were altering course to shadow a convoy out from Gibraltar for the next twenty-four hours. Afterwards the ship would make a call at Plymouth to refuel before going on to dock in Liverpool. This suited me fine with the odds-on chance of getting overnight leave, and quite a few others as well who had homes in the Plymouth area.

Wednesday the 9th: We picked up the convoy of 76 ships and took up station. On Thursday, torpedo carrying enemy aircraft also found the convoy and tried to get close enough to attack with their 'tin fish'. 'Gambia' opened fire with everything it had, joined by all the guns on the other ships. The strong barrage beat off the attack without loss but the possibility of further attacks meant everyone staying on full alert. In fact having a 'pop' at the enemy planes was a welcome break to ease the daily monotony. Friday the 11th: At 2200hrs. 'Gambia' left the convoy and set a course for Plymouth, arriving at 1400hrs. on the 12th. Before turning upriver to berth, there was the exhilarating sensation of passing the breakwater and seeing clearly the people watching on Plymouth Hoe. Like a homesick schoolboy I felt pangs of emotion at surviving to return home. I started to think back to the youngsters maimed and drowned on 'Dorsetshire' that would never be coming home, I was one of the lucky survivors. Except for their families they were just an official number to be soon forgotten. Nobody was going to get over excited about an extra few hundred corpses on the seabed far away from home, certainly not the politicians.

Fortunately H.M.S. Gambia's return to 'Guzz' coincided with summertime, a bonus for sailors returning to the British climate from the tropics. It gave them a fighting chance to get properly acclimatised before the cold weather set in. The gold from South Africa was quickly taken ashore, apparently unnoticed by the crew. I casually asked around if anyone had seen it go but nobody I spoke to had. Luckily I was watch ashore on the day we arrived and I was granted all night leave. Weeks before I had made myself a smaller version of a canvas kit bag and packed it with the presents for the family, regretting the loss of my other souvenirs when H.M.S.Dorsetshire was sunk. After a Custom's check I lost no time getting to the station to catch the train to Torquay. A thousand and one thoughts flooded my mind as the train clickety-clacked away the few miles. The old 'flames' would need a little charming and a few plausible excuses to explain my lack of letter writing. With any luck they would have married by now or taken up with a 'Yank', either way I wouldn't have to face them. My eyes stayed glued to the carriage window as I savoured the familiar scenes of the South Devon countryside. If nothing else, this was worth fighting for. The cows and sheep grazing peacefully in the fields made the war seem a long way away, in reality it was very close for civilians and servicemen alike with the bombing.

After a change of buses from Torre Station into town and out the other way I stood at the front door, straightened my uniform, stood tall, and pressed the bell. It never entered my head there would not be someone at home to welcome me. When Mother opened the door she was speechless, unusual for her. It was obvious I was the last person she expected to be confronted with, which was understandable. The day before a letter I had written from Australia had arrived and the family assumed I was still down-under, beneath the Southern Cross. Instead here was the sailor boy home from the sea and as ever ready for a meal. As always Mother got her priorities right. After the hugging and kissing she immediately reached for the large frying pan and started cooking me something. Later when the rest of the family arrived the 'front' room sounded more like a bear garden with everyone talking at the same time asking, and answering, questions. If the short time at home was a sample of what I could expect when I returned for a weeks leave, then it couldn't come quick enough. Mother fussed over me like a loving hen with a new chick, Father wanted to know everything about everything, and the rest of the family asked ceaseless questions about the places I had been. The pleasure of distributing the presents made me feel like a latter day Santa Claus, and I loved it.

There was an air raid during the evening but no bombs were dropped. Father, considered to be an authority on such matters, adjudged the bombers were just passing over their intended target this time would be either Plymouth or Exeter. His war service had been in France and Germany during the First World War with the Army but he had a good working knowledge of the other Services, especially the Navy. Having been born in the naval town of Devonport, his insight into the Senior Service was remarkable at times. An avid reader of books, coupled with a retentive memory, he was an formidable debater on issues that affected the country. His two pet hates were Americans and Winston Churchill. He had a low opinion of the man he thought had achieved position and power by privilege and not with brains. According to him Churchill was responsible for the mismanagement of the Allied Forces during the First War when thousands of lives were lost unnecessarily in botched campaigns such as the Dardanelles. Strangely enough I also heard this opinion of Churchill voiced for the same reason when I was in Australia. The Anzacs suffered terrible losses from the expedition that was irresponsibly prepared and badly carried out. I never argued, suspecting that Father resented the high society Churchill had been born into, a life that differed dramatically from his own humble origins. Pictures of the Prime Minister smoking big cigars, when tobacco was scarce was another annoying factor. Father loved his pipe but could never get enough to fill it and was suspicious of those who could.

The evening at home didn't allow me time to do much except enjoy the company of the family and exchange pleasantries with the neighbours. There would be opportunities to sample the delights of the town and it's activities when I came back soon on a weeks leave. Mother had me up early the next morning to enjoy a good breakfast before I set off back to the ship. The train was forced to stop just outside Plymouth and everyone had to get off to finish the journey by bus, the line had been damaged by enemy aircraft. It was only as the buses picked their way around mounds of smouldering rubble that I realised what a terrible bashing Plymouth must have had during the night. The centre of the city looked a devastated shambles with rescue workers busily going around and through the debris, putting out fires and looking for casualties. Devonport, when I got to it, appeared to have favoured better this time, all the roads were open to traffic. My good fortune to have escaped the unpleasant events of the night did not go unnoticed. I got to the top of the gangway, remembering to turn aft and salute, to be greeted by comments of " You jammy '*Š#@* " from a group of weary eyed matelots. " We've been up all night while you've been in your bloody flea bag ". I gave them all a sympathetic and compassionate reply befitting a sailor. " Bloody hard luck Jan, my heart bleeds for each and every one of you". Down in the Mess I got the full story of the raid. First German pathfinders dropped flares to light up the area, some over the ship. This was for the incoming bombers to easily find their targets. They followed with Mines and bombs to cause havoc and destruction, mostly to the city centre. By an unbelievable stroke of luck the big oil terminal on the other side of the river escaped damage, it would have been disastrous if the storage tanks had been set on fire.

Another air raid on Monday evening, promising a repeat of Sunday's attack, didn't materialize and we were stood down. On Tuesday June 15th. H.M.S.Gambia was refuelled and ready for sea. At 1100hrs. we cast off and slipped down the river, leaving the grieving city behind. The next day we arrived in the river Mersey and went straight into Gladstone Dock. Liverpool's dockland was teeming with every type of ship, mostly merchantmen unloading the supplies necessary for the country's survival. It would be difficult to over emphasise the importance of the port as one of the nation's major lifelines for continuing the war. One messmate, a true 'Scouser', could hardly contain himself at the thought of sailing into his hometown. He came from a long line of Merseyside dockers with entrepreneurial ability, and compulsive urge, to 'appropriate' anything of value that could be moved in a dockyard. 'Scouse's dockyard connections stemmed from a large mafia style family of uncles with many self interests. From his telling the yard was a hotbed of pilfering practises that included skimming off from the various cargoes being unloaded. Another often-used ploy was to drop the odd case of goods to burst open. Set aside as badly damaged freight to be assessed and recorded, some of it mysteriously disappeared before the end of the shift. The disclosures of our 'artful' dodger messmate, and his extensive repertoire of amusing antidotes, kept us amused for hours. His itch to uphold the legacy he had inherited from his kinsfolk became evident a couple of days later when the ship was provisioning. On a couple of occasions 'Scouse' vanished from the victualling party detailed to carry in boxes of canned baked beans. I didn't think much about it until he turned up in the Mess that evening with a large bunch of bananas and a net of oranges for the lads. Nobody in their right mind, and certainly no one familiar with a 'Scousers' thinking would ask where the fruit came from. It was obvious to all that he had traded the baked beans for it.

Knowing that we were the second batch to go on a weeks leave Dave and I decided to take advantage of all-night shore leave and explore the city. A telephone call for me on the shore line altered all that. I was puzzled how anyone could possibly know I was in Liverpool, more so as we had only just arrived in port. Racing down the ladders to the exchange I picked up the phone with some trepidation but got a pleasant surprise. The voice at the other end was a girl friend who had joined the WRENS. My first question was how did she know I was in England and more so in Liverpool. She didn't want to say too much on the telephone except to tell me she was stationed at H.M.S.Gosling near Warrington. I found out later she was in the communication centre and well briefed on the movements of warships. Dave didn't take kindly to having our arrangements changed because of a WREN but he had to admit a choice between him and her was a foregone conclusion, he even lent me a couple of pounds for 'extras'. There would be plenty of other times when we would go ashore together and sink a few pints. 'Jennie Wren' arranged for us to meet outside the main entrance of Lime Street station the next day when I was watch ashore. All the way there I practised plausible excuses why I had not answered all her letters. In the end I decided it was best to tell lies or cloud the issue. Smartly turned out I got there early to show my good intent and eyed everyone approaching to make sure I didn't miss her. When an attractively youthful WREN walked up and said 'hallo' I couldn't believe my good fortune. She looked so different, I think it was the uniform and the fact she had blossomed into a lovely young lady since I had last seen her in civilian clothes. I complimented her on her appearance but when I told her she had the fragrance of freshly picked primroses on a spring morning she burst out laughing and said I had used that line on her when we first met.

Stationed at Warrington she had a fairly good knowledge of Liverpool, the ideal person to chaperone me around to see the sights. The elegance of the fine buildings and shops could not disguise the fact that Liverpool was a seaport with a long and distinguished maritime history. It was a busy bustling place in a constant state of flux. The local gentry rubbed shoulders with Lascars, Chinese, and Negros as part of their everyday business life. Judging from the number of scruffs wanting a few coppers, the city had more than it's fair share of 'bums' from the lower pecking order of humanity. Filled with the exuberance of youth, 'Jennie Wren' and I had a fabulous day before it was time for her to get the train back to Warrington. With nothing in the King's Rules and Admiralty Instructions to forbid it we strolled close together arm in arm, and with so much to catch up on we chattering nonstop. She said she would telephone me the following day to find out when we could meet again. After seeing her safely on her journey I booked into the local Seaman's Mission to get a bed for the night. The warden asked me if I had been there before and when I said I hadn't he warned me to tie my clothes in a bundle and take them into bed with me. He also said it would be wise to step legs of the bed into my shoes, otherwise they might not be there in the morning. 'Jennie' rang early the next day and I told her that a pal had offered to stand in for me and I could get into town that day. She said she could do the same and so it went on for the rest of the time I was in Liverpool, except for the week I spent at home. I was totting up a lot of favours from pals, deputizing that would have to be reciprocated at some future time.

A couple of days before going home on leave, six of us decided to smuggle out extra tobacco for the family. It was decided that if we intended taking out much more than the official ration we would be wise to have a word with 'Scouse' for advice. He said it could be managed and to leave it to him. The driver of the truck getting us out undetected, he warned us, would expect something in the way of 'smokes' for himself. We all agreed it was a reasonable request for the risk he was taking. Knowing the time for the liberty muster in the barn-like structure on the dockside, the driver would pull up on the road outside away from the prying eyes of the police on the main gate. He couldn't hang about so we had to be on time otherwise he would drive on. When the men formed up in four long lines it was expected the officer would want to get it over and done with in a minute or two. Instead he began scrutinizing each individual as he slowly passed down the ranks at a snail's pace. When the truck was heard pulling up we knew time was running out fast for us. Nerves jangled as the minutes ticked away and the officer was only half way through with the inspection. I agonised knowing he couldn't possibly finish in time before the truck was forced to move on. With the extra contraband we were carrying we could not take the risk of walking past the M.O.D. police on the gate. With a sinking feeling of despair, convinced we would end up in cells, I looked to Scouse for inspiration only to see him smiling; the nerve of the sod. On reflection I suppose I should have had more faith in his intuition and acumen.

He gave an acknowledging nod pointing to the small door at the rear, and with the officer at the other end of a line, Scouse took off. With discreet caution the rest of us followed when the opportunity arose. The other lads told us later that they tried to close the gaps we left but not before the officer noticed and gave them a good rollicking for not being properly 'fell in'. The castigation they didn't mind but a threat to keep them there all day if necessary until they smartened themselves up did, fortunately it turned out to be only a threat. Outside we sprinted to the truck and clambered on board with out loot before Scouse dropped and secured the tarpaulin over the tailboard. Crouched in silence we held our breath knowing that the next few minutes were crucial if we were to escape the wrath of the navy. The driver pulled up at the main gates to be checked out by the police. From the laughter and conversation on first name terms, one could only assume the policeman and the driver were well acquainted with each other. After a cheery 'so-long' the truck drove through the gates and dropped us off near the station, only Scouse was near home. Our collection for the driver was well received with his assurance that he was available anytime for a repeat run on the same terms.

On the first day out after arriving home I was pleased to see that Torquay and the surrounding district had escaped lightly from enemy bombing, with one notable exception. That was the tragic bombing of St.Marychurch parish church on Sunday May 30th.1943, shortly before I came on leave. A Sunday School was in progress when the enemy bombers struck, killing three teachers and twenty-one children as well as injuring others and demolishing the church. Rescuers of all kinds, but especially men from the RAF clawed through the rubble with their bare hands hoping to find children. It was an isolated incident of it's kind but one that enraged the local people, an anger that would not be forgotten for a long time. My sister was able to give me a first hand account because she was on the scene soon afterwards. Peter my youngest brother, the tail end of the family, was lucky that Sunday. If the attack had taken place on a weekday he would have been in Hartop Infants school, near the church, when it was also hit by a bomb. Instead he was walking on Babbacombe Downs with my sister and her RAF boyfriend. They wondered what was happening when the airman suddenly flung them both to the ground, not realising at first that he was shielding them with his body as the German planes swooped in low over the sea before dropping their bombs a few hundred yards up the road. When my sister looked up she saw everyone else on the Downs lying down flat hugging the grass for safety. My father had a lot of praise for the young airman's actions when he took my sister and brother home. The Palace Hotel, being used as an RAF hospital was hit as were a few residential properties around the area. On Teignmouth Road an enemy plane crashed on two houses destroying them, but the tribulations of war in Torquay and it's casualties could not be compared with places like Plymouth and Exeter where the people suffered terribly over a prolonged period.

For the next week I revelled in Mother's home cooking and the peaceful environment despite the few air raid warnings. Mother had the ability to make a meal out of a little bit of this and a little bit of that. She had a good contact for getting a plentiful supply of rabbits that she cooked to taste like chicken. I didn't go out for a drink with my father because he was never one to frequent pubs. He was a hard parent to us when we were young but he had his good points too. I never heard him swear or curse, or take the name of the Lord in vain. He was reputed to have been a 'drinker' in his youth but in my lifetime he was the opposite. He did suffer a 'chip' on his shoulder that came about through age. When he went to join up for war service at the outbreak of hostilities he was turned down as too old, miffed would be a polite word for how he felt. With his background of a Warrant Officer who had seen action in the First World War, he assumed the authorities would welcome him with open arms. He automatically viewed anyone without a white stick as a Conscientious Objector until proven otherwise. I couldn't help thinking that he got a lot of reflected glory from the fact that he had two sons, out there as he put it doing their 'bit' for the country. Not like some he said he could mention and often did. Unfortunately there was still no news of my brother Joe somewhere in Japanese hands. All the family went out of their way to make me relax and feel comfortable. My sister with her wide knowledge of whose who, briefed me on the available 'nice' girls, and insisted she introduce me to them. Her recommendations were a blessing with only a week at home, time was of the essence, not to be unnecessarily squandered sifting and sorting dubious pick-ups masquerading as vestal virgins. It was also wise to chose a girl from the local area to avoid wearily tramping miles across Torbay after taking one home to Paignton, late at night when the buses had stopped running.

Locally, St.Marychurch had two popular pleasure spots for socialising. Segregated into separate and distinct venues, both provided regular well supported dances. American servicemen congregated exclusively at the Links Hotel (now the Snooty Fox) while British servicemen made St.Marychurch Town Hall their own. Demarcation lines, mutually agreed and rigidly observed, kept the two camps apart to avoid fighting. It was the time when British Forces regarded the Americans more as surrogate enemies than allies. Overpaid, over sexed and over here, was the derogatory term commonly used to describe our brothers-in-arms. Woe betide the intellectually inept, foolhardy enough to wander into another's territory, they could be guaranteed a hostile reception at the very least. Girls frequenting the Links Hotel were often typecast as 'common', and 'tarred' by many locals as the 'fur coat and no knickers brigade'. They were accused of being 'easy', only wanting the goodies the Yanks had to offer in the way of, amongst other things, nylons, candy, money and cigarettes. Being labelled as 'Goodtime Girls' with a virginity rating of zero was an unkind slur on their characters that many future GI brides could rightly refute. Those young ladies in terror of becoming pregnant were well advised to resist all inducements to frequent the blacked-out shop doorways and dark alleys in Fore Street after a dance. Invitations to go for a late night walk invariably meant finding a secluded patch of dry grass to lie down on with an intensity of purpose.

Every day of my leave was a bonus to be relished. Therapeutically it was a resounding success. Jitterbugging the evenings away with a pretty girl was a sure fire way of forgetting guns, ammunition and enemy submarines. Female perfume had soon eradicated the smells of sweaty matelots and cordite fumes, not too surprisingly the days sped away. It puzzled me why people always asked exactly the same question, "Hallo. When are you going back", just as you were arriving home on leave. I don't think anything was meant by it, perhaps it merely replaced the customary comment about the weather but there was better ways of greeting a homecomer. Now I was going back and not with any passion to serve King and Country. I spent the last night with the family, it would have been insensitive not to have done so. I have to admit I would have preferred a last fling to the rendering of 'In the Mood' but certain codes of behaviour had to be observed and I stayed at home and chatted. My sister told me that Father had made sure the wireless accumulator was fully charged before I came on leave so that I could listen to the broadcasts if I wanted to; a special privilege. She went to great pains to point out that he had replaced the on/off knob that he usually kept in his pocket to stop anyone else using the wireless set without his permission. His high-handedness caused a certain resentment because he never went to have the accumulator recharged when it was running low, he always sent one of the family.

I met up with a crowd of my own ilk on the train, sailors going back from leave, and the lively conversation made the journey more acceptable. As I walked up the gangway and took my station card from the board, the sweet bouquet of female company was a distant memory. It was replaced with the oily smell of Gladstone Dock. The refit was well under way and like all refits it produced noise and dirt as workers of all kind cut, welded, chipped, hammered and painted.
A mammoth floating crane was brought into place, one of only two in the British Isles, to lift out a turret complete with guns and barbet and swing it ashore into a specially built steel cradle. The operation resembled a dentist extracting a tooth with long roots. It was one of the hundreds of jobs to be carried out before the ship was ready for sea again.

At a higher plane, New Zealand had approached the British government with a suggestion that H.M.S.Gambia should become part of the New Zealand navy to replace 'Leander' when the refit was completed. The request was quickly accepted and on the 22nd.September 1943, 'Gambia' was recommissioned as a HMNZ ship and 'Leander' reverted to the Royal Navy. It was also the day that I ceased to be a part of H.M.S.Gambia's ships' company and set off south to walk through the portals of H.M.S.Drake.

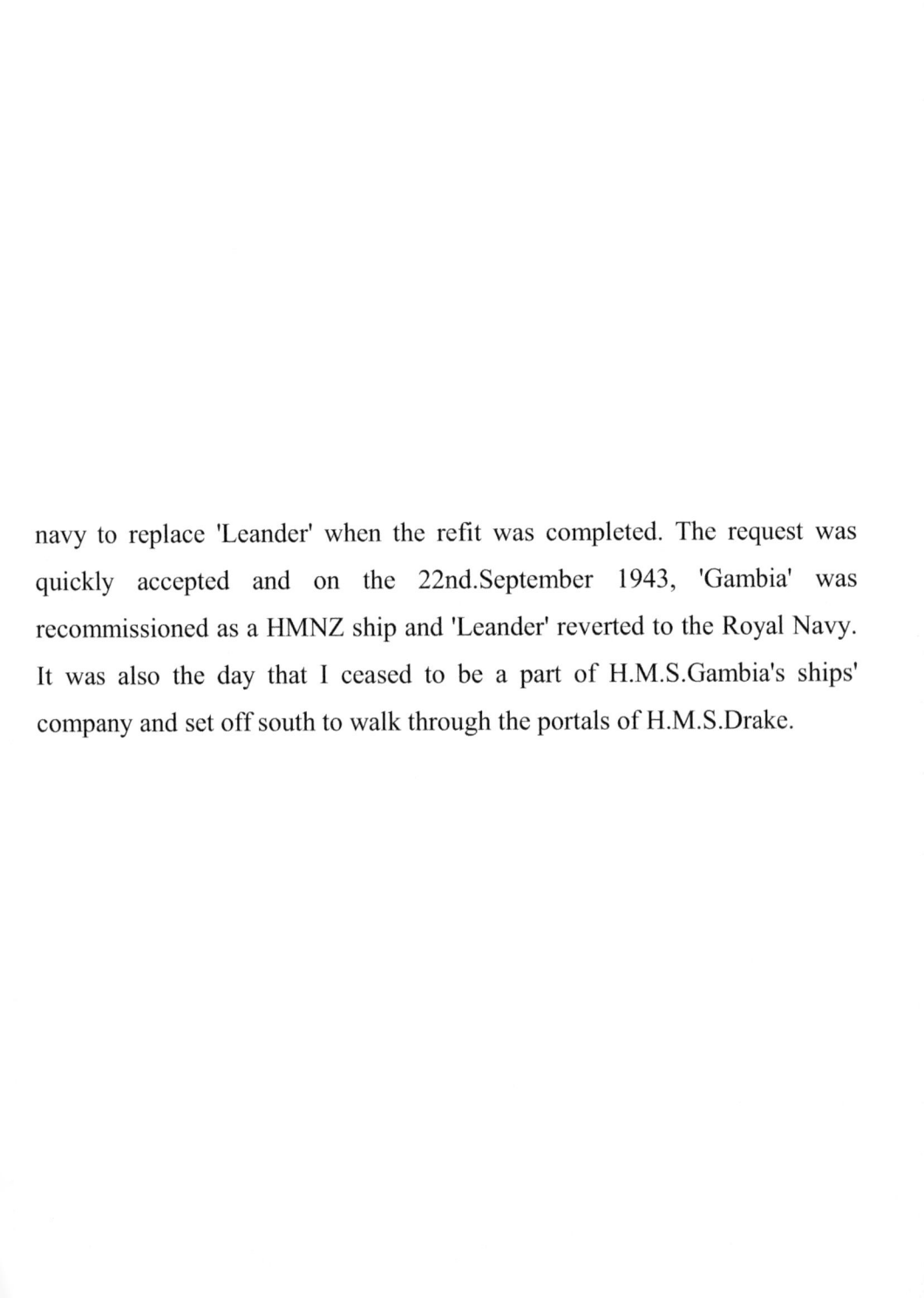

30 HMS Drake - Devonport

On September 22nd.1943 I checked in to H.M.S. Drake with my hammock and kit bag to be allocated a Mess number and told to report for work detail the following morning. It felt strange to be back in Plymouth, and stranger still to be shore based. The beating of waves against the ships' bows, breathing in salt laden air, endless expanses of sea, weary watchkeeping and the ever presence of danger, they all seemed so distant as I walked down the road to my billet. Taking in the grey granite buildings displaying about as much cheerfulness as a London Underground station during the rush hour, I thanked my lucky stars I hadn't spent time in the barracks, just the couple of days in transit after the sinking of H.M.S. Courageous.

The Mess was empty when I got there, except for a seaman gunner leaning leisurely on a sweeping brush. He was obviously the messdeck 'dodger' and I ignored him to get on with stowing my gear. I knew he was eyeing me with inquisitive interest and after a few minutes he began to quizzically cross-examine me about myself. Failing to become any wiser he changed tack from nosey-parker to helpful contemporary. Normally I am allergic to hustlers but he made a sustained effort to be pleasant. He said his name was Ted and asked me if I was going to the 'pictures' that evening. He was never going to be a 'shore-going opo' but he seemed likeable enough and could be useful, not the usual toe-rag found on the end of a brush. I confided in him that I was green as far as the barrack life was concerned and had never realised 'Drake' had a cinema. It was the cue for him to air his extensive knowledge about the ins and outs of the depot. He took it upon himself to enlighten me on all things necessary for trouble free living in the stone frigate. I gathered he had done about as much sea time as Big Ben and had no particular desire to experience seasickness before being demobbed. When I mentioned I had to report for work detail the next day he clued me up on the skulduggery of job allocation. Being naive about the 'fiddles', wangles and self interest that went on in the barracks I appreciated the words of advice from someone so well versed.

That evening I went with my new found friend to the barrack cinema. Well lit and laid out with tip-up seats on two floors it exceeded all my expectations. To add to the overall ambience, NAFFI girls went along the aisles selling a limited range of confectionery, ice creams, and cigarettes from trays hung around their necks. After paying for our tickets we settled into our seats and waited for the curtain to go up. Ted said I would know when the film was about to start because a bell rang to warn the girls the lights were about to go down. This was the signal for them to make their way to the safe area at the rear of the cinema. The precautionary measure was for their own protection. Apparently there had previously been trouble when darkness allowed high-spirited matelots to 'feel' the girls and get away with it. Now a strong naval patrol was positioned at the back, on guard and ready to arrest anyone misbehaving. I was sceptical that a strong patrol presence was necessary, it seemed irrational anyone would 'touch up' the girls with a couple of Petty Officer 'Crushers' about. Later the bell rang and I watched the girls scurrying aft, mindful of the lurking dangers.

Four nights later I experienced first hand why protecting the opposite sex was essential. The bell rang as usual and the girls moved back, with the exception of one usherette. Held up sorting out a query about change, probably by a preconceived ploy, she was just coming up the aisle when it went dark. An outburst of hysterical screaming suddenly drowned out the introductory music. When the house lights came on again it revealed a distraught girl going around in circles as a Petty Officer led patrol raced to her assistance. She was too distressed to make a positive identification and made matters worse by waving her arms around accusing everyone of being the culprit. In the confusion the sweet tray had ended up around her back adding a comical aspect to the bizarre situation. It was impossible to pinpoint the guilty party or parties from the array of choirboy faced innocents sitting upright and silently disassociating themselves from any breach of discipline. Under the circumstances the P.O. had no choice but to escort the girl outside to recover and let the film continue. Apparently she claimed she had been 'felt' several times by many hands in a matter of seconds, making it impossible for her to defend herself against the eager gropers.

The day after arriving in the depot I reported for duty and joined the work queue. Forewarned by Ted about the under the counter dealings I kept my eyes and ears wide open. Sure enough, I saw a seaman a few ahead of me put his hand on the counter and move it towards the Leading Seaman who took something from him. I didn't actually see any money but I knew something irregular was going on. When it was my turn I stared straight at the killock to let him know I was aware of his scam. I gave my name and as he ran down the worksheet I waited quietly to see if he had the courage to put me on a coaling party. What the outcome of the confrontation might have been is anyone's guess because it was cut short. A Petty Officer in the office looked up from his desk and let out a howl of surprise " Well I'll be damned, young Cannon ". I instantly recognised 'Knocker' White my old Divisional Petty Officer on H.M.S. Dorsetshire. I was as taken aback as him and all I could say was "Hello P.O., long time no see". "Come in here, where have you been, what are you doing here, why haven't you picked up your rate (P.O. rank)". His questions didn't wait for answers as he rattled on excitedly. Curious eyes followed me as I went into the office to be treated to a mug of tea. I sat chatting to him for some time as he wanted to know everything that had happened to me since our ship was sunk. Eventually he went across the room, picked up a telephone, and talked intensely into it for a few minutes. He came back scribbled a note and told me to take it to the Chief Petty Officer steward at the Flag Officers residence. After shaking my hand again for the umpteenth time he said " Come and see me again son. You've done your sea time for now, let some of these other *#Š"!?@ get some in ".

I took the chitty to the CPO and he turned me over to a Leading Hand to be shown the ropes. It soon became obvious that my new berth had been created for me by Petty Officer White and not because of a vacancy. It was a perk number, on the 'Staff' and safe from interference by depot personnel. Back in the Mess that evening Ted thought I was a 'jammy sod' having landed a number he would give his eye teeth for. He even had the nerve to ask if I could put a word in for him with 'Knocker' White. The work was mostly domestic and extremely boring, the smell of mansion polish instead of salt air was alien to my nostrils. A couple of days later I went back to the office to do the unthinkable and asked Petty Officer White to take me off the job. I had not sought special favours from an old shipmate even if his intention was to keep me out of trouble. He went berserk when I asked him, calling me some awful names that he didn't really mean. When he finally calmed down he told me to go back to my work and he would see what he could do as a compromise.

During my few days in the barracks I had the unusual experience of being 'picked up' by a NAFFI girl. Unusual, because most local girls working with the Navy kept sailors at arms length unless they were married to them. It happened when I bought something from the NAFFI shop. Checking my change I noticed I had more money than when I went in. Ted followed me out and I told him about the mistake, saying I was going back because she would be short in her till. He looked at me in an old-fashioned way and burst out laughing. "You've cracked it old Jan, she fancies you. It's the 'come on' so go for it". My learned friend continued. "Go in tomorrow to make sure. If she does it again it means she wants you to take her out. It's a known fact some of them do it". Out of curiosity I went to be served by the same girl. Sure enough she lingered long enough to say she was called Pauline and unattached. She lived locally and was free that weekend, that is if I was too. I didn't enlighten her that all my free time was going to be spent at home in Torquay, where I had very positive expectations with the opposite sex. I noticed others taking an amusing interest in our mating game and feigned embarrassment to break off the conversation, saying I would see her again but without making a commitment. She had over paid me again and I felt a twinge of guilt leading her to expect some returns for her contribution to my finances. On reflection she wasn't a bad looking girl but all of twenty-five and too old for me. It was galling having to put up with a leering Ted who preened himself on his acumen of all things 'Drake'. If he said, "I told you so" once he said it a thousand times that day to annoy me.

Petty Officer White, true to his word, sent for me to say arrangements had been made for me to go on a Torpedo course at H.M.S. Defiance. His general tone was one of regret that I hadn't taken his advice and stayed in the safety of the senior officer's residence. At least he stopped calling me a stupid young +#Š"*!< for not listening to reason. I packed my kit, bid Ted farewell, and caught the next pinnace up the river to the torpedo school. H.M.S. Defiance at Wilcove presented itself as a mishmash establishment, consisting of three big ships of the sailing era moored together and a large collection of single storey buildings ashore. The outward appearance of the hulks belied the excellent technical and efficiently run courses that demanded high standards. Most of the academic work and the messing facilities were on the floating part of the depot. The electrical and torpedo training, known as Whitehead, was mainly carried out in the classrooms and workshops ashore. I enjoyed the course from the start and that made it easier to learn and remember the information in textbooks. 'Red inks' (Recommendations) for the coloured drawings and diagrams that filled my exercise books helped to fuel my enthusiasm. When a Torpedo Lieutenant paid me a special compliment on a section of detailed illustrations that included Shunt, Compound, and Series motors and a ships' Ring Main system, I knew I belonged here.

To ensure a constant supply of defaulters to peel the never decreasing mountain of potatoes for the ships' galley, punishment was meted out for seemingly minor offences. One dinner hour with a little time to spare, four of us went over the fence into the field adjoining the shore base hoping to catch some of the pheasants we had seen roaming about. It never entered our heads what we would do with them if we caught any. Poaching proved not to be one of our strongest attributes. The moment we approached the birds sped away and so did the time, making us two minutes late for an afternoon lecture. All four, with different pleas of mitigation, got the same punishment. A week of our free periods on 'jankers' that inevitably meant the 'spud bashing' detail with a few other offenders. Squatting around in a circle chatting as we peeled, the conversation was never lacking, except for one lonesome looking character who defrocked potato after potato without uttering a word. On the second evening I purposely sat next to him and asked him an outright question to break the ice. "What are you here for Jan". "I'm two and two", meaning he was second-class for leave and conduct, usually a punishment during probation after a spell in the brig. The follow-up to a jail sentence was intended to finally purge the offender of his wrongdoing. At first he was reluctant to discuss his misconduct but with a little gentle coaxing he opened up and spilled out his tale of woe.

Newly married he was unfortunate to be drafted overseas to the Eastern Fleet, and away from home for some time. Still fresh from his marriage vows and being a natural homemaker he allotted the maximum allowances to his young bride. To make a little extra money he started a dhobi 'firm' on board washing other peoples dirty laundry and hammocks and bedcovers. On top of that he penny-pinched to save as much as possible from what was left of his meagre pay to send money home, convinced by his wife's letters that she was putting it to good use for their future. When mail started arriving from his mother hinting that his wife was bestowing favours on another, he told his mother not to write to him again. The same happened when his sister wrote implying someone was sharing his wife's affections. He would not believe what they were telling him and put it down to petty jealousy on their behalf. In due course his ship returned to the UK and he got home leave. The usual procedure for him was to telephone his mother, because at the time she was the only one in the family with a phone, and tell her to let his wife know he was coming. Because of the fall-out with his mother he decided to go straight home and give his wife a pleasant surprise.

Travelling from Devonport to Yorkshire with delays on the railway line, it was late when he got there. A light was still on in an upstairs window so he let himself in and shouted out to say it was him downstairs. Hearing a commotion he called out again to allay any fears that he might be mistaken for an intruder. A man he recognised came out of the bedroom carrying his clothes and made to get past him on the stairs, then his wife appeared in a state of undress and started screaming. He grabbed the lover and threw him over the banister then rushed down to knock seven bells of hell out of him. While he was extracting retribution from the yelling boyfriend, his wife dashed out of the house and took off. He found out later that she had gone up the street to take refuge at her parents. In a frenzy of uncontrolled rage he went berserk. Letting go of the fancy-man he went to the shed where he knew he kept an axe, a saw and a hammer. Armed with the tools he set about destroying everything he had worked and saved for. Smashing the pottery and glassware was easy, sawing the wardrobes and dining room table in half was much more difficult. Only blind fury gave him the strength to saw the furniture into pieces. He was about three-quarters of the way hacking through the sideboard when the police arrived and arrested him for the vicious assault on his wife's beau. A complaint had been made and they were duty bound to respond.

After two nights in the local constabulary cells he was collected by a naval police patrol and returned to the Provost Establishment in Devonport to await trial and sentencing. Everyone dealing with the case sympathised with him, even the Captain passing sentence told him that he would have done much the same under similar circumstances, but the law had to be upheld.
All the pent up emotions came flooding out as the tale of misery unfolded. At times he was too upset to carry on but we all remained silent until he could continue. The conclusion was that he served his time behind bars without incident and was now finishing his probationary period before being reinstated to first class for leave and conduct when he could apply for leave again and draw some pay. The confessional over there was still one important ingredient missing to complete the story. It was the answer to a question on all our minds, but with a reluctance to ask it. What did he intend doing about his wife ? Eventually someone did and got a reply that astonished us all. " I still love her very much and I'd have her back tomorrow if she would have me to start over again ". Listening to the others, the consensus of opinion was that he should go home and knock seven bells out of her as well and take the consequences, but he just shook he his head in disagreement.

It was a nice feeling when the 'jankers' finished and I could get ashore. With an excuse to celebrate I took the first opportunity to catch a liberty boat down to Flagstaff Steps and the bus into the city with a crowd from my class to prop up a bar. Knowing the company I was keeping I realised this could mean raising hell and high water before the proprietor threw us out or sent for the naval patrol. It was amazing how complacent my contemporaries had become about air raids. The wail of a siren didn't even merit a pause in conversation and certainly not to hasten down a pint or take cover. Only once did I see a sign of alarm, caused by an individual who had perfected the sound of a whistling bomb. A group of us were sitting around one night discussing various topics during a heavy air raid when the idiot did his impression of the missile coming down right on us, it was so realistic everyone ducked under the table before realising it was a sham. The culprit was grabbed and wrestled to the deck and for a moment I thought he was about to get a 'bunch of fives' in the mouth. However tempers quickly cooled and he got off with a warning that if he did it again he would be minus a few teeth when he went home the next time.

My 'Jennie Wren' travelled down from Warrington one weekend to spend it with me. I took it as a measure of her feelings and momentarily had a surge of ego. That was until the terrible realisation registered that she was very serious about our relationship. We had a wonderful few days before I saw her off at the station for the return journey. When she started to shed a few tears it confirmed my suspicions that she didn't see our association as a casual affair. We never met again, mainly due to where the Navy sent us, although we did correspond regularly for some time. Eventually that tailed off and we lost contact, perhaps she met and married a much nicer guy.

January 11th.1943 it was my 21st.birthday. The day, as if by magic, I became a man in the eyes of the law and officially allowed to draw a rum ration. Boyhood days were over, my manhood days beginning, and there was still a war to fight. Sitting by the side of Smeaton's tower on Plymouth Hoe I allowed myself a little time to reflect on the past. Through a haze of memory I saw phantom ships and their ghostly crews slipping silently down the Tamar, outward bound never to return. Courageous, Barham, Repulse, Royal Oak, Cornwall, and the Hermes, to name but a few. So many great ships now lying on the ocean bed with the remains of good men. Had I actually been in their company, had I really been to the Pacific and back. Would I ever visit far away places again to mix with different peoples and strange customs. Would I ever again serve with the likes of the men and boys who fought and died that Easter Sunday when H.M.S. Dorsetshire was destroyed by Japanese dive-bombers. Comrades I was proud to have served with who never came home, Murtagh, Edmunds, Jones and the many others. It was a chilling reminder of ones fragile mortality, notably in wartime, with the day to day possibility of being cut short from fulfilling some of the things you wanted to achieve in this world.

I had no doubt that the Allies would win the war but history will always challenge the price for winning. "Was it too high"? That is the question that can only be answered in time by those who experienced the pain of seeing close friends die. Until then, those who go down to the sea in the ships of the Royal Navy will continue to sail the oceans of the world with pride in their calling.

What happened to me next, and particularly for the subsequent part of my war, is the sequel to this story. It has to keep for the telling on a cold winters night around a well lit fire with a glass of hot rum in my hand and a captive audience. Suffice to say it was a few years after hostilities ceased before I went overseas again, albeit in different circumstances on secondment. It was a different tour of duty, one that gave me the opportunity of seeing and hearing the majesty of Niagara Falls on the Atlantic side of Canada before crossing the Rockies to see the great logging rafts floating down the mighty Fraser River on the Pacific side. It was the chance for me to dive in the crystal blue waters of the Bahamas, tussle with the sporting fish of the Caribbean until the rod bent to near breaking, and watch the high rolling Americans lose their thousands of dollars in the opulence of the Paradise Island Casino. The official tour of duty allowed me time to travel in the remote parts of the Yucatan to visit Indian villages, to explore the wonders of the ancient Maya temple cities, especially sites like Chichen Itza. Before that happened of course there was a war to fight and finish; but that is the story for the cold winters night.

Some Nautical Colloquialisms ~ Glossary

A1	First Class
Ackers	Money
Acting Green	Pretending innocence
Adrift	Absent. Admiralty Pattern. Admiralty specification.
Ancient Mariner.	Seagull (contains soul of departed sailor)
Aggies	Dame Agnes Weston's homes for sailors
All at Sea	Disorganised. Confused
All Night In.	No night watch.
Andrew	The Navy. The name derived from Andrew Miller who press-ganged so many men into the navy, people said he owned it.
Ash Can.	Depth Charge
Avast	Stop. Hold fast.
Bagshanty	House of ill repute
Barrack Stanchion	Someone serving lots of time ashore
Bear-up.	Keep smiling
Belay	Cancel (belay the last pipe)
Between the Devil & Deep Blue Sea.	The 'devil' was an area between the gunwale and the sea on wooden ships, where it was precarious to work; ie below the 'devil'.
Bible	Seamanship Manual
Bibles	Holystones
Big Wigs	Senior officers (they wore full wigs in 17th-18th)
Bilge	Rubbish. Nonsense.
Blackie	Blacksmith
Blast	Told off. A telling off.
Blue	Pay day
Blue Watermen.	Deep sea mariners.
Boats	Destroyers. Submarines.
Bottle	Telling off. Reprimand.
Bootneck	Royal Marine. Bullock. Turkey.
Bombay Oyster.	Egg, milk, and castor oil mixture.
Bond Free.	Duty Free. Tax Free.
Bones	Ships' doctor

Bone	Steal.
Bone-up	Polish up. Swot up.
Brig	Cells
Burma Road.	Rice pudding
Bullets.	Dried peas.
Burn.	Have a smoke
Buffer	Boatswain's mate
Bubbly	Rum. Nelson's blood.
Bunghole	Cheese
Bunkers	Idiotic
Burgoo	Porridge. (originally a coarse boiled oatmeal sweetened with molasses
Bunting.	Signalman
Bubble & Squeak	Hash made from leftovers
Bullocks	Men of the former Royal Marine Artillery
Bundlemen	Married men
Buzz	Rumour
Cag	Discuss. Argue
Cackle the Fat.	Talk too much. Chatter.
Cackleberries.	Eggs.
Call	A Boatswain's whistle
Cap Tally	Froth on a pint of beer.
Carry the can	Taking the blame
Cast Loose	Let fly. Strike out
Chatty Chats	Chatham rating
Char	Tea
Charlie	Reveile
Chippy Chap.	Shipwright.
Chow	Food
Chock-a-block.	Fed up. Bored. Chocker
Chuffs & Puffs	Chiefs and Petty Officers
Clewed up	Briefed. Aware of. Knowledgeable
Club Swinger.	Physical Training Instructor
Copper-bottomed.	Well founded. First class. Reputable
Crabfat	Dark grey paint
Crash down	A nap. A sleep
Crossing the Bar.	What a sailor does when he dies.
Crusher	Regulating Petty Officer. Ships' policeman.
Dab Dab	Rating
Davy Jones Locker	Bottom of the sea.

Dead Marine.	An empty beer bottle.
Dhobing	Washing clothes.
Dhobi-itch	Irritation caused by not rinsing clothing.
Ditty Box	Small wooden box for personal items
Dipped	Failed an examination
Dodger	Sweeper. Cleaner.
Drag	Have a smoke
Draw	Take the rum issue
Drink	The sea. (in the drink, in the sea)
Drip	Grumble. Complain.
Dummy Run	Rehearsal. Practise run.
Fanny	Mess utensil for carrying rum
Fanny Adams	None. Nothing.
Fender Belly	Fat sailor. One with big belly.
Fiddlers Green.	Where a sailor goes when he dies.
Figgy Duff	Suet pudding
Flannel	Ingratiating talk. Humbug. 'Soft Soap'.
Flake out	Collapse
Flap	Panic. Undue haste.
Flea Bag	Hammock
Flat-aback	Wearing hat on the back of head.
Foo-foo barge	Non-alcohol drink.
Gong	Medal.
Grog	Rum.
old 'Grog'	Admiral Vernon. (he introduced rum into the navy)
Gulpers	Large part of a tot of rum.
Guzz	Devonport.
Hardlayers	Hardship money paid on small ships.
Harry Freemans.	Free of charge. Something for nothing.
Hard Tack	Ships' dry biscuit.
Harry Tates	Something of a joke.(Harry Tate was a comedian)
Head Down	To get some sleep.
Heads	Ships' lavatories.
Hogwash	The Sea. Oggin. Drink. Briny.
Hicks	Mah Jong.
Hook	Leading Seaman.
Housey-housey	Bingo. Tombola.
Jack Dusty	Stores assistant.
Jack Strop	Truculent sailor.
Jam	Luck.

Jago's Mansion.	The dining hall in the barracks.
Jankers	Punishment.
Janner	Devonport rating of Westcountry origin.
Jaunty	The Master at Arms.(corruption of gendarme)
Jeep	Idiot. (used mainly in Training Ship)
Jenny.	Jenny Wren. A WREN rating.
Jewing	Tailoring. Sewing clothing.
Jimmy the One.	The First Lieutenant.
Jollies	Royal Marine.
Jonah	Person who brings bad luck.
Joss	Luck.
Jug	Cells.
Ki or Kye	Cocoa. (introduced into the navy in 1832)
Killick	Leading Seaman. Hook.
Kipper	Two faced and no guts.
Larboard	Portside. (from the Italian word 'laborda')
Lay Aft with Cap.	Fall in on the Quarterdeck to be charged.
Leathernecks.	Royal marines.
Left-footer.	Roman Catholic.
Liberty	Leave less than one full day.
Lobs	Warning. (short for 'Look out Boys')
Lower Deck Lawyer.	A Lower Deck know-all.
Make your number	Introduce yourself in a new mess.
Maties	Dockyard workers.
Matelot	Sailor.
Mess Traps	Food utensils on the Mess-deck.
Mungy	Food.
Mudhook	Anchor.
Neaters	Undiluted rum.
Nelson's Blood.	Rum.
Nozzer	New recruit. Untrained sailor
North-easter.(NE).	Not entitled. no pay entitlement
Nutty	A chocolate bar
Oggie Waffler.	A Westcountry sailor. A janner
Oggin	The Sea. Hogwash. Drink. Briney
Old Rope	Well used. Well worn
Oppo	Pal. Opposite number
Outrageous.	H.M.S. Courageous
Paybob	Paymaster
Peggie	'Cook of the Mess' on small ships

Pig	An officer. (mostly used pre-war)
Pipe	Bosun's whistle. Bosun's Call
Pipe Down	Shut up. Last pipe call of the day
Pledge taking the.	Becoming teetotal
Pilot	Ships' Navigator
Perique	Leaf tobacco rolled in canvas and tied with spunyard
Pongo	A soldier
Pussers	Admiralty pattern. Regulation issue
Pussers Dirk.	Seaman's regulation issue knife
Pussers Hard.	Regulation issue soap
Queen Bee	Senior WRENS officer
Rabbits	Ships' stores pilfered for taking ashore.
Rabbit Bag	Bag for taking suspect goods ashore
Rate, picking up	Promotion to Petty Officer
Rattle in the	On a charge.
Red Ink	A good mark to your credit
Red Lead	Tomato soup
Rig	Dress
Rogues Salute	Gun fired on the morning of Court Martial
Round the Buoy	Another helping
Rubber	A loan. A sub
Rub Up	A refresher course. To cram for exams
Rum Rat	Someone with an insatiable appetite for rum
Runners	Smugglers
Sea-daddy	Boys instructor
Set	Beard
Scouse	A Liverpudlian
Scouse	A dish of minced beef and stewed vegetables
Scran	Food
Scran Bag	Bag for stray clothing. A scruffy person
Scrub	Cancel. Forget it. Erase
Scrambled Egg.	Gold braid on an officer's cap
Scuppers	Someone always after tots of rum
Seven Beller	Watchkeeper's leave to 1130hrs.
Shellback	Seasoned mariner
Shanghai Runner.	Small roasted chicken. A Weihai Runner
Show a Leg	Get a move on.
Sippers	A sip of rum
Sin Bosun	Ships' Parson. Sky Pilot
Skate	Someone always in trouble

Slops	Ships' clothing store
Slide	Butter or margarine
Snob	Shoe repairer
Snottie	Midshipman. Wart. Crab. Wonk.
Snotties Nurse.	Senior Lieu. responsible for Midshipmen.
Soft Tack	Bread
Soft Number	An easy job of work. Easy duty
Spell	Short period of duty
Spurious	H.M.S. Furious
Sprog	Young recruit
Spliced	Married
Square Rig	Ratings uniform
Squeeze	Handout. Gratuitous gift. Charity
Squeeze Band.	Ships' Band made up of oddments
Stone Frigate.	A shore establishment
Strippey	Three good conduct badge Able Seaman
Strongers	Mixture of soda crystals and water
Stroppy	Aggresive. Truculent
Swallow the Anchor	Leave the sea. Retire ashore
Swing the Lead	Shirk. Malinger
Tailor Made	Cigarettes made by a tobacco company
Ticket	Discharge papers. (getting your ticket)
Tally	Name
Tids for Leave.	Getting everything neat and tidy for going home
Tiddy-oggie	A pasty
Tiffey	Artificer. Shipwright
Tiddley	Neat. Smart. (Misuse of the word tidily)
Tin Fish	Torpedo
Tittler	Tobacco for hand rolling cigarettes
Topsides	On deck. Aloft
Torps	Torpedo Gunner
Torpoint Chicken	Selfish person. Self first person
Tot	Daily issue of rum
Trick	A spell on watch
Two Blocks	The limit of a person's patience. Fed up
Turret Rat	Turret sweeper. Turret cleaner
Two and two	Second class for leave and conduct
Uckers	Sophisticated game of Ludo
Uproarious	H.M.S. Glorious
Up Homers	'Fostered' by a family ashore

Up the Board.	A game of cribbage
Warming the Bell	Finish early. Put the clocks on.
Wet	Stupid
Wet as a Brush.	Very stupid
Work Up	Training crew of a newly commissioned ship
Wobbly Rs'	Ships of the Royal Sovereign battleship class

Some nicknames

Name	Nickname	Name	Nickname
Bailey	Bill	Lee	Tansey
Beech	Nutty	Martin	Pincher
Bell	Daisy or Dinger	Miller	Dusty
Black	Nigger	Moore	Pony
Carpenter	Chippy	Murphy	Spud
Clark	Nobby	Pitts	Zassu
Collins	Jumper	Palmer	Pedlar
Day	Happy	Smith	Smudger
Freeman	Harry	Tate	Harry
Green	Jimmy	Ward	Sharkey
Gunn	Ben	White	Chalky or Knocker
Harding	Tosh	Williams	Bungey
James	Jimmy	Woods	Slinger
Knight	Bogie	Wright	Shiner

The U-29

To conclude this episode of my boyhood life at sea it seems only appropriate to mention something about the enemy who gave me my first experience of warfare and baptism of fire. This dubious honour fell to the German submarine U-29 captained by the then Kapitanleutnant Otto Schuhart already referred to in a previous chapter. The U-29 had the distinction of sinking the first British warship, the aircraft carrier H.M.S. Courageous, in the 1939 – 1945 conflict. Unlike so many of the other 1154 U-boats commissioned during the war, 998 were sunk and another 217 scuttled, it had the added distinction that it never suffered any loss of men from a crew of 39 due to accident.

U-29 was a type 7A boat with a maximum speed of 17knots laid down in Bremen on January 2nd. 1936. It survived the war to be scuttled in Küptemuhlen Bay on May 4th. 1945. The wreck of the submarine was finally broken up in 1946.

OTTO SCHUHART
Otto Schuhart was born on 1st.April 1909 in Hamburg and joined the Reichmarine in 1929 as a commissioned officer. Between 2nd September 1938 and 29th.October 1938 he captained the U-boat U8.

From the 10th.December 1938 and 3rd.April 1939 he captained the U25 and from the 4th.April 1939 until the 2nd.January 1941. U-boat U29. He completed 7 patrols and 222 days on the U29 and credited with sinking 12 allied ships with a total of 85,265tons.

For his part in sinking H.M.S. Courageous he was awarded the Knight's Cross on May 16th 1940. The crew of the U29 were also decorated for their part in the sinking. Later Otto Schuhart was in charge of submarine officer training. He finally retired in September 1967 with the rank of Kapitan Zur See (Captain) from the German Navy and he died in March 1990.

Printed in Great Britain
by Amazon